THE
ADDRESS
BOOK

Other Books by Michael Levine

The Corporate Address Book

The Music Address Book

The Environmental Address Book

The Kid's Address Book

Guerrilla PR

Lessons at the Halfway Point

Take It from Me: Practical and Inspiring
Advice from the Celebrated and the Successful

THE
ADDRESS
BOOK

How to Reach Anyone Who *Is* Anyone

MICHAEL LEVINE

A Perigee Book

Every effort has been made to provide the most current mailing addresses. Addresses, however, do change, and neither the publisher nor the author is responsible for misdirected or returned mail.

We regret that when this book went to press it was too late to include the names of recently elected United States public officials.

A Perigee Book
Published by The Berkley Publishing Group
A member of Penguin Putnam Inc.
375 Hudson Street
New York, New York 10014

First printing of the ninth edition: April 1999

ISBN 0-399-52487-8
ISSN 1090-0101

Published simultaneously in Canada.

The Penguin Putnam Inc. World Wide Web site address is
http://www.penguinputnam.com

Printed in the United States of America

10 9 8 7 6 5 4 3 2 1

Acknowledgments

I'm lucky. I get to say publicly to the special people in my life how much they mean to me. To each of them, my appreciation for their help with this book and, most of all, their unwavering friendship and love.

My literary agent, Alice Martell.

My friends at Putnam, where I have been published since 1984.

My father, Arthur O. Levine, stepmother, Marilyn, and sister, Patty.

My special friends Bill Calkins, Richard Imprescia, Karen Karsian, Michael Lamont, Richard Lawson, Nancy Mager, John McKillop.

Special thanks to Robin Page for commitment to excellence in the researching of this book.

THE
ADDRESS
BOOK

A

And none will hear the postman's knock without a quickening of the heart. For who can bear to feel himself forgotten?

—W. H. AUDEN, from "Night Mail"

Aadland, Beverly
PO Box 1115
Canyon Country, CA 91350
Actress

Aaron, Hank
PO Box 4064
Atlanta, GA 30302
Former baseball player

Aaron, Tommy
PO Drawer 545
Buford, GA 30518
Golfer

AARP (American Association for Retired Persons)
601 E St. NW
Washington, DC 20049
Web site: http://www.aarp.org/
E-mail: member@aarp.org
Joseph S. Perkins, president
Association for senior citizens

ABBA
Postbus 3079
NL4700 GB
Roosendaal
The Netherlands
Pop group

Abbot Laboratories
100 Abbott Park Rd.
Abbott Park, IL 60064
Web site: http://
www.abbott.com
Duane L. Burnham, CEO
Drug manufacturer

Abbot & Costello Fan Club
PO Box 2084
Toluca Lake, CA 91610

Abbott, Bruce
4526 Wilshire Blvd.
Los Angeles, CA 90010
Actor

Abbott, Gregory
PO Box 68
Bergenfield, NY 07621
Singer

ABC Entertainment
2040 Ave. of the Stars
Century City, CA 90067
or
77 W. 66th St., 9th Fl.
New York, NY 10023
Ted Harbert, president
Major television network

Abdul, Paula
14755 Ventura Blvd., #1–710
Sherman Oaks, CA 91403
or
12434 Wilshire Blvd., #770
Los Angeles, CA 90024
Singer, dancer, choreographer
Birthday: 6/19/62

Abdul-Jabbar, Kareem
2049 Century Park E.,
    Ste. 1200
Century City, CA 90067
Former basketball player

Abdullah the Butcher
1000 S. Industrial Blvd.
Dallas, TX 75207
Wrestler

Abelson, Amanda
E-mail:
    manda@martingny.ai.mit.edu
Hypercard programmer

Above the Line Agency
9200 Sunset Blvd., #401
Los Angeles, CA 90069
Rima Greer, agent
*Agency that handles directors;
    clients include Irvin Kershner,
    Ryan Rowe, and John Hopkins*

Abraham, F. Murray
40 5th Ave., #2C
New York, NY 10011
Actor
Birthday: 10/24/39

Abrams, Rhonda
E-mail: rhonda@ideacafe.com
Business planning expert

Abramson, Leslie Hope
4929 Wilshire Blvd., #940
Los Angeles, CA 90010
*Attorney who represented Erik
    Menendez*

**Academy of Motion Picture
    Arts and Sciences (AMPAS)**
8949 Wilshire Blvd.
Beverly Hills, CA 90210
Web site: http://www.ampas.org/
E-mail: ampas@ampas.org
Robert Rehme, president
*Film organization; awards the
    Oscars*

**Academy of Television Arts
    and Sciences (ATAS)**
5220 Lankershim Blvd.
North Hollywood, CA 91601
Web site: http://
    www.emmyonline.org/
*TV organization; awards the
    Emmys*

**Acadiana Symphony
    Association**
412 Travis St.
Lafayette, LA 70503
Web site: http://
    cust.iamerica.net/symphony/
E-mail:
    symphony@iamerica.net
Xiao-Lu Li, conductor
Orchestra

**ACCESS: A Security
    Information Service**
1511 K St. NW, #643
Washington, DC 20005
E-mail: access@4access.org

Accuracy in Media, Inc.
4455 Connecticut Ave. NW,
    #330
Washington, DC 20008
Attn: Joseph Wilson
E-mail: joew@aim.org
Web site: http://www.aim.org/
*Group concerned with fairness,
    balance, and accuracy in news
    reporting*

AC/DC
46 Kensington Ct.
London W8 5DP
England
Rock group

Ace Hardware
2200 Kensington Ct.
Oak Brook, IL 60523
David F. Hodnik, CEO
Wholesalers

Ace of Base
Siljernark Gardsvagern 2
17152 Stockholm
Sweden
Music group

Acid Test
83 Riverside Dr.
New York, NY 10024
Music group

Acker, Sharon
6310 San Vicente Blvd., #401
Los Angeles, CA 90048
Actress

**Action on Smoking and Health
(ASH)**
2013 H St. NW
Washington, DC 20006
Web site: http://ash.org/
John F. Banzhaf III, executive
director
*Nation's oldest and largest
antismoking organization, and
the only one which regularly
takes legal action to fight
smoking and protect the rights
of nonsmokers*

Actors and Others for Animals
5510 Cahuenga Blvd.
North Hollywood, CA 91607
Cathy Singleton, executive
director
*Protection group for the welfare of
animals*

Actors' Equity Association
165 W. 46th St.
New York, NY 10036
Web site: http://hipp.gator.net/
aea.html
Ron Silver, president
Stage actors' union

Acuff, Roy
Grande Ole Opry
2804 Opryland Dr.
Nashville, TN 37214
Country singer

Adair, Deborah
9300 Wilshire Blvd., #555
Beverly Hills, CA 90212
Actress
Birthday: 5/23/52

Adair, Red
PO Box 747
Bellville, TX 77418
*Owns company that puts out oil
well fires*

Adams, Bryan
146 N. LaBrea Ave.
Hollywood, CA 90028
Web site: http://
www.bryanadams.com/
Singer, songwriter
Birthday: 11/5/59

Adams, Cecil
E-mail:
ezotti@merle.acns.nwu.edu
Columnist

Adams, Cindy
1050 5th Ave.
New York, NY 10028
Actress/Columnist

Adams, Don
2160 Century Park E.
Los Angeles, CA 90067
Actor, writer, director
Birthday: 4/19/?

Adams, Douglas
E-mail:
  76206.2507@compuserve.com
  or adamsd@cerf.net
Author, The Hitchhiker's Guide
  to the Galaxy

Adams, Geoff
E-mail: gadams@eng.umd.edu
Desktop textures programmer

Adams, Joey
1050 5th Ave.
New York, NY 10028
Actor, writer, director
Birthday: 1/06/11

Adams, Maria
247 S. Beverly Dr., #102
Beverly Hills, CA 90212
Actress

Adams, Mason
900 5th Ave.
New York, NY 10021
Actor
Birthday: 2/26/19

Adams, Maude
11901 Sunset Blvd., #214
Los Angeles, CA 90049
or
1939 Century Park W., #403
Los Angeles, CA 90067
Model, actress
Birthday: 2/12/45

Adams, Scott
E-mail: scottadams@aol.com
Web site: http://
  www.unitedmedia.com/
  comics/dilbert/
Cartoonist, creator of "Dilbert"

Adams, Tom
29–31 Kings Rd.
London SW3
England
Actor

ADC Band
17397 Santa Barbara
Detroit, MI 48221
Music group

Ad Council
261 Madison Ave., 11th Fl.
New York, NY 10016-2303
Web site: http://135.145.55.19/
Lea Werbel, media outreach
  assistant
E-mail: media_materials
  @adcouncil.org
*Nonprofit volunteer organization
  that conducts public service
  advertising*

Adjani, Isabelle
B.P. 475–07
F-75327 Paris
France
or
2 Rue Lord Byron
75008 Paris
France
Actress
Birthday: 6/27/55

Trace Adkins Fan Club
PO Box 121889
Nashville, TN 37212

Adler, Margot
c/o National Public Radio
2025 M St. NW
Washington, DC 20036
News correspondent

Adoption Support Center, Inc.
6331 N. Carrolton Ave.
Indianapolis, IN 46220
Web site: http://
  www.adoptionsupport.com/
Julie Craft, cofounder,
  president
E-mail:
  jcraft@adoptionsupport.com
*International information network
  for adoptees and birth/adoptive
  parents*

Adrian Symphony Orchestra
110 South Madison
Adrian, MI 49221
Web site: http://www.aso.org/
E-mail: aso@lni.net
David Katz, conductor

Advocacy Institute
1707 L St. NW, #400
Washington, DC 20036
Web site: http://
www.advocacy.org/
E-mail: info@advocacy.org
*Dedicated to strengthening the
capacity of public interest and
social and economic justice
advocates to influence and
change public policy*

**Advocates for Highway and
Auto Safety**
750 1st St. NE, #901
Washington, DC 20002
Web site: http://
www.saferoads.org/
Joan Claybrook, consumer
cochair
Dedicated to traffic safety

Advocates for Youth
1025 Vermont Ave. NW, #200
Washington, DC 20005
Web site: http://
www.advocatesforyouth.org/
E-mail:
info@advocatesforyouth.org
James Wagoner, president
*Creates programs and promotes
policies which help young people
make informed and responsible
decisions about their sexual and
reproductive health*

Aerosmith
PO Box 4668
San Francisco, CA 94101
or
584 Broadway, #1009
New York, NY 10012
Rock group

Aetna
151 Farmington Ave.
Hartford, CT 06156
Web site: http://
www.aetna.com
Richard L. Huber, CEO
Life and health insurance

AFLAC
1932 Wynnton Rd.
Columbus, GA 31999
Web site: http://www.aflac.com
Daniel P. Amos, CEO
Life and health insurance

Africa Fund, The
50 Broad St., Ste. 711
New York, NY 10004
Web site: http://
www.prairienet.org/acas/
afund.html
E-mail: africafund@igc.org
*Works for a positive U.S. policy
toward Africa and supports
human rights, democracy, and
development*

African-American Institute
1625 Massachusetts Ave. NW,
Ste. 400
Washington, DC 20036
Web site: http://
www.igc.apc.org/ia/mb/
aai.html
*A nonprofit, multiracial,
multiethnic organization whose
mission is to promote African
development, primarily through
education and training*

Agassi, Andre
ATP Tour North America
200 ATP Tour Blvd.
Ponte Vedra Beach, FL 32082
Tennis player
Birthday: 4/29/70

AGCO
4205 River Green Pkwy.
Duluth, GA 30096
Web site: http://
  www.agcocorp.com
Robert J. Ratliff, CEO
Manufacturer of farm equipment

Agency, The
1800 Ave. of the Stars
Los Angeles, CA 90067
Emile Gladstone, Jerry
  Zeitman, Walter Van Dyke,
  Walter Morgan, and Nick
  Mechanic, agents
Agency that handles directors

Agony Column
Cosmopolitan
224 W. 54th St.
New York, NY 10019
Attn: Irma Kurtz
Magazine advice column

Aid Association for Lutherans
4321 N. Ballard Rd.
Appleton, WI 54919
John O. Gilbert, CEO
*Life and health insurance
  (mutual)*

Aikman, Troy
PO Box 630227
Irving, TX 75063
Football player
Birthday: 1/21/66

Ailes, Roger
440 Park Ave. S.
New York, NY 10016
Producer, director

Aimee, Anouk
201 rue du Faubourg St.
  Honore
75008 Paris
France
Actress
Birthday: 4/27/32

Ainge, Danny
2910 N. Central
Phoenix, AZ 95012
Basketball player

Airborne Freight
3101 Western Ave.
Seattle, WA 98121
Web site: http://www.airborne-
  express.com
Robert S. Kline, CEO
Mail, package, freight delivery

Air Products & Chemicals
7201 Hamilton Blvd.
Allentown, PA 18195
Web site: http://
  www.airproducts.com
Harold A. Wagner, CEO
Chemicals

Air Supply
14755 Ventura Blvd., #1-710
Sherman Oaks, CA 91403
Music group

Air Touch
1 California St.
San Francisco, CA 94111
Web site: http://
  www.airtouch.com
Samuel Ginn, CEO
Telecommunications

Emperor Akihito
The Palace
1-1 Chiyoda-Chiyoda-Ku
Tokyo
Japan
Emperor of Japan

Alabama
PO Box 529
Ft. Payne, AL 35967
Country music group

Al-Anon Family Group Headquarters, Inc.
1600 Corporate Landing Pkwy.
Virginia Beach, VA 23454
Web site: http://www.al-anon.alateen.org/
Support group for families of alcoholics

Alateen
Al-Anon Family Group Headquarters, Inc.
1600 Corporate Landing Pkwy.
Virginia Beach, VA 23454
Web site: http://www.al-anon.alateen.org/alalist_usa.html
For young people whose lives have been affected by someone else's drinking

Albano, Lou
PO Box 3859
Stamford, CT 06905
Wrestler, manager

Albee, Edward
PO Box 697
Montauk, NY 11954
Playwright

Crown Prince Albert
Palais de Monaco
Boite Postal 518
Monte Carlo
Monaco
Crown prince of Monaco

Albert, Eddie
1930 Century Park W., #403
Los Angeles, CA 90067
Actor
Birthday: 4/22/09

Albertsons
250 Parkcenter Blvd.
Boise, ID 83706
Gary G. Michael, CEO
Food and drug stores

Albright, Lola
PO Box 250070
Glendale, CA 91225
Actress
Birthday: 7/20/24

Albright, Madeleine
1318 34th St. NW
Washington, DC 20007
Secretary of State

Alcoa
425 6th Ave.
Pittsburgh, PA 15219
Web site: http://www.shareholder.com/alcoa
Paul H. O'Neill, CEO
Metals

Alcoholics Anonymous
475 Riverside Dr.
New York, NY 10115
Web site: http://www.alcoholics-anonymous.org/
Support group for alcoholics

Alda, Alan
Martin Bregman Productions, Inc.
641 Lexington Ave.
New York, NY 10022
Actor
Birthday: 1/28/36

Aldrin, Buzz
Starcraft Enterprise
233 Emerald Bay
Laguna Beach, CA 92651
or
2101 NASA Rd. 1
Houston, TX 77058
Former astronaut

Alexander, Daniele
PO Box 23362
Nashville, TN 37202
Country music singer

Alexander, Denise
345 N. Maple Dr., #361
Beverly Hills, CA 90210
Actress

Alexander, Jane
1100 Pennsylvania Ave. NW,
#520
Washington, DC 20506
Actress
Birthday: 10/28/?

Alexander, Jason (Jay Scott Greenspan)
151 El Camino Dr.
Beverly Hills, CA 90212
Actor
Birthday: 9/23/59

Alexander, Lamar
1109 Owen Pl. NE
Washington, DC 20008
Politician

Alexander, Shana
156 5th Ave., #617
New York, NY 10010
News correspondent

Alexandria Symphony Orchestra
PO Box 11014
Alexandria, VA 22312
Web site: http://www.cais.com/
webweave/symphony.htm
Kim Allen Kluge, music
director, conductor
Marcia N. Speck, executive
director

Alexis, Kim
343 N. Maple Dr., #185
Beverly Hills, CA 90210
Supermodel

Alfonso, Kristian
c/o *Days of Our Lives*
3000 W. Alameda Ave.
Burbank, CA 91523
or
345 Maple Dr., #185
Beverly Hills, CA 90210
Soap opera star

Ali, Muhammad (Cassius Clay)
PO Box 187
Berrien Springs, MI 49103
Boxing champion
Birthday: 1/17/42

Allan, Jed
PO Box 5302
Blue Jay, CA 92317
Actor

Allard, J.
E-mail: jallard@microsoft.com
Microsoft TCP/IP specialist

Allegheny Teledyne
1000 Six PPG Pl.
Pittsburgh, PA 15222
Richard P. Simmons, CEO
Metals

Allegiance
1430 Waukegan Rd.
McGaw Park, IL 60085
Web site: http://
www.allegiance.net
Lester B. Knight, CEO
Healthcare

Allen, Corey
8642 Hollywood Blvd.
Los Angeles, CA 90069
Actor, writer, director

Deborah Allen's Front Row Friends
PO Box 120849
Nashville, TN 37212
Fan club

Allen, Elizabeth
PO Box 243
Lake Peekskill, NY 10537
Actress

Allen, Joan
40 W. 57th St.
New York, NY 10019
Actress

Allen, Jonelle
8730 Sunset Blvd., #480
Los Angeles, CA 90069
Actress, singer

Allen, Karen
PO Box 237
Monterey, MA 01245
or
PO Box 5617
Beverly Hills, CA 90212
Actress
Birthday: 10/05/51

Allen, Marty
11365 Ventura Blvd., #100
Studio City, CA 91604
Comedian

Allen, Nancy
PO Box 6
Sky Forest, CA 92385
Actress
Birthday: 6/24/50

Allen, Rex Jr.,
PO Box 120501
Nashville, TN 37212
Country music singer

Allen, Rex Sr.,
PO Box 430
Sonoita, AZ 85637
Country music singer

Allen, Robert
32 Ave. of the Americas
New York, NY 10013
Business leader

Allen, Steve (Stephen Valentine Patrick William Allen)
15201-B Burbank Blvd.
Van Nuys, CA 91411
Television comedian, author, pianist, songwriter
Birthday: 12/26/21

Allen, Tim (Tim Allen Dick)
7920 Sunset Blvd., #400
Los Angeles, CA 90046
or
1122 S. Robertson Blvd., #15
Los Angeles, CA 90035
E-mail:
    HI.Tim@refuge.cuug.ab.ca
Actor
Birthday: 6/13/53

Allen, Woody
930 5th Ave.
New York, NY 10018
Actor, comedian, director
Birthday: 12/01/35

Alley, Kirstie
132 S. Rodeo Dr., #300
Beverly Hills, CA 90212
Actress
Birthday: 1/12/55

All-4-One
11693 San Vicente Blvd., #550
Los Angeles, CA 90049
Web site: http://www.otb1.com/
    all-4-one/
Music group

Alliance for Aging Research
2021 K St. NW, #305
Washington, DC 20006
Web site: http://207.78.88.3/
    aar/
Organization promoting medical research on aging

Alliance for Justice
1601 Connecticut Ave. NW,
 #601
Washington, DC 20009
Web site: http://www.afj.org/
E-mail: alliance@afj.org
*National association of
 environmental, civil rights,
 mental health, women's
 children's, and consumer
 advocacy organizations*

Alliance to Save Energy
1725 K St. NW, #509
Washington, DC 20006
Contact: Rozanne Weissman
Web site: http://www.ase.org/
*Nonprofit coalition of business,
 government, environmental, and
 consumer leaders promoting
 efficient use of energy*

Allied Signal
101 Columbia Rd.
Morristown, NJ 07962
Web site: http://
 www.alliedsignal.com
Lawrence A. Bossidy, CEO
Trucking company

Allman Brothers
40 W. 57th St.
New York, NY 10019
Music group

Allmerica Financial
440 Lincoln St.
Worcester, MA 01653
Web site: http://
 www.allmerica.com
John F. O'Brien, CEO
P & C insurance

Allred, Gloria
6300 Wilshire Blvd., #1500
Los Angeles, CA 90048–5016
Attorney

Allstate
2775 Sanders Rd.
Northbrook, IL 60062
Web site: http://
 www.allstate.com
Jerry D. Choate, CEO
Insurance

Alltel
1 Allied Dr.
Little Rock, AR 72202
Web site: http://www.alltel.com
Joe T. Ford, CEO
Telecommunications

Almost Persuaded
PO Box 727
Rossville, GA 30741
Country music group

Alonso, Maria Conchita
PO Box 537
Beverly Hills, CA 90213
Actress
Birthday: 11/30/56

All Saints
72 Chancellor's Rd.
London W6 9SG
England
Music group

Alpert, Hollis
PO Box 142
Shelter Island, NY 11964
Writer

Alpert, Dr. Richard
PO Box 1558
Boulder, CO 80306
Psychologist

Alt, Carol
111 E. 22nd St., #200
New York, NY 10010
or
9169 Sunset Blvd.
Los Angeles, CA 90069
Actress

Altman, Robert
502 Park Ave., #15G
New York, NY 10022
Writer, producer, director

Alumax
3424 Peachtree Rd. NE
Atlanta, GA 30326
Web site: http://
   www.alumaxnet.com
Allen Born, CEO
Metals

Alva, Luigi
via Moscova 46/3
20121 Milano
Italy
Tenor

Alvin & the Chipmunks
122 E. 57th St., #400
New York, NY 10003
Animated singing group

Amanpour, Christiane
25 rue de Ponthieu
75008 Paris
France
Broadcast journalist

Amazing Rhythm Aces
555 Chorro St., #A-1
San Luis Obisbo, CA 93401
Music group

Ambrosia
245 E. 54th St.
New York, NY 10022
Music group

Amerada Hess
1185 6th Ave.
New York, NY 10036
John B. Hess, CEO
Petroleum refining

Ameren
1901 Chouteau Ave.
St. Louis, MO 63103
Web site: http://www.ue.com
Charles W. Mueller, CEO
Gas and electric utilities

America
345 N. Maple Dr., #300
Beverly Hills, CA 90210
Music group

**American-Arab Anti-
   Discrimination Committee
   (ADC)**
4201 Connecticut Ave. NW,
   #500
Washington, DC 20008
Web site: http://www.adc.org/
   index4.html
E-mail: adc@adc.org
Naila Asali, chairperson
*Civil rights organization committed
   to defending the rights of people
   of Arab descent and promoting
   their rich cultural heritage*

**American Association of
   English Handbell Ringers**
1055 E. Centerville Station Rd.
Dayton, OH 45459
Vic Kostenko, executive
   director
E-mail: TheAGEHR@aol.com

**American Association of
   University Women (AAUW)**
1111 16th St. NW
Washington, DC 20036
Web site: http://www.aauw.org/
E-mail: info@mail.aauw.org
Janice Weinman, executive
   director
*Promotes education and equity for
   women and girls through
   research; fellowships and grants;
   activism; voter education; and
   support for sex discrimination
   lawsuits*

American Cancer Society
1599 Clifton Rd. NE
Atlanta, GA 30203
Web site: http://
www.cancer.org/frames.html
Joann Schellenbach, senior
director, Media Relations
Lynne Camoosa, director,
Medical and Scientific
Communications
Emily Smith, director,
Communications and Public
Relations Advocacy

American Cinematographer
PO Box 2230
Hollywood, CA 90078
Web site: http://
www.cinematographer.com/
magazine/
*Magazine for cinematographers/
editors*

**American Civil Liberties Union
(ACLU)**
122 Maryland Ave. NE
Washington, DC 20002
Web site: http://www.aclu.org/
Steven R. Shapiro, legal
director of the national
ACLU
Advocate of individual rights

**American Conservative Union
(ACU)**
1007 Cameron St.
Alexandria, VA 22314
Attn: David A. Keene
Web site: http://
www.conservative.org/
E-mail: acu@conservative.org
Thomas R. Katina, executive
director
*The nation's oldest conservative
lobbying organization; its
purpose is to effectively
communicate and advance the
goals and principles of
conservatism*

**American Council for Capital
Formation**
1750 K St. NW, #400
Washington, DC 20006
Web site: http://www.accf.org/
E-mail:
awilkes@mindspring.com
Charles E. Walker, chairman
(former Deputy Secretary of
the Treasury)
*Research and publications by the
ACCF and ACCF Center for
Policy Research on tax,
regulatory, and environmental
issues*

**American Council on
Education**
1 Dupont Cir., #800
Washington, DC 20036
Web site: http://
www.ACENET.edu/
Stanley O. Ikenberry, president
*The nation's umbrella higher
education association*

**American Council on Science
and Health**
1995 Broadway, 16th Fl.
New York, NY 10023
Web site: http://www.acsh.org/
Elizabeth M. Whelan, president
E-mail: whelan@acsh.org
Publisher, Priorities: For Long
Life and Good Health
*A consumer education and
advocacy group directed and
advised by over 250 American
and Canadian physicians and
scientists*

American Dietetic Association
216 W. Jackson Blvd.
Chicago, IL 60606
Web site: http://
www.eatright.org/
Polly Fitz, president

American Electric Power
1 Riverside Plaza
Columbus, OH 43215
Web site: http://www.aep.com
E. Linn Draper, Jr., CEO
Gas and electric utilities

American Enterprise Institute for Public Policy Research
1150 17th St. NW
Washington, DC 20036
Web site: http://www.aei.org/
E-mail: webmaster@aei.org
Christopher C. DeMuth, president
Dedicated to preserving and strengthening the foundations of freedom—limited government, private enterprise, vital cultural and political institutions, and a strong foreign policy and national defense—through scholarly research, open debate, and publications

American Express
200 Vesey St.
New York, NY 10285
Web site: http://www.americanexpress.com
Harvey Golub, CEO
Diversified financials

American Family Insurance Group
6000 American Pkwy.
Madison, WI 53783
Dale F. Mathwich, CEO
Insurance

American Farm Bureau Federation
600 Maryland Ave. SW, #800
Washington, DC 20024
Web site: http://www.fb.com/
E-mail: davec@fb.com
David P. Conover, administrator
Dean R. Kleckner, president
The voice of agriculture

American Federation of Government Employees
80 F St. NW
Washington, DC 20001
Web site: http://www.afge.org/splash/splash.htm
Bobby L. Harnage, national president
The largest federal employee union, representing some 600,000 federal and D.C. government workers nationwide

American Federation of State, County and Municipal Employees (AFSCME)
1625 L St. NW
Washington, DC 20036
Web site: http://www.afscme.org/
E-mail: webmaster@afscme.org
Gerald W. McEntee, international president
Nation's largest public employee and health care workers union

American Federation of Teachers (AFT)
555 New Jersey Ave. NW
Washington, DC 20001
Web site: http://www.aft.org//index.htm
E-mail: AskAFT@aol.com
Sandy Feldman, president

American Financial Group
1 E. 4th St.
Cincinnati, OH 45202
Web site: http://www.amfn.com
Carl H. Lindner, CEO
Insurance

American Gas Association
1515 Wilson Blvd.
Arlington, VA 22209
Web site: http://www.aga.com/
Julie Stewart, communications
E-mail: jstewart@aga.com
*Represents 181 local natural gas
utilities that deliver gas to 54
million homes and businesses in
all fifty states*

American General
2929 Allen Pkwy.
Houston, TX 77019
Web site: http://www.agc.com
Robert M. Devlin, CEO
Life and health insurance

"American Gladiators"
10203 Santa Monica Blvd.
Los Angeles, CA 90067
Web site: http://
www.americangladiators.com/
E-mail: whoever@bellsouth.net
Television series

American Home Products
5 Giralda Farms
Madison, NJ 07940
Web site: http://www.ahp.com
John R. Stafford, CEO
Pharmaceuticals

American International Group
70 Pine St.
New York, NY 10270
Web site: http://www.aig.com
Maurice R. Greenberg, CEO
P & C insurance

American Jewish Congress
2027 Massachusetts Ave. NW
Washington, DC 20036
Web site: http://
www.ajcongress.org/
E-mail: washrep@ajcongress.org
Jack Rosen, president
*Considered the legal voice of the
American Jewish community*

American League of Lobbyists
PO Box 30005
Alexandria, VA 22310
Web site: http://www.alldc.org/
E-mail: info@alldc.org
Elaine Acevedo FTD, president
E-mail:
eacevedo@compuserve.com
*A national organization founded
in 1979 dedicated to serving
government relations and public
affairs professionals*

**American Legislative Exchange
Council**
910 17th St. NW, 5th Fl.
Washington, DC 20006

American Library Association
50 E. Huron St.
Chicago, IL 60611
Web site: http://www.ala.org/
E-mail: linda.wallace@AL.org
Barbara J. Ford, president
E-mail: BJFORD@VCU.EDU
*World's oldest, largest, and most
influential library association; a
leader in defending intellectual
freedom and promoting the
highest quality library and
information services*

**American Medical Association
(AMA)**
515 N. State St.
Chicago, IL 60610
Web site: http://
www.ama-assn.org
Percy Wootton, president
*Dedicated to promoting the art and
science of medicine and the
betterment of public health*

American Postal Workers Union
1300 L St. NW
Washington, DC 20005
Web site: http://www.apwu.org/
Moe Biller, president
The largest postal union, representing 366,000 union members in the United States

American Public Health Association
1015 15th St. NW, #300
Washington, DC 20005
Web site: http://www.apha.org/
E-mail: comments@apha.org.
Mohammad N. Akhter, executive director
The oldest and largest organization of public health professionals in the world, representing more than 50,000 members from over 50 occupations of public health

American Rivers
1025 Vermont Ave., #720
Washington, DC 20005
Web site: http://www.amrivers.org/
E-mail: amrivers@amrivers.org
Leigh Askew, associate director of Foundations
E-mail: laskew@amrivers.org
National river-conservation organization whose mission is to protect and restore America's river systems and to foster a river stewardship ethic

American Security Council
1155 15th St. NW, #1101
Washington, DC 20005
Political organization

American Tort Reform Association
1850 M St. NW, Ste. 1095
Washington, DC 20036
Web site: http://aaabiz.com/atra/
E-mail: lleclair@atra.org
Sherman Joyce, president
A national advocate of lawsuit reform

American Trial Lawyers Association (ATLA)
1050 31st St. NW
Washington, DC 20007
E-mail: help@atlahq.org
Promotes justice and fairness for injured persons, safeguards victims' rights—particularly the right to trial by jury

American Veterinary Medical Association
1101 Vermont Ave. NW, #710
Washington, DC 20005
Web site: http://www.avma.org/
E-mail: 74232.57@compuserve.com
Diana Tomasek, online managing editor for the AVMA Web site

Americans for Democratic Action (ADA)
1625 K St. NW, #210
Washington, DC 20006
Web site: http://kogod-b9.battellel.american.edu/ada.htm
E-mail: adaction@Ix.netcom.com
Pioneered the development and promotion of a national liberal agenda of public policy formulation and action

Americans for Indian Opportunity
681 Juniper Hill Rd.
Bernalillo, NM 87004
E-mail:
lharris@CARINA.unm.edu

American Society of Cinematographers (ASC)
PO Box 2230
Hollywood, CA 90078
Web site: http://
www.cinematographer.com/

American Society of Composers, Authors and Publishers (ASCAP)
1 Lincoln Plaza
New York, NY 10023
Website:http://www.ascap.com/
Marilyn Bergman, ASCAP
president and chairman of
the board
The only performing rights licensing organization in the United States whose board of directors is made up entirely of writers and music publishers elected by and from its membership

American Society of Composers, Authors and Publishers (ASCAP), Atlanta
(Not a membership office)
541–400 10th St. NW
Atlanta, GA 30318
Web site: http://
www.ascap.com/

American Society of Composers, Authors and Publishers (ASCAP), London
8 Cork St.
London W1X 1PB
England
Web site: http://
www.ascap.com/

American Society of Composers, Authors and Publishers (ASCAP), Los Angeles
7920 Sunset Blvd., Ste. 300
Los Angeles, CA 90046
Website:http://www.ascap.com/

American Society of Composers, Authors and Publishers (ASCAP), Miami
844 Alton Rd., Ste., 1
Miami Beach, FL 3313
Web site: http://www.ascap.com

American Society of Composers, Authors and Publishers (ASCAP), Nashville
2 Music Sq. W.
Nashville, TN 37203
Website:http://www.ascap.com/

American Society of Composers, Authors and Publishers (ASCAP), Midwest
1608 W. Belmont Ave., Ste. 200
Chicago, IL 60657
Web site: http://
www.ascap.com/

American Society of Composers, Authors and Publishers (ASCAP), Puerto Rico
1519 Ponce de Leon Ave., Ste. 505
Santurce, PR 00909
Web site: http://
www.ascap.com/

American Standard
1 Centennial Ave.
Piscataway, NJ 08855
Web site: http://
www.americanstandard.com
Emmanuel A. Kampouris, CEO
Industrial and farm equipment

American Stores
709 S. Temple
Salt Lake City, UT 84102
Victor L. Lund, CEO
Food and drug stores

AmeriSource Health
300 Chester Field Pkwy.
Malvern, PA 19355
Web site: http://
www.amerisrc.com
R. David Yost, CEO
Wholesale pharmaceuticals

Ameritech
30 S. Wacker Dr.
Chicago, IL 60606
Web site: http://
www.ameritech.com
Richard C. Notebaert, CEO
Telecommunications

Ames, Trey
15760 Ventura Blvd., #1730
Encino, CA 91436
Actor

Amgen, Inc.
1840 Dehavilland Dr.
Thousand Oaks, CA 91320
Web site: http://
wwwext.Amgen.com/cgi-bin/
genobject
Gordon M. Binder, chairman
and CEO
Kevin W. Sharer, president and
COO
*One of the world's largest
biotechnology companies*

AmHS Institute
400 N. Capitol St. NW, #590
Washington, DC 20001

Amick, Madchen
9200 Sunset Blvd., #625
Los Angeles, CA 90069
Actress

Amin, Idi
Box 8948
Jidda 21492
Saudi Arabia
Former dictator of Uganda
Birthday: 1/1/25

Amnesty International, USA
322 8th Ave.
New York, NY 10001
Web site: http://
www.amnesty-usa.org/
E-mail: LRack/leg@igc.apc.org
Roberto A. Quezada, Web site
coordinator
E-mail: rquezada@aiusa.org
*Works to free all prisoners of
conscience detained anywhere for
their beliefs or because of their
ethnic origin, sex, color, or
language, who have not used or
advocated violence*

Amoco
200 E. Randolph Dr.
Chicago, IL 60601
Web site: http://
www.amoco.com
H. Laurance Fuller, CEO
Petroleum refining

Amos, Deborah
c/o National Public Radio
2025 M St. NW
Washington, DC 20036
News correspondent

Amos, John
PO Box 18764
Encino, CA 91416
or
Box 587
Califon, NJ 07830
Actor

Amos, Tori (Myra Ellen Amos)
PO Box 8456
Clearwater, FL 34618
Singer, songwriter
Birthday: 8/22/64

AMP
470 Friendship Rd.
Harrisburg, PA 17111
Web site: http://www.amp.com
William J. Hudson, CEO
Electronics, electrical equipment

AMR
4333 Amon Carter Blvd.
Fort Worth, TX 76155
Web site: http://
www.amrcorp.com
Robert L. Crandall, CEO
Airline

Anbinder, Mike
E-mail: mha@baka.ithaca.ny.us
Author journalist

Anderson, Barbara
PO Box 10118
Santa Fe, NM 87504
Actress

Anderson, Bill
PO Box 888
Hermitage, TN 37076
Country music singer

Anderson, Brett
E-mail:
76646.3722@compuserve.com
Author, journalist

Anderson, Gillian
151 El Camino Dr.
Beverly Hills, CA 90212
Actress

Anderson, John
PO Box 810
Smithville, TN 37166
Country music singer

Anderson, John B.
World Federalist Association
418 7th Street, SE
Washington, DC 20003
E-mail: wfa@igc.apc.org
*Former presidential candidate and
current president of the World
Fedralist Association*

Anderson, Lewis
E-mail: andersol
@server2.health.state.mn.us
Mac shareware author

Anderson, Louie
8033 Sunset Blvd., #605
Los Angeles, CA 90046
Comedian

Anderson, Lynn
PO Box 90454
Charleston, SC 29410
Country music singer

Anderson, Richard Dean
12049 Century Park E.,
Ste. 2500
Los Angeles, CA 90067
or
8942 Wilshire Blvd.
Beverly Hills, CA 90211
Actor
Birthday: 1/23/50

Anderson, Terry
50 Rockefeller Plaza
New York, NY 10020
News correspondent

Andress, Ursula
Via Francesco Siacci 38
00197 Roma
Italy
Actress
Birthday: 3/19/36

Andretti, John
PO Box 59244
Indianapolis, IN 46259
Race car driver

Andretti, Mario
53 Victory Ln.
Nazareth, PA 18604
Race car driver
Birthday: 2/28/40

HRH Prince Andrew
Suninghill Park
Windsor
England
Son of Queen Elizabeth
Birthday: 2/19/60

Andrews, Andy
PO Box 17321
Nashville, TN 37217
Country music singer

Andrews, Julie
PO Box 491668
Los Angeles, CA 90049
Actress, singer
Birthday: 10/1/35

Angell, David
E-mail:
   dangell@shell.portal.com
Author, journalist

Angelou, Maya
Wake Forest University
PO Box 7314
Winston-Salem, NC 27109
Poet

Angels, The
PO Box 3864
Beverly Hills, CA 90212
Music group

Angelyne
PO Box 3864
Beverly Hills, CA 90212
Billboard siren

Anglade, Jean-Hughes
151 El Camino Dr.
Beverly Hills, CA 90212
Actress

Angle, Jim
c/o National Public Radio
2025 M St. NW
Washington, DC 20036
News correspondent

Anh, Le Duc
c/o Council of Ministers
Bac Thao, Hanoi
Vietnam
President of Vietnam

Anheuser-Busch
1 Busch Pl.
St. Louis, MO 63118
Web site: http://
   www.anheuser-busch.com
August A. Busch III, CEO
Beverages

Aniston, Jennifer
5750 Wilshire Blvd., #580
Los Angeles, CA 90036
Actress

Anixter
4711 Golf Rd.
Skokie, IL 60637
Web site: http://
   www.anixter.com
Robert W. Grubbs, Jr., CEO
Wire and cable wholesalers

Anka, Paul
10573 W. Pico Blvd., #159
Los Angeles, CA 90064
Singer, songwriter
Birthday: 7/30/41

Annan, Kofi
799 United Nations Plaza
New York, NY 10017
*Secretary-general of the United
   Nations*

HRH Princess Anne
Gatcombe Park
Gloucestershire
England
Daughter of Queen Elizabeth

Ann-Margret (Ann-Margret Olson)
5664 Cahuenga Blvd., #336
North Hollywood, CA 91601
Actress
Birthday: 4/28/41

Ant, Adam (Stewart Goddard)
503 The Chambers
Chelsea Harbour
Lots Rd.
London SW10 0XF
England
Singer
Birthday: 11/3/54

Anthem Insurance
120 Monument Cir.
Indianapolis, IN 46204
L. Ben Lytle, CEO
Life and health insurance

Anthrax
15 Haldane Crescent
Piners Heath
Wakefield WF1 4TE
England
Heavy metal group

Anti-Defamation League (ADL)
823 United Nations Plaza
New York, NY 10017
Web site: http://www.adl.org/
E-mail: webmaster@adl.org
David H. Strassler, national
   chairman
*Fighting anti-Semitism through
   programs and services that
   counteract hatred, prejudice,
   and bigotry*

Anton, Susan
16830 Ventura Blvd., #300
Encino, CA 91436
Actress
Birthday: 10/12/50

Anwar, Gabrielle
253 26th St., #A-203
Santa Monica, CA 90402
Actress
Birthday: 2/4/70

Aoki, Rocky
8685 N.W. 53rd Ter.
Miami, FL 33166-4591
Food entrepreneur

Aon
123 N. Wacker Dr.
Chicago, IL 60606
Web site: http:/www.aon.com
Patrick G. Ryan, CEO
Diversified financials

Apollonia (Kotero)
8383 Wilshire Blvd., #614
Beverly Hills, CA 90211
Actress

Apple Computer
1 Infinite Loop
Cupertino, CA 95014
Web site: http://
   www.apple.com
Steven P. Jobs, CEO
Computers, office equipment

Applied Materials
3050 Bowers Ave.
Santa Clara, CA 95054
Web site: http://
   www.appliedmaterials.com
James C. Morgan, CEO
Electronics, semiconductors

Aquino, Corazon
c/o Pius XVI Ctr.
UN Manila
Philippines
Former president of the Philippines

Arab American Institute
918 16th St. NW, Suite 601
Washington, DC 20006
E-mail: aaijzogby@delphi.com
*The Arab American Institute is
   dedicated to the Arab American
   community's involvement in the
   political process.*

Arafat, Yassir
Gaza City
Gaza Strip
Palestine
Israel
President of Palestine

Aramark
1101 Market St.
Philadelphia, PA 19107
Joseph Neubauer, CEO
Diversified outsourcing services

Archer, Anne
c/o Ilene Feldman Agency
8730 Sunset Blvd., #490
Los Angeles, CA 90069
Actress

Archer Daniels Midland
4666 Faries Pkwy.
Decatur, IL 62526
Web site: http://
   www.admworld.com
G. Allen Andreas, CEO
Food

Archerd, Army
c/o *Daily Variety*
5700 Wilshire Blvd., #120
Los Angeles, CA 90036
Columnist

Arens, Moshe
49 Hagderat
Savyon
Israel
Politician

Arias, Oscar
Apdo 8-6410-1000
San Jose
Costa Rica
*Former president of Costa Rica
   and Nobel Peace Prize winner*

Arinze, Francis Cardinal
Piazza San Calisto 16
00153 Roma
Italy
Cardinal

Arkin, Adam
2372 Veteran Ave., #102
Los Angeles, CA 90064
Actor

Arkin, Alan
21 E. 40th St., #1705
New York, NY 10016
or
c/o William Morris Agency
151 S. El Camino Dr.
Beverly Hills, CA 90212
Actor
Birthday: 3/26/34

Arledge, Roone
1330 Ave. of the Americas
New York, NY 10019
Former President, ABC News

Armani, Giorgio
Palazzo Durini 24
20122 Milano
Italy
Fashion designer
Birthday: 7/11/34

Armatrading, Joan
27 Queensdale Pl.
London W11
England
Singer, guitarist
Birthday: 12/9/50

Armstrong, Anne
Armstrong Ranch
Armstrong, TX 78338
Politician

Armstrong, Bess
151 El Camino Dr.
Beverly Hills, CA 90212
Actress

Army of Lovers
78 Stanley Gardens
London W3 7SN
England
Music group

Arnaz, Lucie
PO Box 636
Cross River, NY 10536
Actress
Ricky and Lucy's daughter

Arness, James (James Aurness)
PO Box 49003
Los Angeles, CA 90049
Actor
Birthday: 5/26/23

Arnold, Eddy
PO Box 97
Brentwood, TN 37024
Country singer

Arnold Tom
500 S. Sepulveda Blvd., #400
Los Angeles, CA 90049
Actor, comedian, producer
Birthday: 3/6/59

Arquette, Patricia
9560 Wilshire Blvd., #516
Los Angeles, CA 90212
Actress
Birthday: 4/8/68

Arrested Development
9380 S.W. 72nd St., #B-220
Miami, FL 33174
Music group

Arrow Electronics
25 Hub Dr.
Melville, NY 11747
Web site: http://
   www.arrow.com.
Stephen P. Kaufman, CEO
Wholesale electronics

Arts & Entertainment
235 E. 45th St.
New York, NY 10017
Cable network

Ash, Mary Kay
16251 Dallas Pkwy.
Dallas, TX 75248

Ashdown, Paddy
House of Commons
London SW1 AAA
England
Politician

Asheville Symphony Orchestra
PO Box 2852
Asheville, NC 28802
Alice Jolly, general manager
Robert Hart Baker, music
   director

Ashford & Simpson
254 W. 72nd St., #1A
New York, NY 10023
Musical group

Asia America Symphony
1440 W. 178th St.
Gardena, CA 90248
Heiichiro Ohyama, music
   director
E-mail: asso@earthlink.net

**Asian American Journalists
   Association**
1765 Sutter St., #1000
San Francisco, CA 94115
Web site: http://www.aaja.org/
   front.html
E-mail: National@aaja.org
Benjamin Seto, national
   president
*Seeks to increase employment of
   Asian American print and
   broadcast journalists; assist high
   school and college students
   pursuing journalism careers;
   encourage fair, sensitive, and
   accurate news coverage of Asian
   American issues; and provide
   support for Asian American
   journalists*

Asleep at the Wheel
PO Box 463
Austin, TX 78767
Country music group

Asner, Ed
12400 Ventura Blvd., #371
Studio City, CA 91604
E-mail:
72726.357@compuserve.com
Actor
Birthday: 11/15/29

Al-Assad, Hafez
Office of the President
Damascus
Syria
President of Syria

Assante, Armand
367 Windsor Hwy.
New Windsor, NY 12553
Actor
Birthday: 10/4/49

Associated Builders and Contractors
1300 N. 17th St., 8th Fl.
Roslyn, VA 22209
Web site: http.//www.abc.org
Scott Brown, director of communications
E-mail: brown@abc.org
A national trade association representing over 19,000 contractors, subcontractors, material suppliers, and related firms from across the country and from all specialties in the construction industry

Association for Community Based Education
1805 Florida Ave. NW
Washington, DC 20009
Membership is composed of community activist organizations, including many that operate literacy projects

Association for the Advancement of Mexican Americans
6001 Gulf Frwy. #B-3, #165
Houston, TX 77023

Association of Independent Commercial Producers (AICP)
11 E. 22nd St., 4th Fl.
New York, NY 10010
Web site: http://www.aicp.com/
E-mail: AICPHO@aol.com
Represents commercial production companies

Astin, John
PO Box 49698
Los Angeles, CA 90049
Actor, writer, director
Birthday: 3/30/30

Astin, Sean
c/o Samantha Crisp
William Morris Agency
151 S. El Camino Dr.
Beverly Hills, CA 90212
Actor

AT&T
32 6th Ave.
New York, NY 10013
Web site: http://www.att.com
C. Michael Armstrong, CEO
Telecommunications company

Atkins, Chet
1013 17th Ave. S.
Nashville, TN 37212
Guitarist
Birthday: 6/20/24

Atlantic Ritchfield
515 S. Flower St.
Los Angeles, CA 90071
Web site: http://www.arco.com
Michael R. Bowlin, CEO
Petroleum refining

Attenborough, Lord Richard
Old Friars
Richmond Green
Surrey
England
Writer, producer
Birthday: 8/29/23

Auermann, Nadja
c/o Elite Models
Via San Vittóre 40
10-20123 Milano
Italy
Supermodel

Autry, Gene
5858 Sunset Blvd.
Los Angeles, CA 90028
*Actor, founder of Gene Autry
    Western Museum*
Birthday: 9/29/07

Avery, Margaret
PO Box 3493
Los Angeles, CA 90078
Actress

Avery, Dennison
150 N. Orange Grove Blvd.
Pasadena, CA 91103
Web site: http://www.
    averydennison.com
Charles D. Miller, CEO
Labels, office supplies

Avon
1345 6th Ave.
New York, NY 10105
Web site: http://www.avon.com
James E. Preston, CEO
Cosmetics and soaps

Awsome
10 Bourlit Close
London W1T 7PJ
England
Music Group

Axton, Hoyt
1102 17th Ave. S., #401
Nashville, TN 37212
Singer, songwriter

Ayes, Ebony
4060 Peachtree Rd., Ste. #D241
Atlanta, GA 30319
Porn star

Aykroyd, Dan
1180 S. Beverly Dr., #618
Los Angeles, CA 90035
Actor, writer
Birthday: 7/1/52

If you want to know your true opinion of someone, watch the effect produced in you by the first sight of a letter from him.

—Schopenhauer

Babbitt, Bruce
Department of the Interior
5169 Watson St. NW
Washington, DC 20016
Secretary of the Interior

Babock, Barbara
c/o CBS/MTM Studios
4020 Radford Ave.
Studio City, CA 91604
Actress

Babyface (Kenneth Edmonds)
8255 Beverly Blvd.
Los Angeles, CA 90048
Singer, songwriter, producer
Birthday: 1958

Baby's
1545 Archer Rd.
Bronx, NY 10462
Music group

Baby Spice (Emma Bunton)
1790 Broadway, 20th Fl.
New York, NY 10019
Singer, member of the Spice Girls

Bacall, Lauren (Betty Perske)
1 W. 72nd St., #43
New York, NY 10023
or
151 El Camino Dr.
Beverly Hills, CA 90212
Actress
Birthday: 9/16/24

Bachman-Turner Overdrive
1505 W. 2nd Ave., #299
Vancouver, BC V6H 3Y4
Canada
Musical group

Back Week Festival in Evanston
PO Box 6133
Evanston, IL 60204
Contact: Barbara Bennett
Richard Webster, music
    director

Backstage West
5055 Wilshire Blvd.
Los Angeles, CA 90025
Web site: http://
    www.backstage.com/
Steve Elish, publisher
Magazine for actors

Backstreet Boys
7380 Sand Lake Rd., #350
Orlando, FL 32819
Music group

Bacon, Kevin
9830 Wilshire Blvd.
Beverly Hills, CA 90212
or
PO Box 668
Sharon, CT 06069
Actor
Birthday: 7/8/58

Bader, Diedrich
c/o "The Drew Carey Show"
4000 Warner Blvd.
Burbank, CA 91522
Actor

Badham, John
c/o Elkins and Elkins
16830 Ventura Blvd., #300
Encino, CA 91436
Movie director

Baez, Joan
PO Box 1026
Menlo Park, CA 94026
Singer
Birthday: 1/9/41

Bailey, F. Lee
1400 Centre Park Blvd., #909
W. Palm Beach, FL 33401
Attorney
Birthday: 6/10/33

Bailey, Razzy
PO Box 62
Geneva, NE 68361
or
c/o Marilyn Schultze, fan club
   president
PO Box 11950
Nashville, TN 37222
E-mail: razzypres@hotmail.com
Country singer

Baillie & the Boys
PO Box 121185
Arlington, TX 76012
Country music group

Baio, Scott
4333 Forman Ave.
Toluca Lake, CA 91602
Actor
Birthday: 9/22/61

Baker, Carrol
PO Box 48059
Los Angeles, CA 90048
Actress
Birthday: 11/15/25

Baker, Howard, Jr.
PO Box 8
Huntsville, TN 37756
Former senator
Birthday: 11/15/25

Baker, James A., III
1299 Pennsylvania Ave. NW
Washington, DC 20004
Former Secretary of State

Baker, Janet Abbott
450 Edgeware Rd.
London W2
England
Mezzo-soprano

Baker, Lisa
c/o Playboy Enterprises
9242 Beverly Blvd.
Beverly Hills, CA 90210
Model

Baker, Tom
2–4 Noel St.
London W1V 3RB
England
Actor known as "Dr. Who"
Birthday: 1/20/34

Baker Hughes
3900 Essex Ln.
Houston, TX 77027
Web site: http://
   www.bakerhughes.com
Max L. Lukens, CEO
Industrial and farm equipment

Bakker, Jim (James O.)
PO Box 94
Largo, FL 33649
TV evangelist in PTL scandal
Birthday: 1/2/40

Bakula, Scott
9560 Wilshire Blvd., #500
Beverly Hills, CA 90212
or
15300 Ventura Blvd., #315
Sherman Oaks, CA 91403
Actor
Birthday: 10/9/55

Baldwin, Adam
PO Box 5617
Beverly Hills, CA 90210
Actor
Birthday: 2/27/62

Baldwin, Alec (Alexander Rae Baldwin III)
132 Rodeo Dr., #300
Beverly Hills, CA 90212
Actor
Birthday: 4/3/58

Baldwin, Daniel
c/o William Morris Agency
151 S. El Camino Dr.
Beverly Hills, CA 90212
Actor

Baldwin, Stephen
8730 Sunset Blvd., #490
Los Angeles, CA 90069
Actor
Birthday: 1966

Baldwin, William
955 S. Carrillo Dr., #200
Los Angeles, CA 90048
Actor
Birthday: 1963

Ballard, Kaye
PO Box 922
Rancho Mirage, CA 92270
Singer

Ballard, Roger
PO Box 46305
Baton Rouge, LA 70895
Country music singer

Baltimore Gas & Electric
39 W. Lexington St.
Baltimore, MD 21201
Web site: http://www.bge.com
Christian H. Poindexter, CEO
Gas and electric utilities

Bama Band
c/o Rob Battle, Enterprises
  Artists
819 18th Ave. S.
Nashville, TN 37203
Country music group

Banc One Corp.
100 E. Broad St.
Columbus, OH 43271
Web site: http://
  www.bankone.com
John B. McCoy, CEO
Commercial bank

Bancroft, Anne (Anna Maria Italiano)
20th Century Fox
Box 900
Beverly Hills, CA 90213
Actress
Birthday: 91/7/31

Band, The
121 N. San Vicente Blvd.
Beverly Hills, CA 90211
Musical group

Bandar, Prince Sultan-al-saud
601 New Hampshire NW
Washington, DC 20037
*Saudi Arabia's ambassador to the
  United States*

Banderas, Antonio
9830 Wilshire Blvd.
Beverly Hills, CA 90212
Actor
Birthday: 1960

Bando, Sal
c/o Milwaukee Brewers
Milwaukee County Stadium
Milwaukee, WI 53214
Baseball player

Bani-Sadr, Abol Hassan
Auvers-sur-Oise
France
Former president of Iran

BankAmerica Corp.
555 California St.
San Francisco, CA 94104
Web site: http://
www.bankamerica.com
David A. Coulter, CEO
Commercial bank

BankBoston Corp.
100 Federal St.
Boston, MA 02110
Web site: http://www.bkb.com
Charles K. Gifford, CEO
Commercial bank

Bankers Trust of New York
130 Liberty St.
New York, NY 10006
Web site: http://
www.bankerstrust.com
Frank N. Newman, CEO
Commercial bank

Bank of New York
48 Wall St.
New York, NY 10286
Web site: http://
www.bankofny.com
Thomas A. Renyi, CEO
Commercial bank

Banks, Ernie
c/o Chicago Cubs
1060 W. Addison St.
Chicago, IL 60613
Former baseball player

Banks, Tyra
170 5th Ave., #1000
New York, NY 10010
Actress, model
Birthday: 12/3/73

Banshees, The
127 Aldersgate St.
London EC1
England
Music group

Barbeau, Adrienne
PO Box 1839
Studio City, CA 91614
or
9255 Sunset Blvd., #515
Los Angeles, CA 90069
Actress
Birthday: 6/11/45

Barbiera, Paula
PO Box 20483
Panama City, FL 32411
*Model, O. J. Simpson's ex-
girlfriend*

Bardot, Brigitte
La Madrague
83990
St. Tropez
France
Actress
Birthday: 9/28/34

**Barker, Bob (Robert William
Barker)**
5757 Wilshire Blvd., #206
Los Angeles, CA 90036
Host of "The Price Is Right"
Birthday: 12/12/23

Barker, Clive
PO Box 691885
West Hollywood, CA 90069
Author

Barkin, Ellen
c/o Creative Artists Agency
9830 Wilshire Blvd.
Beverly Hills, CA 90212
Actress
Birthday: 4/16/54

Barkley, Charles
10 Greenway Plaza E.
Houston, TX 77277
Basketball player

Barlow, Gary
c/o BMG Records Ltd.
Bedford House
69–79 Fulham High St.
London SW6 4JW
England
*Musician, former member of
    Take That*
Birthday: 1/20/71

Barnard, Dr. Christian
Box 6143, Welgemoed 7538
Capetown
South Africa
Heart surgeon

Barnes, Binnie
838-B. N. Doheny Dr.
Los Angeles, CA 90069
Actress
Birthday: 3/25/?

Barnes, Priscilla
8428-C Melrose Pl.
W. Hollywood, CA 90069
Actress
Birthday: 12/7/56

Barnes & Noble
122 5th Ave.
New York, NY 10011
Web site: http://
    www.BarnesandNoble.com
Leonard Riggio, CEO
Bookseller

Barnett Banks
50 N. Laura St.
Jacksonville, FL 32202
Hugh L. McColl, Jr., CEO
Commercial bank

Barney
300 E. Bethany Rd.
Box 8000
Allen, TX 75002
Dinosaur

Baros, Dana
151 Merrimac St., 4th Fl.
Boston, MA 02114
*Boston Celtics guard (height 5'
    11")*
Birthday: 4/13/67

Barr, Julie
420 Madison Ave., #1400
New York, NY 10017
Actress

Barrichello, Rubens
c/o Stewart Grand Prix Ltd.
16 Tanners Dr.
Blakelands
Milton Keynes MK14 5BW
England
Professional Formula-1 driver

Barris, Chuck
17 E. 76th St.
New York, NY 10021
TV producer

Barrows, Sydney Biddle
210 W. 70th St.
New York, NY 10023
Alleged madam

Barry, Dave
1 Herald Plaza
Miami, FL 33101
E-mail:
    733314.722@compuserve.com
Humorist, columnist

Barry, Gene
10100 Santa Monica Blvd.,
    #2490
Los Angeles, CA 90067
Actor
Birthday: 6/14/22

Barry, Marion
161 Raleigh St. SE
Washington, DC 20032
Former mayor of Washington, DC
Birthday: 3/6/36

Barrymore, Drew
1122 S. Robertson Blvd., #15
Los Angeles, CA 90035
Actress
Birthday: 2/22/75

Baryshnikov, Mikhail
9830 Wilshire Blvd.
Beverly Hills, CA 90212
Ballet dancer, actor
Birthday: 1/28/48

Basinger, Kim
9830 Wilshire Blvd.
Beverly Hills, CA 90212
Actress
Birthday: 12/8/53

Bassey, Shirley
24 Ave. Princess Grace, #1200
Monte Carlo
Monaco
Singer
Birthday: 1/8/37

Bateman, Justine
11288 Ventura Blvd., #190
Studio City, CA 91604
Actress
Birthday: 2/19/66

Bates, The
Sickingerstr. 6–8
34117 Kassel
Germany
Music group

Bates, Kathy (Kathleen Doyle Bates)
121 N. San Vicente Blvd.
Beverly Hills, CA 90211
Actress
Birthday: 6/28/48

Battle, Kathleen
165 W. 57th St.
New York, NY 10019
Opera singer
Birthday: 8/13/48

Baxter, Meredith
151 El Camino Dr.
Beverly Hills, CA 90212
or
10100 Santa Santa Monica
  Blvd., #700
Los Angeles, CA 90067
Actress
Birthday: 6/21/47

Baxter International
1 Baxter Pkwy.
Deerfield, IL 60015
Web site: http://
  www.baxter.com
Vernon R. Loucks, Jr., CEO
Scientific, photo, control equipment

"Baywatch"
5433 Beethoven St.
Los Angeles, CA 90066
Web site: http://
  www.baywatchtv.com/
E-mail:
  feedback@baywatchtv.com
TV series

Bay City Rollers
27 Preston Grange Rd.
Preston Pans E.
Lothian
Scotland
Rock band

Bayh, Birch
1575 I St. NW, #1025
Washington, DC 20005
Former senator

Bazelon Center for Mental Health Law
1101 15th St. NW, #1212
Washington, DC 20005
Web site: http://
  www.bazelon.org/
E-mail: bazelon@nicom.com
*Legal advocacy for the civil rights
  and human dignity of people
  with mental disability*

Beach Boys, The
Brother Entertainment
4860 San Jacinto Cir., #F
Fallbrook, CA 92028
Music group

Beals, Jennifer
14755 Ventura Blvd., #710
Sherman Oaks, CA 91403
Actress
Birthday: 12/19/63

Beard, Amanda
1 Olympic Plaza
Colorado Springs, CO 80909
Olympic gold medalist swimmer

Bear Stearns
245 Park Ave.
New York, NY 10167
Web site: http://
   www.bearstearns.com
James E. Cayne, CEO
Securities

Beastie Boys
c/o Morris
1325 Ave. of the Americas
New York, NY 10019
Rap group

Beatty, Warren (Henry Warren Beaty)
9830 Wilshire Blvd.
Beverly Hills, CA 90212
Actor, Shirley MacLaine's brother
Birthday: 3/30/37

Beavis & Butt-Head
1515 Broadway, #400
New York, NY 10036

Beck
c/o Geffen Records
9130 Sunset Blvd.
Los Angeles, CA 90069
Music group

Beck, Marilyn
PO Box 11079
Beverly Hills, CA 90210
Columnist, critic

Beck, Rufus
Lamontstr. 9
81679 München
Germany
Actor

Becker, Boris
Nusslocherstr. 51
65181 Leimen
Germany
Tennis player
Birthday: 11/22/67

Becton Dickinson
1 Becton Dr.
Franklin Lakes, NJ 07417
Web site: http://www.bd.com
Clateo Castellini, CEO
Scientific, photo, control equipment

Bed & Breakfast
c/o Live Music and
   Entertainment
Rothenbaumchaussee 209
20149 Hamburg
Germany
Music Group

Bedelia, Bonnie
c/o ICM
8942 Wilshire Blvd.
Beverly Hills, CA 90211
Actress

Bee Gees, The
20505 U.S. Hwy. 19 N., #12–290
Clearwater, FL 33764
Web: http://www.beegees.net
E-mail: beegees@beegees.net
Music group

Beene, Geoffrey
550 7th Ave.
New York, NY 10018
Fashion designer

Begley, Ed, Jr.
Sterling/Winters Company
1900 Ave. of the Stars, #1640
Los Angeles, CA 90067
Actor
Birthday: 9/16/49

Bell, Archie
PO Box 11669
Knoxville, TN 37939
Singer

Bell, Catherine
c/o JAG Productions
5555 Melrose Ave.
Mae West Bldg., #152
Los Angeles, CA 90038
Actress

Bell, Darryl
9255 Sunset Blvd., #515
W. Hollywood, CA 90069
Actor

Bell, Felicia
"General Hospital"
c/o ABC-TV
4151 Prospect Ave.
Hollywood, CA 90027
Actress

Bell, Wendell
Yale University
PO Box 208265
New Haven, CT 06520
*Professor emeritus of sociology at
    Yale University, and author of*
Foundations of Future
Studies, *Volumes 1
    and 2*

Bellamy Brothers
PO Box #801
San Antonio, FL 33576
or
13917 Restless Ln.
Dade City, FL 33525
Country music group

Bell Atlantic
1095 6th Ave.
New York, NY 10036
Web site: http://
    www.bellatlantic.com
Raymond W. Smith, CEO
Telecommunications

Bellini
Schulterblatt 58
20357 Hamburg
Germany
Music group

BellSouth
1155 Peachtree St. NE
Atlanta, GA 30309
Web site: http://
    www.bellsouthcorp.com
F. Duane Ackerman, CEO
Telecommunications

Belmondo, Jean-Paul
9 rue des Sts.-Peres
75006 Paris
France
Actor
4/9/?

Belushi, Jim
8033 Sunset Blvd., #88
Los Angeles, CA 90046
Actor

Belzer, Richard
9000 Sunset Blvd., #1200
Los Angeles, CA 90069
Comedian, actor

Benatar, Pat
26644 30th St.
Santa Monica, CA 90403
Singer
Birthday: 1/19/52

Beneficial
301 N. Walnut St.
Wilmington, DE 19801
Web site: http://
    www.bnlcorp.com
Finn M. W. Caspersen, CEO
Financial corporation

Ben Folds Five
PO Box 1028
Chapel Hill, NC 27514-1028
Web site: http://
  www.bffweb.com
E-mail: bffmail@aol.com
Music group

Benji
242 N. Canon Dr.
Beverly Hills, CA 90210
Acting dog

Bennett, Cornelius
Buffalo Bills
1 Bills Dr.
Orchard Park, NY 14127
Football player

Benson, George
Turner Management Group
3500 W. Olive Ave., #900
Burbank, CA 91505
Singer
Birthday: 3/2/43

Benson, Jodi
c/o Special Artists Agency
345 N. Maple Dr., #302
Beverly Hills, CA 90210
Attn: Marcia Hurwitz
Actress

Benson, Joe
PO Box 12464
La Crescenta, CA 91224
Web site: http://
  www.unclejoe.com
Los Angeles radio personality

Benson, Robby (Robby Segal)
PO Box 1305
Woodland Hills, CA 91364
Actor, writer, director
Birthday: 1/21/55

Berenger, Tom
PO Box 1842
Beaufort, SC 29901
Actor
5/31/50

Berg, Matraca
c/o Darin Murphy
The William Morris Agency
2100 West End Avenue
Nashville, TN 37203
Web site: www.matraca.com
*1997 Country Music Awards
  award winner*

Bergen, Candice
151 El Camino Dr.
Beverly Hills, CA 90212
Actress
Birthday: 5/9/46

Bergen Brunswick
4000 Metropolitan Dr.
Orange, CA 92868
Web site: http://
  www.bergenbrunswig.com
Donald R. Roden, CEO
Health care supplier

Berger, Gerhard
c/o Benetton Formula Ltd.
Whiteways Technical Centre
Enstone
Chipping Norton
Oxon OX7 4EE
England
Professional Formula-1 driver

Berkeley, Elizabeth
12400 Ventura Blvd., #122
Studio City, CA 91604
Actress

Berkowitz, David
#78A1976
Sullivan Corr. Fac., Box AG
Fallsburg, NY 12733
Convicted killer, "Son of Sam"
Birthday: 6/1/53

Berkshire Hathaway
1440 Kiewit Plaza
Omaha, NE 68131
Warren E. Buffett, CEO
P & C insurance (stock)

Berle, Milton
10750 Wilshire Blvd., #1003
Los Angeles, CA 90024
Comedian, actor
Birthday: 7/12/08

Bernadotte, Princess Marianne
Villagatan 10
Stockholm
Sweden

**Bernadotte af Wisborg Count
   Lennart**
Insel Mainau
78465
Konstanz
Germany
Honorary President, Professor
   Count Lennart Bernadotte
   of Wisborg, Mainau Castle of
   the Committee for the
   Meetings of Nobel Laureates
   in Lindau

Bernard, Crystal
10866 Wilshire Blvd.
Los Angeles, CA 90024
Actress

Bernsen, Corbin
3500 W. Olive, #920
Burbank, CA 91505
Actor

Berra, Yogi
PO Box 462
Caldwell, NJ 07006
Former baseball player

Berry, Chuck
Berry Park
Buckner Rd.
Wentzville, MO 63385
Singer, songwriter
Birthday: 10/18/26

John Berry's Pack
1807 N. Dixie, Ste. 116
Elizabethtown, KY 42701
Country music fan club

Berry, Ken
4704 Cahuenga Blvd.
North Hollywood, CA 91602
Actor
Birthday: 11/3/33

Bertinelli, Valerie
12711 Ventura Blvd., #490
Studio City, CA 91604
Actress
Birthday: 4/23/60

Besson, Luc
c/o Les Films du Dolphin
25 rue Ives Toudic
75010 Paris
France
Film director
Birthday: 3/18/59

Best, James
PO Box 621027
Oviedo, FL 32762
Actor
Birthday: 7/26/26

Best, Pete
8 Hyman's Green
W. Derby
Liverpool 12
England
Former Beatle
Birthday: 11/24/41

Best Buy
7075 Flying Cloud Dr.
Eden Prairie, MN 55344
Web site: http://
   www.bestbuy.com
Richard M. Schulze, CEO
Electronics retailer

Best Foods
700 Sylvan Ave.
Englewood Cliffs, NJ 07632
Web site: http://
   www.bestfoods.com
Charles R. Shoemate, CEO
Food producer

Bethlehem Steel
1170 8th Ave.
Bethlehem, PA 18016
Web site: http://
  www.bethsteel.com
Curtis H. Barnette, CEO
Metals

Beverly Enterprises
1200 S. Waldron Rd.
Fort Smith, AR 72903
Web site: http://
  www.beverlynet.com
David R. Banks, CEO
Health care

Beverly Hills Hotel, The
9641 Sunset Blvd.
Beverly Hills, CA 90210
(310) 276-2251
Hotel

B. F. Goodrich
4020 Kinross Lakes Pkwy.
Richfield, OH 44286
Web site: http://
  www.bfgoodrich.com
David L. Burner, CEO
Aerospace

B-52's, The
PO Box 60468
Rochester, NY 14606
Music group

B. G. Prince of Rap
c/o Allstars Music
Hundshager Weg 30
68623 Hofheim
Germany
Rap artist

Bhumibol Adulyadej, King
Villa Chitralada
Bangkok
Thailand
King of Thailand

Biafra, Jello (Eric Boucher)
PO Box 419092
San Francisco, CA 94141
*Former lead singer of the punk
  rock band Dead Kennedys*

Bialik, Mayim
8942 Wilshire Blvd.
Beverly Hills, CA 90211
Actress
Birthday: 12/12/75

Biffi, Giacomo Cardinal
Archives Covado
Via Altabella 6
40126 Bologna
Italy
Cardinal

Biggs-Dawson, Roxann
1999 Ave. of the Stars, #2850
Los Angeles, CA 90067
*Actress, plays Lt. B'Elanna Torres
  on "Star Trek: Voyager"*

Big Mountain
c/o Giant Records
8900 Wilshire Blvd., #200
Beverly Hills, CA 90211
Music group

Bijan
699 5th Ave.
New York, NY 10022
Fashion designer

Bikel, Theodore
1131 Alta Loma, Ste. 523
W. Hollywood, CA 90069
Musician
Birthday: 5/2/24

Billingsley, Barbara
PO Box 1588
Pacific Palisades, CA 90272
*Actress, played Beaver's mother on
  "Leave It to Beaver"*
Birthday: 12/22/22

Bindley Western
10333 N. Meridian St.
Indianapolis, IN 46290
Web site: http://
 www.bindley.com
William E. Bindley, CEO
*Largest wholesale distributors of
 pharmaceuticals, health and
 beauty care products, and home
 health care products in the
 United States*

Bingham, Traci
5433 Beethoven St.
Los Angeles, CA 90066
Actress on "Baywatch"

Bird, Larry
RR #1 Box 77A
West Baden Springs, IN 47469
Indiana Pacers basketball coach
Birthday: 12/7/56

Bishop, Stephen
c/o Miles Hymes
18321 Ventura Blvd., #580
Tarzana, CA 91356
Singer/Songwriter

Bisset, Jacqueline
c/o Guttman Associates
118 S. Beverly Dr.
Beverly Hills, CA 90212
Actress

B.J.'s Wholesale Club
1 Mercer Rd.
Natick, MA 01760
Web site: http://
 www.bjswholesale.com
John J. Nugent, CEO
Food and drug stores

Black, Clint
PO Box 299386
Houston, TX 77299
or
6255 Sunset Blvd., #111
Hollywood, CA 90028
Country singer, songwriter
Birthday: 2/4/62

Black, Karen (Karen Ziegler)
3500 W. Olive Ave., #1400
Burbank, CA 91505
Actress
Birthday: 7/1/42

Black & Decker
701 E. Joppa Rd.
Towson, MD 21286
Web site: http://
 www.blackanddecker.com
Nolan D. Archibald, CEO
*Tools, industrial and farm
 equipment*

Black Crowes, The
888 7th Ave., #602
New York, NY 10107
Music group

Blackhawk
PO Box 121804
Nashville, TN 37212
Country music group

Black Oak Arkansas
1487 Red Fox Run
Lilburn, GA 30247
Music group

Blackstone, Harry, Jr.
11075 Santa Monica Blvd.,
 #275
Los Angeles, CA 90025
Magician

Blackwood, Nina
c/o Angelwood
23705 Vanowen St., #111
West Hills, CA 91307
Singer

Blair, Linda
8033 Sunset Blvd., #204
Los Angeles, CA 90046
Actress
Birthday: 1/22/59

Blair, Tony
10 Downing St.
London SW1
England
Prime Minister of Great Britain

Blakely, Susan
N. Rodeo Dr., #15–111
Beverly Hills, CA 90210
Actress
Birthday: 9/7/50

Blakley, Ronee
8033 Sunset Blvd., #693
Los Angeles, CA 90046
Actress, singer

Blanda, George
PO Box 1153
LaQuinta, CA 92253
Former football player

Blass, Bill
550 7th Ave.
New York, NY 10018
Fashion designer
Birthday: 6/22/22

Blasters, The
555 Chorro St., #A-1
San Luis Obispo, CA 93401
Rock band

Bledsoe, Drew
c/o New England Patriots
Route 1
Foxboro, MA 02035
Football player

Bledsoe, Tempestt
PO Box 7217
Beverly Hills, CA 90212
Actress
Birthday: 8/1/73

Blood, Sweat & Tears
43 Washington St.
Groveland, MA 021834
Music group

Bloodsworth-Thomason, Linda
9220 Sunset Blvd., #311
Los Angeles, CA 90069
Film producer

Blount, Lisa
5750 Wilshire Blvd., #580
Los Angeles, CA 90036
Actress

Blount, Mel
RD 1 Box 91
Claysville, PA 15323
Former football player

Blow Monkeys
370 City Rd.
London EC1 V2QA
England
Music group

Blue, Vida
PO Box 1449
Pleasanton, CA 94566
*Former baseball player; charges $9
    for trading card, $5 for 3×5*

Blues Traveler
PO Box 1128
New York, NY 10101
Home page: http://
    www.bluestraveler.com
E-mail: blackcatz@earthlink.net
Rock band

Blue System
Metzendorfer Weg
21224 Rosengarten
Germany
Music group

Blume, Judy
40 E. 48th St., #100
New York, NY 10017
Author
Birthday: 2/12/38

Blur
20 Manchester Sq.
London W1A 1ES
England
Music group

Blyth, Ann
PO Box 9754
Rancho Santa Fe, CA 92067
Actress
Birthday: 8/16/28

Boaz, David
Cato Institute
1000 Massachusetts Avenue NW
Washington, DC 20001
E-mail: dboaz@cato.org
Author, executive vice president of the Cato Institute

Bobek, Nicole
c/o U.S. Figure Skating
  Association
20 1st St.
Colorado Springs, CO 80906
Figure skater

Bocho, Steven
10201 W. Pico Blvd.
Los Angeles, CA 90064
Producer, screenwriter
Birthday: 12/16/43

Boeing
7755 E. Marginal Way S.
Seattle, WA 98108
Web site: http://
  www.boeing.com
Philip M. Condit, CEO
Aerospace

Bogguss, Suzy
PO Box 7535
Marietta, GA 30065
Country singer

Bogues, Mugsy
c/o Golden State Warriors
Oakland Coliseum Arena
7000 Coliseum Way
Oakland, CA 94621
Basketball player

Boice, Dr. James
1935 Pine St.
Philadelphia, PA 19103
Theologian

Boise Cascade
1111 W. Jefferson St.
Boise, ID 83702
Web site: http://www.bc.com
George J. Harad, CEO
Forest and paper products

Bologna, Joseph
16830 Ventura Blvd., #326
Encino, CA 91436
Actor, writer, director
Birthday: 12/30/38

Bolton, Michael
PO Box 679
Branford, CT 06516
Singer
Birthday: 2/26/?

James Bonamy Fan Club
PO Box 587
Smyrna, TN 37167
Country music fan club

Bond, Samantha
Pebro House
13 St. Martin's Rd.
London SW9 0SP
England
Actress

Bonds, Barry
9595 Wilshire Blvd., #711
Beverly Hills, CA 90212
Baseball player

**Bonds, Gary "U.S" (Gary
  Anderson)**
2011 Ferry Ave., #U-19
Camden, NJ 08104
Singer
Birthday: 6/6/39

Bon Jovi
250 W. 57th St., #603
New York, NY 10107
Rock group

Bon Jovi, Jon (Jon Bongiovi)
250 W. 57th St., #603
New York, NY 10107
Rock singer
Birthday: 5/10/60

Bono (Paul Hewson)
4 Windmill Ln.
Dublin, 2
Ireland
Singer, songwriter
Birthday: 5/10/60

Bono, Chastity
PO Box 960
Beverly Hills, CA 90213
Sonny and Cher's daughter
Birthday: 3/4/69

Book of Love
12 Charles St., #5A
New York, NY 10019
Music group

Booker T & the MGs
59 Parsons St.
Newtonville, MA 02160
Music group

Boone, Larry
c/o Gene Ferguson
PO Box 23795
Nashville, TN 37212
Musician

Boone, Pat
9200 Sunset Blvd., #1007
Los Angeles, CA 90069
Singer
Birthday: 6/1/34

Betty Boop Fan Club
6024 Fullerton Ave., #2
Buena Park, CA 90621

Boothe, Powers
PO Box 9242
Calabasas, CA 91372
Actor

Boothroyd, Betty
House of Commons
London SW1A 0AA
England
*First woman speaker of the House
of Commons*

Borden
180 E. Broad St.
Columbus, OH 43215
C. Robert Kidder, CEO
Food producer

Borg, Bjorn
1 Eneview Plaza, #1300
Cleveland, OH 44144
Tennis player
Birthday: 6/7/56

Borge, Victor
Fieldpoint Park
Greenwich, CT 06830
Pianist, comedian
Birthday: 1/3/09

Boston
PO Box 6191
Lincoln Center, MA 01773
Music group

Bostwick, Barry
1640 S. Sepulveda Blvd., #218
Los Angeles, CA 90025
Actor
Birthday: 2/24/46

Bosworth, Brian
17383 Sunset Blvd., #250
Pacific Palisades, CA 90272
Actor
Birthday: 3/9/65

**Boston Modern Orchestra
Project**
PO Box 391342
Cambridge, MA 02139
Web site: http://www.bmop.org/
E-mail: bmop@bmop.org
Gil Rose, music director

Boston Symphony Orchestra/
Boston Pops Orchestra
Symphony Hall
Boston, MA 02115
Web site: http://www.bso.org/

Boucher, Phillippe
c/o Los Angeles Kings
3900 W. Manchester Blvd.
Inglewood, CA 90305
Hockey player

Boulez, Pierre
Psotlach 22
76481 Baden-Baden
Germany
Conductor, composer

Boutros-Ghali, Boutros
Ave. El nil
Giza
Cairo
Egypt
*Former secretary-general of the
United Nations*
Birthday: 11/14/22

Bowen, Christopher
37 Berwick St.
London W1V 3RF
England
Actor

Boxcar Willie
HCR 1, Box 7085
Branson, MO 65616
Country singer

Boxer, Barbara
2112 Hart Office Bldg.
Washington, DC 20510
California senator

Boxleitner, Bruce
PO Box 5513
Sherman Oaks, CA 91403
Actor
Birthday: 5/12/50

Boxtops, The
2011 Ferry Ave., #U-19
Camden, NJ 08104
Music group

Boy George (George O'Dowd)
7 Pepy's Court
84 The Chase
Clapham
London SW4 0NF
England
Singer, songwriter, author
Birthday: 6/14/61

Boy Howdy
c/o Club Howdy
PO Box 570784
Tarzana, CA 91357-0784
Country music group

Boyle, Peter
c/o Innovative Artists
1999 Ave. of the Stars, #2850
Los Angeles, CA 90067
Actor
Birthday: 1/18/33

Boyz, The
c/o Tripple-M-Musik
Postfach 38 01 49
14111 Berlin
Germany
Music group

Boyzone
9 Whitefriars Aungier St.
Dublin, 2
Ireland
Music group

Boyz II Men
5750 Wilshire Blvd., #300
Los Angeles, CA 90036
Vocal group

• **Bozo the Clown**
c/o WGN Television
2501 Bradley Place
Chicago, IL 60618

Bracco, Lorraine
130 W. 57th St., #5E
New York, NY 10019
Actress
Birthday: 11/30/54

Bradford, Barbara Taylor
450 Park Ave.
New York, NY 10022
Author

Bradlee, Benjamin
3014 N St. NW
Washington, DC 20007
Journalist

Bradley, Ed
c/o "60 Minutes"
555 W. 57th St.
New York, NY 10019
News correspondent

Bradshaw, John
2412 South Blvd.
Houston, TX 77098
*Lecturer and author of self-
improvement books*

Brady, James
1255 I St. NW, #1100
Washington, DC 20005
Former White House press secretary

Brady, Sarah
1255 I St. NW, #100
Washington, DC 20005
Gun control advocate

Branagh, Kenneth
10100 Santa Monica Blvd.,
25th Fl.
Los Angeles, CA 90067
Actor, director
Birthday: 12/10/60

Brandis, Jonathan
11684 Ventura Blvd., #909
Studio City, CA 91604
Actor

Paul Brandt Fan Club
Box 57144 Sunridge Postal
Outlet
Calgary, AB TIV 5TO
Canada
Country singer

Brand X
17171 Roscoe Blvd., #104
Northridge, CA 91325
Music group

Braxton, Toni
3350 Peachtree Rd., #1500
Atlanta, GA 30326
Singer
Birthday: 1968

**Bread for the World/BFW
Institute**
1100 Wayne Ave., #1000
Silver Spring, MD 20910
Web site: http://www.bread.org/
*Citizens' movement seeking justice
for the world's hungry people by
lobbying our nation's decision
makers*

Bream, Julian
122 Wigmore St.
London W1
England
Guitarist

**Brechner Center for Freedom
of Information**
University of Florida
3208 Weimer Hall
PO Box 118400
Gainesville, FL 32611-8400
E-mail: bchamber@jou.ufl.edu
or schance@jou.ufl.edu

Breeders, The
3575 Cahuenga Blvd. W., #450
Los Angeles, CA 90068
Music group

Breedlove, Craig
PO Box 194
Novi, MI 48376
Land speed record setter

Brennan, Eileen
15302 Ventura Blvd., #345
Sherman Oaks, CA 91403
Actress
Birthday: 9/03/35

Brenneman, Amy
9150 Wilshire Blvd., #175
Beverly Hills, CA 90212
Actress
Birthday: 2/4/45

Brenner, David
17 E. 16th St., #3
New York, NY 10003
Comedian
Birthday: 2/4/45

Breslin, Jimmy
Newsday
2 Park Ave.
New York, NY 10016
Author, columnist

Brett, George
PO Box 419969
Kansas City, MO 64141
Former baseball player
Birthday: 5/15/53

BR5-49
9830 Wilshire Blvd.
Beverly Hills, CA 90212
Music group

BR5-49 Fan Club
PO Box 23288
Nashville, TN 37202
Country music fan club

Bridges, Elisa
Playboy Productions
9242 Beverly Blvd.
Beverly Hills, CA 90210
Model

Bridges, Jeff
11661 San Vicente Blvd., #910
Los Angeles, CA 90049
Actor

Bridges, Todd
3518 Cahuenga Blvd. W., #216
Los Angeles, CA 90068
Actor
Birthday: 5/27/65

Bright, Dr. Bill
515 N. Cabrillo Park Dr., #225
Santa Ana, CA 92701
Evangelist

Brill, Charlie
c/o Irv Schechter Agency
9300 Wilshire Blvd., #400
Beverly Hills, CA 90212
Actor

Brillstein, Bernie
Brillstein-Grey Enterprises
9150 Wilshire Blvd.
Beverly Hills, CA 90212
Theatrical and literary agent

Brimley, Wilford
415 N. Camden Dr., Ste. 121
Beverly Hills, CA 90210
Actor
Birthday: 9/27/34

Brinkley, Christie
PO Box 5060
East Hampton, NY 11937
Model, actress
Birthday: 2/2/54

Bristol-Meyers Squibb
345 Park Ave.
New York, NY 10154
Web site: http://www.bms.com
Charles A. Heimbold, Jr., CEO
Pharmaceuticals

Broadcast Music, Inc. (BMI), London
84 Harley House
Marylebone Rd.
London NW1 5HN
England
Web site: http://www.bmi.com/
Music licensing organization

Broadcast Music, Inc. (BMI), Los Angeles
8730 Sunset Blvd., 3rd Fl.
West Los Angeles, CA 90046
Web site: http://www.bmi.com/
Robert Barone, vice president, Operations and Information Technology
E-mail: infotech@bmi.com
Music licensing organization

Broadcast Music, Inc. (BMI), Nashville
10 Music Sq. E.
Nashville, TN 37203
Web site: http://www.bmi.com/
Music licensing organization

Broadcast Music, Inc. (BMI), New York
320 W. 57th St.
New York, NY 10019
Web site: http://www.bmi.com/
Music licensing organization

Broderick, Beth
9300 Wilshire Blvd., #555
Beverly Hills, CA 90212
Actress

Broderick, Matthew
PO Box 69646
Los Angeles, CA 90069
Actor
Birthday: 3/21/62

Brokaw, Tom (Thomas John Brokaw)
NBC News
30 Rockefeller Plaza
New York, NY 10112
E-mail: nightly@nbc.com
Television broadcast executive, correspondent

Brolin, James
PO Box 56927
Sherman Oaks, CA 91413
Actor

Bronson, Charles
PO Box 2644
Malibu, CA 90265
Actor

Brooklyn Bridge
PO Box 63
Cliffwood, NJ 07721
Music group

Brooks, Albert (Albert Einstein)
1880 Century Park E., #900
Los Angeles, CA 90067
Actor, writer, director
Birthday: 7/22/47

Brooks, Foster
315 S. Beverly Dr., #2116
Beverly Hills, CA 90212
Comedian

Brooks, Garth (Troyal Garth Brooks)
3322 W. End Ave., #1100
Nashville, TN 37203
Country singer
Birthday: 2/7/62

Brooks, James L.
8942 Wilshire Blvd.
Beverly Hills, CA 90211
Producer, director, screenwriter
Birthday: 5/9/40

Brooks & Dunn
PO Box 120669
Nashville, TN 37212-0669
Country music duo

Brosnan, Pierce
PO Box 982
Malibu, CA 90265
Actor

Brother, Phelps
PO Box 849
Goodlettsville, TN 37070
Country singer

Brothers, Dr. Joyce
235 E. 45th St.
New York, NY 10017
TV personality, psychologist
Birthday: 10/20/28

Brothers Four, The
1221 Scott Rd.
Burbank, CA 91504
Music group

Brown, Bryan
110 Queen St.
Woollahra, NSW 2025
Australia
Actor
Birthday: 6/23/47

Brown, Denise
PO Box 380
Monarch Bay, CA 92629
Nicole Brown-Simpson's sister

Brown, Georg Stanford
c/o International Artists
8033 Sunset Blvd., #1800
Los Angeles, CA 90046
Actor

Brown, Helen Gurley
1 W. 81st St., #220
New York, NY 10024
Magazine editor

Brown, Jim
1851 Sunset Plaza Dr.
Los Angeles, CA 90069
Actor, former football player
Birthday: 2/17/36

Brown, Jim Ed
PO Box 121089
Nashville, TN 37212
Country singer

Brown, Julie
11288 Ventura Blvd., #728
Studio City, CA 91604
Actress

Brown, Junior
PO Box 180763
Utica, MI 48318
Country music singer

Brown, Marty
PO Box 70
Maceo, KY 42355
Country music singer

Brown, Olivia
c/o David Shapira & Associates
15301 Ventura Blvd., Ste. 345
Sherman Oaks, CA 91403
Actress

Brown, T. Graham
1516 16th Ave. S.
Nashville, TN 37212
Country music singer

Brown, Willie, Jr.
401 Van Ness Ave., #336
San Francisco, CA 94102
E-mail: DaMayor @ci.sf.ca.us
Mayor of San Francisco

Browne, Jann
PO Box 3481
Laguna Hills, CA 92654
Country singer

Browne, Sylvia
35 Dillon Ave.
Campbell, CA 95008
Psychic

Browning, Kurt
11160 River Valley Rd., #3189
Edmonton, AB T5J 2G7
Canada
Ice skater

Browning Ferris Industries
757 N. Eldridge Rd.
Houston, TX 77079
Web site: http://www.bfi.com
Bruce E. Ranck, CEO
Waste management

Bruce, Ed
PO Box 120428
Nashville, TN 37212
Country music singer

Brunswick
1 N. Field Court
Lake Forest, IL 60045
Peter N. Larson, CEO
Transportation equipment

Buchanan, James M.
George Mason University
4400 University Dr.
Fairfax, Virginia 22030
*1986 Nobel Prize winner in
economic science, best known for
such works as* Fiscal Theory
and Political Economy, The
Calculus of Consent, The
Limits of Liberty, Democracy
in Deficit, The Power to
Tax, *and* The Reason of
Rules

Buckinghams, The
620 16th Ave.
S. Hopkins, MN 55343
Music group

Buckley, Betty
420 Madison Ave., #1400
New York, NY 10017
Actress
Birthday: 7/3/47

Buckley, William F., Jr.
150 E. 35th St.
New York, NY 10016
Author, editor
Birthday: 11/24/25

Buffett, Jimmy
c/o Coconut Telegraph
424 A Fleming St.
Key West, FL 33040
*Pop singer; his fans are called
"Parrot Heads"*

Bullock, Sandra
9560 Wilshire Blvd., #500
Beverly Hills, CA 90212
Actress

Bunning, Jim
c/o Baseball Hall of Fame
PO Box 590
Cooperstown, NY 13326
Former baseball player

Bure, Pavel
c/o Vancouver Canucks
100 N. Renfrew St.
Vancouver, BC V5K 3N7
Canada
Hockey player

Burghoff, Gary
9911 W. Pico Blvd., #1200
Los Angeles, CA 90035
or
PO Box 1603
Magalia, CA 95994
Actor

Burke, Delta
1012 Royal St.
New Orleans, LA 70116
Actress
Birthday: 7/30/56

Burlington Northern Santa Fe
2650 Lou Menk Dr.
Fort Worth, TX 76131
Web site: http://www.bnsf.com
Robert D. Krebs, CEO
Railroads

Burnette, Billy
1025 16th Ave. S., Ste. 401
Nashville, TN 37212
Country music singer

Burnett, Carol
PO Box 1298
Pasadena, CA 91031
Actress, comedian

Burnin' Daylight Fan Club
PO Box 180763
Utica, MI 48318
Country music fan club

Burns, Ken
Maple Grove Rd.
Walpole, NH 03608
Documentary filmmaker

Burstyn, Ellen
PO Box 217
Palisades, NY 10964
Actress

Burton, LeVar
Paramount Pictures
15 Columbus Cir., 29th Fl.
New York, NY 10023
or
13601 Ventura Blvd., #209
Sherman Oaks, CA 91423
Actor
Birthday: 2/16/57

Busey, Gary
12424 Wilshire Blvd., #840
Los Angeles, CA 90025
Actor

Bush
10900 Wilshire Blvd., #1230
Los Angeles, CA 90024
Music group

Bush, President George and Barbara
PO Box 79798
Houston, TX 77279
or
9 W. Oak Dr.
Houston, TX 77056
Former President and First Lady
Birthday: Barbara Bush 1/28/25
Birthday: George Bush 1/12/24

Business-Industry Political Action Committee (BIPAC)
1747 Pennsylvania Ave. NW, #250
Washington, DC 20006
Political action committee

Butkus, Dick
c/o Excalibur Marketing Group
523 W. Chapman Ave., #110
Anaheim, CA 92802
Attn: Paula Maki
Former football player

Butler, Brett
PO Box 5617
Beverly Hills, CA 90210
Actress

Butler, Robert
c/o William Morris Agency
151 El Camino Dr.
Beverly Hills, CA 90212
Film director

Buzzi, Ruth
c/o "Sesame Street" (CTW)
1 Lincoln Plaza
New York, NY 10023
Comedian

Byner, Jon
9363 Wilshire Blvd., #212
Beverly Hills, CA 90210
Comedian

Tracy Byrd Fan Club
"Byrd Watchers"
PO Box 7703
Beaumont, TX 77726
Country music fan club

C

A telephone call from a friend is joy—unless you're in the middle of a meal, having a bath or on the point of going out to an engagement for which you are already late. A letter in effect is saying, "I am setting aside some of my time for you alone; I'm thinking of you. This is more important to me than anything that I am doing."

—JOHN GREENALL, *Daily Telegraph*

Caan, James
PO Box 6646
Denver, CO 80206
Actor
Birthday: 3/25/39

Caballe, Montserrat
Via Augusta
59, Barcelona, 08006
Spain
Opera singer

Cactus Brothers
PO Box 120316
Nashville, TN 37212
Country music group

Caesar
Hotel Park Sheraton
870 7th Ave.
New York, NY 10019
Lyricist, composer

Cage, Nicolas (Nicolas Coppola)
PO Box 69646
Los Angeles, CA 90069
Actor
Birthday: 1/7/64

Cain, Dean
9830 Wilshire Blvd.
Beverly Hills, CA 90211
Actor

Caine, Michael
Rectory Farm House
North Stoke
Oxfordshire
England
Actor
Birthday: 3/14/33

California Raisins
PO Box 5335
Fresno, CA 93755
Commercial spokesmen

Callas, Charlie
PO Box 67-B-69
Los Angeles, CA 90067
Comedian, actor
Birthday: 11/30/64

Calley, Lt. William
c/o V. V. Vicks
Cross Country Plaza
Columbus, GA 31906
Involved in the My Lai massacre

Cameron, Candace
PO Box 8665
Calabasas, CA 91372
Actress

Cameron, Kirk
PO Box 8665
Calabasas, CA 91372
Actor
Birthday: 10/12/70

Camp, Shawn
PO Box 121972
Nashville, TN 37212
Country music singer

Campaign for an Effective Crime Policy
918 F St. NW, #505
Washington, DC 20004
Web site: http://
   www.sproject.com/cecp.htm
E-mail: info@crimepolicy.com
Launched in 1992 by a nonpartisan group of criminal justice leaders; encourages a less politicized, more informed debate about one of our nation's most difficult problems

Campaign for U.N. Reform
713 D St. SE
Washington, DC 20003
Web site: http://www.cunr.org/
E-mail: cunr@aol.com

Campbell, Bruce
14431 Ventura Blvd., #120
Sherman Oaks, CA 91423
Actor

Bruce Campbell International Fan Club
BC Central
8205 Santa Monica Blvd., #1-287
Los Angeles, CA 90046
Please include a self-addressed stamped envelope or E-mail janholbrk@aol.com for information.

Campbell, Glen
10351 Santa Monica Blvd., #300
Los Angeles, CA 90025
Singer, songwriter
Birthday: 4/22/36

Campbell, J. Kenneth
9150 Wilshire Blvd. #175
Beverly Hills, CA 90212
Actor

Campbell, Kim
275 Slater St., #600
Ottawa, ON K1P 5H9
Canada
Former Prime Minister of Canada

Campbell, Naomi
Ford Model Management
344 E. 59th St.
New York, NY 10022
Model

Campbell, Neve
c/o "Party of Five"
PO Box 900
Beverly Hills, CA 90213
Actress

Campbell, Stacy Dean
1099 Church St., Ste. 102
Nashville, TN 37203
Country singer

Campbell, Tisha
5750 Wilshire Blvd., #640
Los Angeles, CA 90036
Actress

Campbell Soup
Campbell Pl.
Camden, NJ 08103
Web site: http://
   www.campbellsoups.com
Dale F. Morrison, CEO
Food manufacturer

C&C Music Factory
1700 Broadway, #500
New York, NY 10019
Music group

Candiotti, Tom
c/o Los Angeles Dodgers
1000 Elysian Park Ave.
Los Angeles, CA 90012
Baseball player

Canned Heat
PO Box 3773
San Rafael, CA 94912
Music group

Cannell, Steven J.
7083 Hollywood Blvd.
Hollywood, CA 90028
Author, TV producer

Cannon, Dyan
10351 Santa Monica Blvd.,
#211
Los Angeles, CA 90025
Actress

Cannon, J. D.
9255 Sunset Blvd., # 515
Los Angeles, CA 90069
Actor

Canova, Diana
1800 Ave. of the Stars, #400
Los Angeles, CA 90067
Actress

Canyon
Encore Entertainment
PO Box 1259
Dallas, TX 75065
Country music group

Canyon, Christy
13601 Ventura Blvd.,#218
Sherman Oaks, CA 91423
Actress

Capra, Francis
c/o William Morris Agency
1325 Ave. of the Americas
New York, NY 10019
Actor

Capshaw, Kate
PO Box 869
Pacific Palisades, CA 90272
Actress

Captain and Tennille
PO Box 608
Zephyr Cove, NV 89448
Singing duo

Cara, Irene
8033 Sunset Blvd., #735
Los Angeles, CA 90046
Actress
Birthday: 3/18/59

Cardin, Pierre
59 Rue du Foubourg
St. Honore
75008 Paris
France
Fashion designer
Birthday: 7/7/22

Cardinal Health
5555 Glendon Court
Dublin, OH 43016
Robert D. Walter, CEO
Wholesaler

CARE
151 Ellis St.
Atlanta, GA 30303
Web site: http://www.care.org./
E-mail: info@care.org
*Works to affirm the dignity and
   worth of individuals and
   families in some of the poorest
   communities of the world*

Carey, Harry, Jr.
PO Box 3256
Durango, CO 81302
Actor

Carey, Mariah
PO Box 4450
New York, NY 10101
Singer
Birthday: 3/26/70

Carey, Philip
56 W. 66th St.
New York, NY 10023
Actor

Carlson, Paulette
PO Box 1114
Arvada, CO 80001
Country singer

Carlton, Steve
PO Box 736
Durango, CO 81302
Former baseball player

Carney, Art
RR #20 Box 911
Westbrook, CT 06498
Actor

Carolina Power & Light
411 Fayetteville St.
Raleigh, NC 27602
Web site: http://www.cplc.com
William Cavanaugh III, CEO
Gas and electric utilities

Princess Caroline
80 Ave. Foch
75016 Paris
France
Princess of Monaco
Birthday: 1/23/57

Carpenter, Mary Chapin
7003 Carroll Ave.
Takoma Park, MD 20912
Country singer

Carpenter, Richard
PO Box 1084
Downey, CA 90240
Singer

Carpenter, Scott
PO Box 3161
Vail, CO 81658
Former astronaut

Carr, Vikki
PO Box 780968
San Antonio, TX 78278
Singer
Birthday: 7/19/41

Carradine, Keith
PO Box 460
Placerville, CO 81430
Actor
Birthday: 8/8/49

Carrera, Barbara
PO Box 7876
Beverly Hills, CA 90212
Actress

Carrey, Jim
PO Box 57593
Sherman Oaks, CA 91403
Actor
Birthday: 1/17/62

Carroll, Diahann
PO Box 2999
Beverly Hills, CA 90213
Actress

Carrot Top
c/o Carrot Top, Inc.
Disney-MGM Studios
Lake Buena Vista, FL 32830
Comedian

Carson, Jeff
PO Box 121056
Nashville, TN 37212
Country music singer

Jeff Carson International Fan Club
PO Box 121056
Nashville, TN 37212
Country music fan club

Carter, Carlene
PO Box 120845
Nashville, TN 37212
Country music singer

Carter, Dixie
PO Box 1980
Studio City, CA 91614
Actress

Carter, Jack
11365 Ventura Blvd., #100
Studio City, CA 91604
Comedian

Carter, June
Rt. 12, Box 350
Winston-Salem, NC 27107
Country music singer
Birthday: 6/22/29

Carter, Lynda
PO Box 5973
Sherman Oaks, CA 91413
Actress

Carter, Nell
8484 Wilshire Blvd., #500
Beverly Hills, CA 90211
Actress

Cartland, Barbara
Camfield Place
Hatfield
Hertfordshire
England
Romance writer—over 600 books
Birthday: 7/9/01

Cartwright, Angela
10143 Riverside Dr.
Toluca Lake, CA 91602
Actress

Cartwright, Lionel
27 Music Sq. E., #182
Nashville, TN 37203
Country singer

Carville, James
209 Pennsylvania Ave. SE,#800
Washington, DC 20003
Political commentator

Casals, Rosie
PO Box 537
Sausalito, CA 94966
Tennis player

Case
700 State St.
Racine, WI 53404
Web site: http://
   www.casecorp.com
Jean-Pierre Rosso, CEO
Industrial and farm equipment

Cash, Johnny
Rt. 12, Box 350
Winston-Salem, NC 27107
Country singer
Birthday: 2/26/32

Cash, Rosalind
PO Box 1605
Topanga, CA 90290
Actress

Cash, Rosanne
Side One
1775 Broadway, 7th Fl.
New York, NY 11019
Country singer
Birthday: 5/24/55

Caterpillar
100 N. E. Adams St.
Peoria, IL 61629
Web site: http://
   www.caterpillar.com
Donald V. Fites, CEO
Industrial and farm equipment

Catholics for Free Choice
1436 U St. NW, #301
Washington, DC 20009
Web site: http://
   www.cath4choice.org/
E-mail: cffc@igc.apc.org
Frances Kissling, president
*An independent nonprofit
   organization engaged in policy
   analysis, education, and
   advocacy on issues of gender
   equality and reproductive health*

Cato Institute
1000 Massachusetts Ave. NW
Washington, DC 20001
Web site: http://www.cato.org/
E-mail: cato@cato.org
Edward H. Crane, president
   and CEO
*Promoting public policy based on
   limited government, free
   markets, individual liberty, and
   peace*

Cavett, Dick
109 E. 79th St., #2C
New York, NY 10021
TV host
Birthday: 11/19/36

CBS
7800 Beverly Blvd.
Los Angeles, CA 90036
or
51 W. 52 St.
New York, NY 10019
Web site: http://www.cbs.com
E-mail: marketing@cbs.com
Michael H. Jordan, CEO
Television network

Cendant
6 Sylvan Way
Parsippany, NJ 07054
Web site: http://
www.cendant.com
Henry R. Silverman, CEO
Advertising, marketing

**Center for Defense
Information**
1500 Massachusetts Ave. NW
Washington, DC 20005
Web site: http://www.cdi.org
E-mail: cdi@cdi.org
Rear Adm. Gene R. La
Rocque, USN (Ret.),
president
*Private, nongovernmental research
organization whose directors and
staff believe that strong social,
economic, political, and military
components and a healthy
environment contribute equally
to the nation's security*

**Center for Democracy and
Technology**
1634 Eye St. NW, Ste. 1100
Washington, DC 20006
Web site: http://www.cdt.org/
E-mail: webmaster@cdt.org
Jerry Berman, executive
director
*Nonprofit public interest
organization working for public
policies that advance civil
liberties and democratic values
in new computer and
communications technologies*

**Center for Democratic
Renewal and Education, Inc.**
PO Box 50469
Atlanta, GA 30302
E-mail: cdr@igc.apc.org

**Center for Ethics, Capital
Markets, and Political
Economy**
PO Box 1845 University
Station
Charlottesville, VA 22903
E-mail: cecmpe@jefferson.
village.virginia.edu
E. N. Weaver, Jr., Amata Miller,
and John D. Feldmann,
directors
*Nonprofit organization established
in 1994 to provide a discussion
forum and information resource
for persons who believe that
moral concerns should be taken
into account in economic and
political thinking*

**Center for Governmental
Studies**
California Commission on
Campaign Financing
10951 W. Pico Blvd., #206
Los Angeles, CA 90064
Web site: http://www.cgs.org/
E-mail: center@cgs.org
*Strives to enhance the quality and
quantity of governmental
information available to citizens
through the use of modern
communications technologies,
and to expand the opportunities
of citizens to participate in the
elective and governmental
processes*

Center for Law and Social Policy
1616 P St. NW, #150
Washington, DC 20036
Web site: http://epn.org/
clasp.html
E-mail: info@clasp.org
*Education, policy research, and
advocacy organization seeking to
improve the economic conditions
of low-income families and
secure access for the poor to our
civil justice system.*

Center for Media and Values
1962 S. Shenandoah St.
Los Angeles, CA 90034
Web site: http://
www.tripod.com/jobs_career/
goodworks/jobs/170.html
Elizabeth Thoman, director
*Offers programs and services to
provide leadership for a media
awareness/education movement
in the 1990s; pioneered a new
methodology for media
awareness/analysis/reflection/
action*

Center for Policy Alternatives
1875 Connecticut Ave. NW,
#710
Washington, DC 20009
Web site: http://www.cfpa.org/
Linda Tarr-Whelan, president
*Nonprofit, nonpartisan public
policy and leadership
development center devoted to
community-based solutions that
strengthen families and
communities*

**Center for Research on
Women**
Wellesley College
106 Central St.
Wellesley, MA 02181-8259
Web site: http://
www.wellesley.edu/WCW/
crwsub.html
Contact: Pamela Baker-Webber
E-mail: pbaker@wellesley.edu
*Interdisciplinary community of
scholars engaged in research,
programs, and publications that
examine the lives of women,
men, and children in a
changing world*

Center for Responsive Politics
1320 19th St. NW, #700
Washington, DC 20036
Web site: http://www.crp.org/
index.htm
E-mail: info@crp.org
Thomas R. Asher, chair
*Nonprofit, nonpartisan
organization that specializes in
the study of Congress and
particularly the role that money
plays in its elections and actions*

**Center for Science in the
Public Interest**
1875 Connecticut Ave. NW,
#300
Washington, DC 20009
Web site: http://
www.cspinet.org/
E-mail: cspi@cspinet.org
Bruce Silverglade, director of
Legal Affairs
Caroline Smith DeWaal,
director of Food Safety
*A nonprofit education and
advocacy organization that
focuses on improving the safety
and nutritional quality of our
food supply*

Center for Strategic and Budgetary Assessments
777 N. Capitol St., #710
Washington, DC 20002
Web site: http://
www.csbahome.com/
E-mail: info@csbahome.com
Andrew F. Krepinevich,
executive director
*Independent research institute
established to promote
innovative thinking about
defense planning and
investment for the 21st century*

Center for the New West
600 World Trade Center
1625 Broadway, #600
Denver, CO 80202
Web site: http://
www.newwest.org/
E-mail:
bwurmstedt@newwest.org
Steve Bartolin, president
*Policy research institute focusing
on trade, technology, education,
and the enterprise economy*

**Center for the Study of
Popular Culture**
12400 Ventura Blvd., Ste. 304
Studio City, CA 91604
Web site: http://www.cspc.org/
E-mail: weinkopf@cspc.org
Peter Collier and David
Horowitz, founders
*Nationally known writers, editors,
and political commentators
whose intellectual development
has evolved from early,
influential support for the
New Left and Black Panther
movements to the forefront
of neoconservatism*

**Center for Voting and
Democracy**
6905 5th St. NW, #200
Washington, DC 20012
Web site: http://
www.igc.apc.org/cvd/
E-mail:
FairVote@compuserve.com
Rob Richie, executive director
*Nonprofit organization working to
educate the public about the
impact of different voting
systems on voter turnout,
representation, and
accountability and on the
influence of money in elections*

**Center for Women's Policy
Studies**
1211 Connecticut Ave. NW,
Ste. 312
Washington, DC 20036
Web site: http://
www.centerwomenpolicy.org/
E-mail: cwpsx@aol.com or
HN4066@handsnet.org
Contact: Leslie R. Wolfe
*National nonprofit, multiethnic,
and multicultural feminist
policy research and advocacy
institution that addresses
cutting-edge issues that have
significant future implications
for women*

**Center on Budget and Policy
Priorities**
777 N. Capitol St. NE, #705
Washington, DC 20002
Web site: http://www.cbpp.org/
E-mail: cbpp@clark.net
John R. Kramer, member of
board of directors
*Conducts research and analysis on
a range of government policies
and programs, with an
emphasis on those affecting low-
and moderate-income people*

Center on Children + Families
295 Lafayette St., Ste. 920
New York, NY 10012
Web site: http://
   www.kidsuccess.com/
David G. Roland, president
*Protects children from abuse and
   neglect*

Centex
2728 N. Harwood
Dallas, TX 75201
Web site: http://
   www.centex.com
Laurence E. Hirsch, CEO
Engineering, construction

Central & Southwest
1616 Woodall Rodgers Frwy.
Dallas, TX 75202
Web site: http://www.csw.com
Edgar R. Brooks, CEO
Gas and electric utilities

Cetera, Peter
1880 Century Park E., #900
Los Angeles, CA 90067
Singer, musician
Birthday: 9/13/44

Chabert, Lacey
c/o Fox
10201 West Pico Blvd.
Los Angeles, CA 90035
Actress

Chamberlain, Wilt
c/o Seymour S. Goldberg
11111 Santa Monica Blvd.,
   #1000
Los Angeles, CA 90025-3344
Former basketball player

Champion International
1 Champion Plaza
Stamford, CT 06921
Web site: http://
   www.championpaper.com
Richard E. Olson, CEO
Forest and paper products

Chan, Jackie
145 Waterloo Rd.
Kowloon
Hong Kong, Republic of China
Martial arts actor

Chance, Jeff
c/o The Bobby Roberts
   Company
PO Box 3007
Hendersonville, TN 37077
Country singer

Chao, Rosalind
10100 Santa Monica Blvd.,
   #2500
Los Angeles, CA 90067
Actress
Birthday: 9/23/49

Chaplin, Ben
2–4 Noel St.
London W1V 3RB
England
Actor

Chapman, Cee Cee
PO Box 1422
Franklin, TN 37065
Country singer

Chapman, Mark David
#81 A 3860
Box 149
Attica Correctional Facility
Attica, NY 14011
John Lennon's assassin

Charisse, Cyd
10724 Wilshire Blvd., #1406
Los Angeles, CA 90024
Actress
Birthday: 3/3/23

Charleson, Leslie
c/o "General Hospital"
ABC-TV
4151 Prospect Ave.
Los Angeles, CA 90027
Soap opera star

Charo
PO Box 1007
Hanalei, Kauai
HI 96714
Singer

HRH Prince Charles
Highgrove House
Gloucestershire
England
Prince of Wales
Birthday: 11/14/48

Chase, Chevy
PO Box 257
Redford, NY 10506
or
9056 Santa Monica Blvd., #100
W. Hollywood, CA 90069-5545
Actor

Chase Manhattan Corp.
270 Park Ave.
New York, NY 10017
Web site: http://
   www.chase.com
Walter V. Shipley, CEO
Commercial bank

Chateau Marmont
8221 Sunset Blvd.
Los Angeles, CA 90046
Hotel; John Belushi died here in 1982.

Cheap Trick
3805 Country Rd.
Middleton, WI 53262
Music group

Cher
PO Box 960
Beverly Hills, CA 90213
Singer, actress

Cherokee Nation
PO Box 948 Highway 62
Tahlequah, OK 74465
Web site: http://
   www.cherokee.org/
E-mail: Public_
   Affairs@cherokee.org
Joe Byrd, principal chief

Chesnutt, Mark
PO Box 128031
Nashville, TN 37212
Country singer

Chevron
575 Market St.
San Francisco, CA 94105
Web site: http://
   www.chevron.com
Kenneth T. Derr, CEO
Petroleum refining

Chiao, Leroy
c/o NASA
Johnson Space Center
Astronaut Office/Mail Code
   CB
2101 NASA Road 1
Houston, TX 77058
Astronaut

Chiffons, The
1650 Broadway, #508
New York, NY 10019
Music group

Children's Defense Fund
25 E St. NW
Washington, DC 20001
Web site: http://
   www.childrensdefense.org/
E-mail: cdfinfo@
   childrensdefense.org
Marian Wright Edelman,
   president
A lobby for children's rights

Childs, Andy
PO Box 24563
Nashville, TN 37202
Country singer

Child Welfare League of America
440 1st St. NW, #310
Washington, DC 20001
Web site: http://www.cwla.org/
E-mail: webweaver@cwla.org
David Liederman, executive director
Membership association of public and private nonprofit agencies that serve and advocate for abused, neglected, and otherwise vulnerable children

Chong, Rae Dawn
c/o Metropolitan Talent Agency
4526 Wilshire Blvd.
Los Angeles, CA 90010
Actress
Birthday: 2/28/61

Chordettes, The
150 E. Olive Ave., #109
Burbank, CA 91502
Music group

Chow, Amy
c/o West Valley Gymnastics School
1190 Del Ave., #1
Campbell, CA 95008-6614
or
c/o U.S. Gymnastics Federation
201 S. Capitol Ave., Ste. 300
Indianapolis, IN 46225
Gymnast

Christensen, Helena
c/o Marilyn Gaulthiar Agence
62 boulevard Sebastopol
75003 Paris
France
Supermodel

Chrysler
1000 Chrysler Dr.
Auburn Hills, MI 48326
Web site: http://www.chryslercorp.com
Robert J. Eaton, CEO
Motor vehicles and parts

CHS Electronics
2000 N.W. 84th Ave.
Miami, FL 33122
Web site: http://www.chse.com
Claudio Osorio, CEO
Electronics wholesaler

Chubb
15 Mountain View Rd.
Warren, NJ 07061
Web site: http://www.chubb.com
Dean R. O'Hare, CEO
P & C insurance (stock)

Chuck Wagon Gang
PO Box 140571
Nashville, TN 37214
Music group

Chumbawamba
43 Brook Green
London W6 7EF
England
Music group

Chung, Connie
1 W. 72nd St.
New York, NY 10023
Newscaster
Birthday: 8/20/46

Cigna
1 Liberty Pl.
Philadelphia, PA 19192
Web site: http://www.cigna.com
Wilson H. Taylor, CEO
Life and health insurance (stock)

Cinergy
139 E. 4th St.
Cincinnati, OH 45202
Web site: http://
 www.cinergy.com
James E. Rogers, CEO
Gas and electric utilities

Circuit City
9950 Maryland Dr.
Richmond, VA 23233
Web site: http://
 www.circuitcity.com
Richard L. Sharp, president
 and CEO
*Nation's largest retailer of major
 appliances and brand-name
 consumer electronics*

Cisco Systems
170 W. Tasman Dr.
San Jose, CA 95134
Web site: http://www.cisco.com
John T. Chambers, CEO
*Electronics, network
 communications*

Citicorp
399 Park Ave.
New York, NY 10043
John S. Reed, CEO
Web site: http://
 www.citibank.com
Multinational bank

Citizen Action
1750 Rhode Island Ave. NW,
 #403
Washington, DC 20036
Web site: http://www.fas.org/
 pub/gen/ggg/citizen.html
*Nationwide consumer and
 environmental organization that
 addresses issues on behalf of its
 members*

Citizen Information Center
380 A Ave. or PO Box 369
Lake Oswego, OR 97034
Web site: http://
 www.ci.oswego.or.us/citizen/
 citizen.htm
E-mail:
 webmistress@ci.oswego.or.us
*Organization which helps citizens
 of Lake Oswego, Oregon solve
 city-related problems*

**Citizens Against Government
 Waste**
1301 Connecticut Ave. NW,
 #400
Washington, DC 20036
Web site: http://www.cagw.org/
E-mail: webmaster@cagw
Thomas A. Schatz, president
*Private, nonpartisan, nonprofit
 organization dedicated to
 educating Americans about the
 waste, mismanagement, and
 inefficiency in the federal
 government*

**Citizens' Commission on Civil
 Rights**
2000 M St. NW, #400
Washington, DC 20036
Web site: http://www.ccr.org/
E-mail: citizens@ccr.org
Corrine M. Yu, director and
 counsel
*Established to monitor civil rights
 policies and practices of the
 federal government and seek
 ways to accelerate progress in the
 area of civil rights*

Citizens' Committee for the Right to Keep and Bear Arms
600 Pennsylvania Ave. SE, #205
Washington, DC 20003
Web site: http://
www.ccrkba.org/
E-mail: info@ccrkba.org
Contact: Alan Gottlieb
Dedicated to preserving and protecting the Second Amendment

Citizens for a Sound Economy
1250 H St. NW, #700
Washington, DC 20005-3908
Web site: http://www.cse.org/cse
Paul Beckner, president
Fights for lower taxes and less regulation

Citizens for a Tobacco Free Society (CATS)
8660 Lynnehaven Dr.
Cincinnati, OH 45236
E-mail: Unitednews@aol.com

Citizens for Civil Justice Reform
1747 Pennsylvania Ave. NW, #850
Washington, DC 20006
A political action organization

Citizens for Tax Justice
1311 L St. NW, #400
Washington, DC 20005
Web site: http://www.ctj.org/
Robert S. McIntyre, director
A nonpartisan research and advocacy organization working for a fair, progressive tax system

Citizens Jury
Jefferson Center
1111 3rd Ave. S., #364
Minneapolis, MN 55404
Involves citizens in public policy decision-making

Claiborne, Liz
650 5th Ave.
New York, NY 10019
Fashion designer

● **Clancy, Tom**
PO Box 800
Huntington, MD 20639
Author

Clark, Dick
3003 W. Olive Ave.
Burbank, CA 91505
Television personality

Clark, Joe
707 7th Ave. SW, #1300
Calgary, AB T2P 3H6
Canada
Former Prime Minister of Canada

Clark, Marcia
151 El Camino Dr.
Beverly Hills, CA 90212
Prosecutor in the O. J. Simpson criminal trial

Clark, Roy
3225 S. Norwood
Tulsa, OK 74135
Country singer

Clark, Susan
Georgian Bay Productions
3815 W. Olive Ave., #202
Burbank, CA 91505
Actress

Terri Clark International Fan Club
PO Box 1079
Gallatin, TN 37066
Country singer

Clark USA
8182 Maryland Ave.
St. Louis, MO 63105
Paul D. Melnuk, CEO
Petroleum refining

Clarke, Arthur C.
4715 Gregory Rd.
Colombo
Sri Lanka
Science fiction author

Clay, Andrew Dice
836 N. La Cienega Blvd., #202
Los Angeles, CA 90069
Comedian, actor

Claydermann, Richard
c/o Delphine Records
150 bd. Haussmann
75008 Paris
France
Musician
Birthday: 12/28/53

Clean Air Trust
1625 K St. NW, #725
Washington, DC 20006
Environmental organization

Clean Water Action
1320 18th St. NW, #300
Washington, DC 20036
Web site: http://
www.cleanwateraction.org/
E-mail: CWA@essential.org.
Marguerite Young, national
recruitment coordinator
*Organizes strong grassroots groups,
coalitions, and campaigns to
protect our environment, health,
economic well-being, and
community quality of life*

Cleese, John
82 Ladbroke Rd.
London W11 3NU
England
Comedian, actor
Birthday: 10/27/39

Clemens, Roger
c/o Toronto Blue Jays
The Skydome, 1 Blue Jays Way
Toronto, ON M5V 1J1
Canada
Baseball player
Birthday: 8/4/62

Always Patsy Cline
PO Box 2236
Winchester, VA 22604
Patsy Cline fan club

Clinton, Buddy the Dog
The White House
1600 Pennsylvania Ave.
Washington, DC 20500

Clinton, Chelsea
Stanford University
Wilbur Hall
Palo Alto, CA 94305
Bill and Hillary's daughter

Clinton, Hillary Rodham
The White House
1600 Pennsylvania Ave.
Washington, DC 20500
*First Lady of the United States,
attorney*
Birthday: 10/26/47

Clinton, Socks the Cat
The White House
1600 Pennsylvania Ave.
Washington, DC 20500

Clinton, William Jefferson
The White House
1600 Pennsylvania Ave.
Washington, DC 20500
Home page: http://
www.president@
whitehouse.gov
Birthday: 8/19/46
President of the United States

Cloke, Kirsten
c/o The Gersh Agency
PO Box 5617
Beverly Hills, CA 90210
Actress

Clooney, George
151 El Camino Dr.
Beverly Hills, CA 90212
Actor;
Birthday: 5/6/61

Close, Glenn
9830 Wilshire Blvd.
Beverly Hills, CA 90212
Actress
Birthday: 3/19/47

Clovers, The
Rt. 1, Box 56
Belvedere, NC 90212
Music group

Clower, Jerry
PO Box 121089
Nashville, TN 37212
Storyteller

CMS Energy
330 Town Center Dr.
Dearborn, MI 48126
Web site: http://
    www.cmsenergy.com
William T. McCormick, Jr.,
    CEO
Gas and electric utilities

CNF Transportation
3240 Hillview Ave.
Palo Alto, CA 94304
Web site: http://www.cnf.com
Donald E. Moffitt, CEO
Trucking

**Coalition on Human Needs
    (CHN)**
1000 Wisconsin Ave. NW
Washington, DC 20007
*Alliance of over 100 national
    organizations working together
    to promote public policies that
    address the needs of low-income
    and other vulnerable
    populations*

Coalition to Stop Gun Violence
100 Maryland Ave. NE, #402
Washington, DC 20002
Web site: http://
    www.gunfree.org/
E-mail: noguns@aol.com
Gun ban organization

Coastal
9 Greenway Plaza
Houston, TX 77046
Web site: http://
    www.coastalcorp.com
David A. Arledge, CEO
Petroleum refining

Coasters, The
4905 S. Atlantic Ave.
Daytona Beach, FL 32127
Music group

Coca, Imogene
PO Box 51551
Westport, CT 06881
Actress
Birthday: 11/18/1908

Coca-Cola
1 Coca-Cola Plaza
Atlanta, GA 30313
Web site: http://
    www.cocacola.co
M. Douglas Ivester, CEO (the
    10th chairman of the board
    in the company's history)
Beverages

Coca-Cola Enterprises
2500 Windy Ridge Pkwy.
Atlanta, GA 30339
Web site: http://
    www.cokecce.com
Summerfield K. Johnston, Jr.,
    CEO
Beverages

Cochran, Johnnie L.
2245 W. 28th St.
Los Angeles, CA 90018
Lawyer in O. J. Simpson trial

Cocker, Joe
9830 Wilshire Blvd.
Beverly Hills, CA 90212
Singer
Birthday: 5/20/42

Coe, David Allan
PO Box 270188
Nashville, TN 37227-0188
Country singer

Coen, Ethan
c/o United Talent Agency
9560 Wilshire Blvd., Ste. 516
Beverly Hills, CA 90212
Screenwriter
Birthday: 9/21/57

Coen, Joel
c/o United Talent Agency
9560 Wilshire Blvd., Ste. 516
Beverly Hills, CA 90212
Film director, writer
Birthday: 11/29/54

Cole, Gary
10390 Santa Monica Blvd.,
    #300
Los Angeles, CA 90025
Actor
Birthday: 9/27/50

Coleman, Jack
c/o Innovative Artists
1999 Ave. of the Stars, #2850
Los Angeles, CA 90067
Actor
Birthday: 2/21/58

Colgate-Palmolive
300 Park Ave.
New York, NY 10022
Web site: http://
    www.colgate.com
Reuben Mark, CEO
Soaps, cosmetics

Collie, Mark
PO Box 120311
Nashville, TN 37212
Country singer

Collins, Jackie
PO Box 5473
Glendale, CA 91221
Author
Birthday: 10/4/41

Columbia Energy Group
12355 Sunrise Valley Dr.
Reston, VA 20191
Web site: http://
    www.columbiaenergy.com
Oliver G. Richard III, CEO
Gas and electric utilities

Columbia/HCA Healthcare
1 Park Plaza
Nashville, TN 37203
Web site: http://
    www.columbia.net
Thomas F. Frist, Jr., CEO
Health care

Columbia Tristar Interactive
9046 Lindblad Ave.
Culver City, CA 90232
Richard Glosser, president
E-mail:
    rglosser@sonypictures.com
*Developers of Jeopardy and Wheel
    of Fortune online*

Colvin, Shawn
30 W. 21st St., 7th Flr.
New York, NY 10010
Musician

Combs, Jeffrey
13601 Ventura Blvd., #349
Sherman Oaks, CA 91423
Actor

Comcast
1500 Market St.
Philadelphia, PA 19102
Web site: http://
    www.comcast.com
Brian L. Roberts, CEO
Telecommunications

Comdisco
6111 N. River Rd.
Rosemont, IL 60018
Web site: http://
    www.comdisco.com
Jack S. Slevin, CEO
Computer and data services

Comerica
500 Woodward Ave.
Detroit, MI 48226
Web site: http://
www.comerica.com
Eugene A. Miller, CEO
Commercial banks

Commission on Presidential Debates
601 13th St., #310 S.
Washington, DC 20005
Web site: http://
www.debates.org/
Lewis K. Loss, general counsel

Committee for a Responsible Federal Budget
220½ E Street NE
Washington, DC 20002
E-mail: crfb@aol.com
Bipartisan, nonprofit educational organization committed to educating the public regarding the budget process and particular issues that have significant fiscal policy impact

Committee for Children
2203 Airport Way S., #500
Seattle, WA 98134
Web site: http://
www.cfchildren.org/
E-mail:
webmatron@cfchildren.org
Nonprofit organization dedicated to preventing child abuse and youth violence through developing educational curricula and original research

Committee for Study of the American Electorate
412 New Jersey Ave. SE
Washington, DC 20003
Web site: http://tap.epn.org/
csae/
Maurice Rosenblatt, president
Nonpartisan, nonprofit research institution with a primary focus on issues surrounding citizen engagement in politics

Committee on the Constitutional System
1400 16th St. NW, #502
Washington, DC 20036

Common Cause
2030 M St. NW, #300
Washington, DC 20036
Web site: http://
www.commoncause.org/
Ann McBride, president
Nonprofit, nonpartisan citizen's lobbying organization promoting open, honest, and accountable government

Communications Workers of America (CWA)
501 3rd St. NW
Washington, DC 20001
Web site: http://www.
cwa-union.org/home/
E-mail: cwa@ctsg.com
Morton Bahr, president
Representing North American workers in telecommunications, printing and news media, public service, health care, cable television, general manufacturing, electronics, gas and electric utilities, and other fields

Community Nutrition Institute
910 17th St. NW, #413
Washington, DC 20006
E-mail: cnii@igc.apc.org
Rodney E. Leonard, executive
director and founder
*A leading advocate for consumer
protection food program
development and management,
and sound federal diet and
health policies*

Compaq Computer
20555 SH 249
Houston, TX 77070
Web site: http://
www.compaq.com
Eckhard Pfeiffer, CEO
Computers, office equipment

Compassion in Dying
6312 SW Capitol Hwy.,
Ste. 415
Portland, OR 97201
Web site: http://
www.CompassionInDying.org
E-mail:
info@compassionindying.org
Barbara Coombs-Lee, executive
director
*Organization for people who believe
in the right to die with dignity*

**Competitive Enterprise
Institute**
1001 Connecticut Ave. NW,
#1250
Washington, DC 20036
Web site: http://www.cei.org/
E-mail: info@CEI.org
Dr. William Dunn, president
*A promarket public policy group
committed to advancing the
principles of free enterprise and
limited government*

Competitiveness Policy Council
1726 M St. NW, 3rd Fl.
Washington, DC 20036
Web site: http://www.cpc.gov/
cpc/
Rand V. Araskog and
Claudine Schneider,
Commission members
*A 12-member federal advisory
commission made up of
business, labor, government,
and the public working to
improve U.S. living standards*

Comp USA
14951 N. Dallas Pkwy.
Dallas, TX 75240
Web site: http://
www.compusa.com
James F. Halpin, CEO
Computer retailers

**Computer Associates
International**
1 Computer Associates Plaza
Islandia, NY 11788
Web site: http://www.cai.com
Charles B. Wang, CEO
Computer software

**Computer Professionals for
Social Responsibility**
459 Hamilton Ave., #300, or
PO Box 717
Palo Alto, CA 94302
Web site: http://www.cpsr.org/
E-mail: cpsr@cpsr.org
Aki Namioka, president
E-mail: aki@cpsr.org
*Public-interest alliance of computer
scientists and others concerned
about the impact of computer
technology on society*

Computer Sciences
2100 E. Grand Ave.
El Segundo, CA 90245
Web site: http://www.csc.com
Van B. Honeycutt, CEO
Computer and data services

ConAgra
1 ConAgra Dr.
Omaha, NE 68102
Web site: http://
www.conagra.com
Bruce Rohde, CEO
Food producer

Concern, Incorporated
1794 Columbia Rd. NW, #6
Washington, DC 20009
E-mail: concern@igc.apc.org
Political organization

Concerned Women for America
370 L'Enfant Promenade SW, #800
Washington, DC 20024
Web site: http://www.cwfa.org/
Beverly LaHaye, chairman
National, politically active women's organization, promoting Christian values and morality in family life and public policy

Concord Coalition
1019 19th St. NW, #810
Washington, DC 20005
Web site: http://www.afn.org/~
concord/coalition/
georgia.htm
E-mail:
74431.3225@
compuserve.com
Bipartisan, nonprofit group dedicated to breaking the toxic habit of federal deficit spending—through public education and grass-roots organization

Confederate Railroad
PO Box 128185
Nashville, TN 37212
Country music group

Congressional Accountability Project
1322 18th St. NW, #36
Washington, DC 20036
Web site: http://
www.essential.org/orgs/CAP/
CAP.html
Contact: Gary Ruskin
E-mail: gary@essential.org
Congressional watchdog organization

Congressional Budget Office
U.S. Congress
2nd & D St. SW
Washington, DC 20515
Web site: http://www.cbo.gov/
June E. O'Neill, director
Created by the Congressional Budget and Impoundment Control Act of 1974; mission is to provide the Congress with objective, timely, nonpartisan analyses needed for economic and budget decisions and with the information and estimates required for the congressional budget process

Congressional Quarterly, Inc.
1414 22nd St. NW
Washington, DC 20037
Web site: http://www.cq.com/
E-mail: webmaster@cq.com
Robert W. Merry, president and publisher
A world-class provider of information on government, politics, and public policy

Conlee, John
PO Box 15261
Nashville, TN 37215
Country music singer

Conley, Earl Thomas
PO Box 23552
Nashville, TN 37202
Country singer

Connells, The
901 18th Ave. S.
Nashville, TN 37212
Music group

Connery, Jason
c/o Joy Jameson Ltd.
The Plaza 2/19
535 Kings Rd.
London SW10 OSZ
England
Actor, son of Sean Connery
Birthday: 1/11/63

Connery, Sean
c/o Creative Artists Agency
9830 Wilshire Blvd.
Beverly Hills, CA 90212
Actor
Birthday: 8/25/30

Conrad-Hefner, Kimberly
c/o Playmate Promotions
9492 Beverly Blvd.
Beverly Hills, CA 90210
Hugh Hefner's wife

Conseco
11825 N. Pennsylvania St.
Carmel, IN 46032
Web site: http://
www.conseco.com
Stephen C. Hilbert, CEO
Life and health insurance (stock)

Conservative Caucus
450 Maple Ave. E.
Vienna, VA 22180
Web site: http://
www.conservativeusa.org
E-mail: webmaster@
conservativeusa.org
Howard Phillips, founder and
chairman
*Dedicated to educating citizens
about how we must take action
to restore America to its
constitutionally limited
government*

Consolidated Edison
4 Irving Pl.
New York, NY 10003
Web site: http://
www.coned.com
Eugene R. McGrath, CEO
Gas and electric utilities

Consolidated Natural Gas
625 Liberty Ave.
Pittsburgh, PA 15222
Web site: http://www.cng.com
George A. Davidson, Jr., CEO
Gas and electric utilities

Consolidated Stores
300 Phillipi Rd.
Columbus, OH 43228
Web site: http://
www.cnstores.com
William G. Kelley, CEO
*Specialist retailers, K-B Stores, Big
Lots Odd Lots Stores*

Constantine, Kevin
c/o Pittsburgh Penguins
Civic Arena, Gate 9
Pittsburgh, PA 15219
E-mail: coaches@mail.
pittsburgpenguins.com
Pittsburgh Penguins head coach

Constantine, Michael
1800 Ave. of the Stars, #400
Los Angeles, CA 90067
Actor
Birthday: 5/22/27

**Consumer Energy Council of
America Research
Foundation**
2000 L St. NW, #802
Washington, DC 20036

**Consumer Federation of
America**
1424 16th St. NW, #604
Washington, DC 20036
*Public advocacy and education on
issues that face consumers*

Consumers Union
101 Truman Ave.
Yonkers, NY 10703
Web site: http://
www.consumersunion.org/
Rhoda H. Karpatkin, president
*Mission has been to test products,
inform the public, and protect
consumers*

Continental Airlines
2929 Allen Pkwy.
Houston, TX 77019
Web site: http://
www.flycontinental.com
Gordon M. Bethune, CEO
Airline

Conway, Tim
PO Box 17047
Encino, CA 91416
Actor
Birthday: 11/14/33

Cooper Industries
600 Travis St., Ste. 5800
Houston, TX 77002
Web site: http://
www.cooperindustries.com
H. John Riley, Jr., CEO
Electronics, electrical equipment

Copperfield, David (David Kotkin)
11777 San Vincente Blvd.
Los Angeles, CA 90048
Magician
Birthday: 9/15/56

Corea, Chick
PO Box 39581
Los Angeles, CA 90039
E-mail: CCoreaProd@aol.com
Musician
Birthday: 6/12/41

CoreStates Financial Corp.
Broad & Chestnut Sts.
Philadelphia, PA 19101
Web site: http://
www.corestates.com
Terrence A. Larsen, CEO
Commercial bank

Official Danielle Cormack Fan Club, The
Ephiny of the Amazons
297 Boston Post Rd., Ste. 141
Wayland, MA 01778
Web site: http://
members.aol.com/
dancorfans/index.html
E-mail: DanCorFans@aol.com

Corman, Roger
11611 San Vincente Blvd.
Los Angeles, CA 90049
Film producer

Cornelius, Helen
PO Box 2977
Hendersonville, TN 37077
Country singer

Corning
1 Riverfront Plaza
Corning, NY 14831
Web site: http://
www.corning.com
Roger G. Ackerman, CEO
Building materials, glass

Corporate Express
1 Environmental Way
Broomfield, CO 80021
Web site: http://
www.corporate-express.com
Jirka Rysavy, CEO
Specialist retailers, office products

Cortese, Dan
15250 Ventura Blvd., #900
Sherman Oaks, CA 91403
Actor

Cosby, Bill
PO Box 4049
Santa Monica, CA 90411
Comedian, actor
Birthday: 7/11/37

Costco
999 Lake Dr.
Issaquah, WA 98027
Web site: http://
www.pricecostco.com
James D. Sinegal, CEO
Specialist retailers, warehouse store

Costello, Elvis (Declan Patrick McManus)
9028 Gr. Guest Rd.
Middlesex TW8 9EW
England
Musician
Birthday: 8/25/54

Coulier, David
9150 Wilshire Blvd., #350
Beverly Hills, CA 90212
Actor

Coulthard, David
c/o McLaren International
Ltd.
Woking Business Park
Albert Dr.
Woking
Surrey GU21 5JS
England
Professional Formula-1 driver

Council of State Governments
P.O. Box 11910
Lexington, KY 40578
Web site: http://www.csg.org
E-mail: info@csg.org

Council on Foreign Relations
58 E. 68th St.
New York, NY 10021
E-mail: ppappachan@cfr.org

Counting Crows
c/o DGC
9130 Sunset Blvd.
Los Angeles, CA 90069
Music group

Couric, Katie
NBC
30 Rockefeller Plaza
New York, NY 10122
Broadcast journalist
Birthday: 1/7/57

Courier, Jim
c/o IMG
1 Erieview Plaza, #1300
Cleveland, OH 44114
Tennis player
Birthday: 8/17/70

Cox, DeAnna
818 18th Ave. S.
Nashville, TN 37203
Country singer

Cox Family, The
PO Box 787
Cotton Valley, LA 71018
Country group

Craddock, Billy "Crash"
PO Box 1585
Mt. Vernon, IL 62864
Country singer

Craig, Jenny
PO Box 387190
La Jolla, CA 92038
Diet company founder

Craig, Yvonne
11365 Ventura Blvd., #100
Studio City, CA 91604
Actress

Cramer, Floyd
110 Glancy S., #201
Goodlettsville, TN 37072
Musician

Cranberries, The
c/o Rough Trade Mgmt.
66 Goldborne Rd.
London W10 5PS
England
Music group

Crash Test Dummies
c/o BMG
150 John St., 6th Fl.
Toronto, ON M5V 3C3
Canada
Music group

Craven, Wes
8491 Sunset Blvd., #375
W. Hollywood, CA 90069
Film director
Birthday: 8/2/39

Crawford, Cindy
9056 Santa Monica Blvd., Ste.
 100
Hollywood, CA 90069
Model, actress

Crawford, Michael
7605 Santa Monica Blvd., #644
Los Angeles, CA 90046
Singer
Birthday: 1/19/52

Cray, Robert
Box 170429
San Francisco, CA 94117
Musician

Creamengine
c/o William A. McGrath III
230 Westmar Dr.
Rochester, NY 14624
Music group

Crenna, Richard
c/o Creative Artists Agency
9830 Wilshire Blvd.
Beverly Hills, CA 90212
Actor

Cretien, Jean
24 Sussex Dr.
Ottawa, ON K1M OMS
Canada
Web site: http://pm.gc.ca/mail_
 room/contact_pm/
 index.html-ssi
Prime Minister of Canada

Cristo
48 Howard St.
New York, NY 10013
Artist

Cronenberg, David
184 Cottingham St.
Toronto, ON M4V 1C5
Canada
Film director
Birthday: 3/15/43

Crook, Lorianne
c/o Jim Owens Associates
1515 McGavock St.
Nashville, TN 37203
TV host

Crook and Chase
1525 McGavock St.
Nashville, TN 37203
Talk show hosts

Crosby, David
PO Box 9008
Solvang, CA 93464
Musician
Birthday: 8/14/41

Crosby, Norm
c/o Jono Productions, Inc.
5750 Wilshire Blvd., #580
Los Angeles, CA 90036
Comedian
Birthday: 9/15/27

Crosby, Rob
PO Box 120025
Nashville, TN 37212
Country musician

Cross, Christopher
PO Box 127465
Nashville, TN 37212
Singer

Crowded House
Box 333
Prahan
Victoria 3181
Australia
Music group

Crowe, Cameron
c/o C.A.A.
9830 Wilshire Blvd.
Beverly Hills, CA 90212
Director/producer/screenwriter
Birthday: 7/13/57

Fans of Rodney Crowell
PO Box 120576
Nashville, TN 37212
Country music singer

Crown, Cork & Seal
1 Crown Way
Philadelphia, PA 19106
Web site: http://
  www.crowncork.com
William J. Avery, CEO
Metal products

Cruise, Tom
14755 Ventura Blvd., #1–710
Sherman Oaks, CA 91403
Actor

Cryner, Bobbie
c/o The Erv Woolsey Co.
1000 18th Ave. S.
Nashville, TN 37212
Country singer

Csupo, Gabor
1258 N. Highland Ave.
Hollywood, CA 90038
Web site: http://
  www.klaskycsupo.com
Creator of "Rugrats"

CSX
901 E. Cary St.
Richmond, VA 23219
Web site: http://www.csx.com
John W. Snow, CEO
Railroads

**Culinary Arts Institute of
  Louisiana**
427 Lafayette St.
Baton Rouge, LA 70802
Vi Harrington, founder and
  owner
Cooking school

**Culinary Institute of America
  at Greystone**
2555 Main St.
St. Helena, CA 94574
Roger Riccardi, managing
  director
Cooking school

Cummins Engine
500 Jackson St.
Columbus, IN 47202
Web site: http://
  www.cummins.com
James A. Henderson, CEO
Industrial and farm equipment

Cure, The
c/o Levine & Schneider PR
8730 Sunset Blvd., #600
Los Angeles, CA 90069
Music group

Curtin, Jane
PO Box 1070
Sharon, CT 06069
Actress

Curtis-Hall, Vondie
PO Box 5617
Beverly Hills, CA 90210
Actress

Cusack, John
c/o William Morris Agency
151 S. El Camino Dr.
Beverly Hills, CA 90212
Actor
Birthday: 6/28/66

CVS
1 CVS Dr.
Woonsocket, RI 02895
Web site: http://www.cvs.com
Stanley P. Goldstein, CEO
Food and drug stores

Cypress Amax Minerals
9100 E. Mineral Cir.
Englewood, CO 80112
Web site: http://
    www.cyprusamax.com/
Milton H. Ward, CEO
Mining, crude-oil production

Cypress Hill
151 El Camino Dr.
Beverly Hills, CA 90212
Music group

Cyrus, Billy Ray
PO Box 1206
Franklin, TN 37115
Country singer

D

A letter is a conversation you can hold.

—NANCY BUNNING

D'Abo, Maryam
1680 N. Vine St., #517
Los Angeles, CA 90028
Actress

D'Abo, Olivia
1122 S. Robertson Blvd., #15
Los Angeles, CA 90035
Actress
Birthday: 1/22/67

Daddo, Kathryn
151 El Camino Dr.
Beverly Hills, CA 90212
Actress

Dahl, Arlene
c/o Dahlmark Productions
PO Box 116
Sparkill, NY 10976
Actress
Birthday: 8/11/28

Dalai Lama
Thekchen Choling
McLeod Gunji
Dharamsala
Himachal Pradesh
India
Religious leader
Birthday: 7/6/35

Dalton, Abby
PO Box 100
Mammoth Lakes, CA 03546
Actress
Birthday: 8/11/27

Dalton, Lacy J.
915 Millbury Ave.
La Puente, CA 91746
Country singer

Daltrey, Roger
48 Harley House
Marylebone Rd.
London NW1 5HL
England
Musician
Birthday: 3/1/45

Dana
4500 Dorr St.
Toledo, OH 43697
Web site: http://www.dana.com
Southwood J. Morcott, CEO
Motor vehicles and parts

Dana, Bill
PO Box 1792
Santa Monica, CA 90406
Comedian, actor

Daniel, Davis
PO Box 120186
Nashville, TN 37212
Country singer

Daniels, Charlie
17060 Central Pike
Lebanon, TN 37087
Country singer

Danza, Tony
10202 W. Washington Blvd.
Culver City, CA 90232
Actor
Birthday: 4/21/51

Darden Restaurants
5900 Lake Ellenor Dr.
Orlando, FL 32809
Joe R. Lee, CEO
Food services

Darren, James
PO Box 1088
Beverly Hills, CA 90213
Actor
Birthday: 6/9/36

"Dateline NBC"
Story Suggestions
Room 510
30 Rockefeller Plaza
New York, NY 10112
E-mail: dateline@news.nbc.com
TV newsmagazine

Davies, Gail
PO Box 150586
Nashville, TN 37221
Country singer

Davis, Daniel
c/o TriStar ("The Nanny")
9336 W. Washington Blvd.
Culver City, CA 90232
Actor

Davis, Danny
38 Music Sq. E., #300
Nashville, TN 37203
Country singer

Davis, Jimmie
PO Box 15826
Baton Rouge, LA 70896
Country singer

Davis, Josie
c/o CBS ("The Young and the
   Restless")
7800 Beverly Blvd.
Los Angeles, CA 90036
or
1800 Ave. of the Stars, #400
Los Angeles, CA 90067
Actress

Davis, Linda
PO Box 121027
Nashville, TN 37212
Musician

Davis, Skeeter
PO Box 1288
Brentwood, TN 37209
Country singer

Davis, Stephanie
PO Box 121495
Nashville, TN 37212
Country singer

Dawson, Marco
c/o PGA Tour
112 TPC Blvd.
Ponte Vedra Beach, FL 32082
Golfer

**Day, Doris (Doris von
   Kappelhoff)**
PO Box 223163
Carmel, CA 93922
Actress
Birthday: 4/1/24

Day-Lewis, Daniel
65 Connaught St.
London W2
England
Actor
Birthday: 4/20/58

Dayton Hudson
777 Nicollet Mall
Minneapolis, MN 55402
Web site: http://www.dhc.com
Robert J. Ulrich, CEO
General merchandisers—Marshall
Field's, Target, Mervyn's
California

Dead or Alive
370 City Rd.
London EC1 V8N4
England
Music group

Dean, Billy
c/o Rachel Newsome
PO Drawer T1150
Nashville, TN 37244
Country singer

Dean, Jimmy
8000 Centerview Pkwy., #400
Cordova, TN 38018
Country singer

Dean Foods
600 N. River Rd.
Franklin Park, IL 60131
Web site: http://
www.libertydairy-
deanfoods.com
Howard M. Dean, CEO
Food producer

DeAngelis, Barbara
12021 Wilshire Blvd., #607
Los Angeles, CA 90025
Actress

**Death with Dignity Education
Center**
520 S. El Camino Real, Ste.
710
San Mateo, CA 94402
E-mail: DDEC@aol.com
Charlotte Ross, executive
director
*Organization for people who believe
in the right to die*

Dee, Sandra
10351 Santa Monica Blvd.,
#211
Los Angeles, CA 90025
Actress
Birthday: 4/23/42

Deep Purple
3 E. 54th St., #1400
New York, NY 10022
Music group

Deere
1 John Deere Pl.
Moline, IL 61265
Web site: http://
www.deere.com
Hans W. Becherer, CEO
Industrial and farm equipment

Defenders of Wildlife
1101 14th St. NW, #1400
Washington, DC 20005
Web site: http://
www.defenders.org/
E-mail:
webmaster@defenders.org
Alan W. Steinberg, chairman
of board of directors
*Dedicated to the protection of all
native wild animals and plants
in their natural communities*

Delaney, Kim
3435 Ocean Park Blvd., Ste.
201N
Santa Monica, CA 90405
Actress

Dell Computer
1 Dell Way
Round Rock, TX 78682
Web site: http://www.dell.com
Michael S. Dell, CEO
Computers, office equipment

Del Ray, Martin
c/o Sherry Halton
1223 17th Ave. S.
Nashville, TN 37212
Country singer

Del Rubio Sisters, The
PO Box 6923
San Pedro, CA 90734
Musical group

Delta Airlines
1030 Delta Blvd.
Atlanta, GA 30320
Web site: http://
www.delta-air.com
Leo F. Mullin, CEO
Airline

De Luise, Dom
c/o Page and Ma Business
   Management
11661 San Vicente Blvd., #910
Los Angeles, CA 90049
Actor

**Democratic Congressional
   Campaign Committee**
430 S. Capitol St. SE
Washington, DC 20003
Web site: http://www.dccc.org/
Hon. Martin Frost, chairman
*Devoted to electing a Democratic
   majority in the House of
   Representatives*

**Democratic National
   Committee**
430 S. Capitol St. SE
Washington, DC 20003
Web site: http://
   www.democrats.org/
   index.html
Roy Romer, general chair
*The national party organization
   for the Democratic Party of the
   United States*

**Democratic Senatorial
   Campaign Committee**
430 S. Capitol St. SE
Washington, DC 20003
Web site: http://www.dscc.org/
E-mail: info@dscc.org
Sen. Bob Kerrey, chairman
*A national party committee formed
   by the Democratic members of the
   U.S. Senate to raise funds for
   Democratic U.S. Senate
   candidates throughout the
   country*

Denver, Bob
General Delivery
Princeton, WV 24740
Actor

DePalma, Brian
5555 Melrose Ave.
Ernst Lubitch Annex #119
Los Angeles, CA 90038
Director

Desert Rose Band
PO Box 120186
Nashville, TN 37212
Country music group

DeVito, Danny
PO Box 491246
Los Angeles, CA 90049
Actor

DeWitt, Joyce
101 Ocean Ave., #L-4
Santa Monica, CA 90402
Actress

Dey, Susan
10390 Santa Monica Blvd.,
   #300
Los Angeles, CA 90025
Actress
Birthday: 12/10/52

DeYoung, Cliff
626 Santa Monica Blvd., #57
Santa Monica, CA 90401
Actor

Diamond Rio
PO Box 506
White House, TN 37188-0506
Web site: http://
  www.diamondrio.com
Country music group

**Diana, Princess of Wales
  Memorial Fund**
c/o Fleet Bank
PO Box 30596
Hartford, CT 06150

DiCaprio, Leonardo
9830 Wilshire Blvd.
Beverly Hills, CA 90212
Web site: http://
  www.dicaprio.com
E-mail: webmaster@
  pde.paramount.com
Actor

Dickens, Little Jimmy
Grand Ole Opry
PO Box 131
Nashville, TN 37214
Country musician

Dietl, Helmut
c/o Diana Film
Ainmillerstr. 33
80801 München
Germany
Film director

Diffie, Joe
PO Box 479
Velma, OK 73091
Country singer

Digital Equipment
111 Powdermill Rd.
Maynard, MA 01754
Web site: http://
  www.digital.com
Robert B. Palmer, CEO
Computers, office equipment

Dillards
1600 Cantrell Rd.
Little Rock, AR 72201
Web site: http://
  www.azstarnet.com/dillards
William Dillard, CEO
*General merchandisers, department
  stores*

Diller, Phyllis
11365 Ventura Blvd., #100
Studio City, CA 91604
Comedian

Dillon, Dean
PO Box 935
Round Rock, TX 78680
Country singer

Diniz, Pedro
c/o Arrows/TWR Formula
  One Ltd.
Leafield Technical Centre
Leafield
Whitney
Oxon OX8 5PF
England
Professional Formula-1 driver

Celine Dion
C.P. 65
Repentiguy
PQJ 6A 5H7
Canada

Dire Straits
c/o Damage Mgmt.
16 Lambton Pl.
London W11 2SH
England
Music group

Dirt Band
PO Box 1915
Aspen, CO 81611
Music group

Disney, Roy E.
c/o Shamrock Broadcasting
  Co.
4444 Lakeside Dr.
Burbank, CA 91505
or
500 S. Buena Vista St.
Burbank, CA 91521
Broadcasting executive

Dixiana
PO Box 3569
Greenville, SC 29608
Country music group

Dixie Chicks
c/o The Buckskin Co.
7 Music Cir. N.
Nashville, TN 37203
Country music group

Dole Foods
1365 Oak Crest Dr.
Westlake Village, CA 91361
Web site: http://www.dole.com
David H. Murdock, CEO
Food producer

Dolenz, Mickey
9000 Sunset Blvd., #1200
W. Hollywood, CA 90069
Musician, member of the Monkees
Birthday: 3/19/45

Domingo, Placido
c/o Plácido Domingo
   Sekretariat
Zaunergasse 1–3; Tür 16
1030 Wien
Austria
Tenor
Birthday: 1/21/41

Dominion Resources
901 E. Byrd St.
Richmond, VA 23219
Web site: http://
   www.domres.com
Thomas E. Capps, CEO
Gas and electric utilities

Donner, Richard
4000 Warner Blvd., #102
Burbank, CA 91522
Film director

Douglas, Donna
PO Box 49455
Los Angeles, CA 90049
Actress
Birthday: 9/26/39

Dover
280 Park Ave.
New York, NY 10017
Web site: http://
   www.dovercorporation.com
Thomas L. Reece, CEO
Industrial and farm equipment

Dow Chemical
2030 Dow Ctr.
Midland, MI 48674
Web site: http://www.dow.com
William S. Stavropoulos, CEO
Chemicals

Downey, Roma
PO Box 5617
Beverly Hills, CA 90210
Actress

Dr. Alban
c/o Dr. Records
Drottningholmsvägen 35
11242 Stockholm
Sweden
Singer

Dramalogue
PO Box 38771
Hollywood, CA 90038
Newspaper for actors

Drapper, John T., aka Cap'n Crunch
Web site: http://209.76.144.203/
   crunch/
E-mail crunch@
   webcruncher.woz.org
*Famous pioneer hacker; used
   whistle out of Cap'n Crunch
   cereal box to hack long-distance
   calls*

D:Ream
c/o FXU
"Pumphouse"
71 Fairfield Rd.
London E3 2QA
England
Music group

Dresser Industries
2001 Ross Ave.
Dallas, TX 75221
Web site: http://
 www.dresser.com
William E. Bradford, CEO
Industrial and farm equipment

Driever, Klaus
Medienallee 4
85774 Unterföhring
Germany
Inventor

Driver, Minnie
37 Berwick St.
London W1
England
Actress

Drug Policy Foundation
4455 Connecticut Ave. NW,
 #B500
Washington, DC 20008
Web site: http://
 www.drugpolicy.org/
E-mail: webfeedback@dpf.org
Sher Horosko, executive
 director
*An independent, nonprofit
 organization with over 20,000
 members that publicizes
 alternatives to current drug
 strategies, in the belief that the
 drug war is not working*

DTE Energy
2000 Second Ave.
Detroit, MI 48226
Web site: http://
 www.dteenergy.com
John E. Lobbia, CEO
Gas and electric utilities

Duffy, Patrick
PO Box D
Tarzana, CA 91356
Actor
Birthday: 3/19/49

Duke Energy
422 S. Church St.
Charlotte, NC 28202
Web site: http://www.
 duke-energy.com
Richard B. Priory, CEO
Gas and electric utilities

Dunaway, Faye
PO Box 15778
Beverly Hills, CA 90209
Actress

Dunn, Holly
PO Box 120964
Nashville, TN 37212
Singer

Dunne, Griffin
1501 Broadway, #2600
New York, NY 10036
Actor, director
Birthday: 6/8/55

Duran Duran
PO Box 21
London W10 6XA
England
Music group

Duvall, James
c/o APA
9000 Sunset Blvd., #1200
Los Angeles, CA 90069
Actor

Duvall, Robert
PO Box 520
The Plains, VA 22171
Actor
Birthday: 1/15/31

Dying with Dignity
#706, 188 Eglinton Ave. E.
Toronto, ON M4P 2X7
Canada
Cynthia St. John, executive
 director
Web site: http://www.we 16-489-
 b.apc.org/dwd
E-mail: dwdca@web.apc.org
*A right-to-die society founded in
 1980*

Dylan, Bob
PO Box 870
Cooper Station
New York, NY 10276
Singer, songwriter
Birthday: 5/24/41

Dylan, Jakob
H. K. Management
8900 Wilshire Blvd.
Beverly Hills, CA 90211
Singer

E

A letter is the mind alone without corporeal friend.

—EMILY DICKINSON

Eagle Forum
316 Pennsylvania Ave., Ste. 203
Washington, DC 20003
Web site: http://
www.basenet.net/~eagle/
index.html
E-mail: eagle@eagleforum.org
Phyllis Schlafly, president
*Stands for the fundamental right
of parents to guide the
education of their own children*

Eagleton Institute on Politics
Rutgers University
New Brunswick, NJ 08901
Web site: http://
www.rci.rutgers.edu./
~eagleton/
E-mail:
eagleton@rci.rutgers.edu
Ruth B. Mandel, director
E-mail: rmandel@rci.
rutgers.edu
*Develops new knowledge and
understanding of emerging
topics and themes in American
politics and government in order
to encourage more responsive
and effective leadership*

Earl, Steve
c/o MCA Records
1514 S. St.
Nashville, TN 37212
Country singer

Eastman Chemical
100 N. Eastman Rd.
Kingsport, TN 37660
Web site: http://
www.eastman.com
Earnest W. Deavenport, Jr.,
CEO
Chemicals

Eastman Kodak
343 State St.
Rochester, NY 14650
Web site: http://
www.kodak.com
George M. C. Fisher, CEO
Scientific, photo, control equipment

East-West Center
1777 East-West Rd.
Honolulu, HI 96848
Web site: http://
www.ewc.hawaii.edu/
E-mail:
ewcinfo@ewc.hawaii.edu
Kenji Sumida, president
*A national education and research
institution, and a major
resource of knowledge and
information about Asia and the
Pacific*

Eastwood, Clint
4000 Warner Blvd., #16
Burbank, CA 91522
Actor
Birthday: 5/29/30

Eaton
Eaton Center
Cleveland, OH 44114
Web site: http://
www.eaton.com
Stephen R. Hardis, CEO
Electronics, electrical equipment

Ebert, Roger
PO Box 146366
Chicago, IL 60614
Movie critic
Birthday: 6/18/42

Ebsen, Buddy
PO Box 2069
Palos Verdes Peninsula, CA
90274
Actor
Birthday: 4/2/08

Echlin
100 Double Beach Rd.
Branford, CT 06405
Web site: http://
www.echlin.com
Larry W. McCurdy, CEO
Motor vehicles and parts

Eckersley, Dennis
c/o St. Louis Cardinals
Busch Stadium
250 Stadium Plaza
St. Louis, MO 63126
Baseball player

Economic Policy Institute
1600 L St. NW, #1200
Washington, DC 20036
Web site: http://epinet.org/
E-mail: epi@epinet.org
Jeff Faux, president
*A nonprofit, nonpartisan think
tank that seeks to broaden the
public debate about strategies to
achieve a prosperous and fair
economy*

Eden, Barbara
PO Box 5556
Sherman Oaks, CA 91403
Actress
Birthday: 8/22/34

Edison International
2244 Walnut Grove Ave.
Rosemead, CA 91770
Web site: http://
www.edisonx.com
John E. Bryson, CEO
Gas and electric utilities

**Educators for Social
Responsibility**
23 Garden St.
Cambridge, MA 02138
Web site: http://
www.benjerry.com/esr/
about-esr.html
Laura Parker Roerden,
director of Publications and
Communication
*A national nonprofit organization
dedicated to helping young
people develop the convictions
and skills to build a safe,
sustainable, and just world*

Eggert, Nicole
c/o William Carroll Agency
120 S. Victory Blvd.
Burbank, CA 91502
Supermodel

Eichhorn, Lisa
19 W. 44th St., #1000
New York, NY 10036
Actress
Birthday: 2/4/52

E. I. du Pont de Nemours
1007 Market St.
Wilmington, DE 19898
Web site: http://
www.dupont.com
C. O. Holiday, Jr., CEO
Chemicals

Eisner, Michael
500 S. Buena Vista St.
Burbank, CA 91521
Entertainment executive
Birthday: 4/21/26

Electra, Carmen
c/o MTV
1515 Broadway, #400
New York, NY 10036
Television personality

Electronic Data Systems
5400 Legacy Dr.
Plano, TX 75024
Web site: http://www.eds.com
Lester Alberthal, Jr., CEO
Computer and data services

Electronic Frontier Foundation
1550 Bryant, #725
PO Box 170190
San Francisco, CA 94117
Web site: http://www.eff.org
E-mail: eff@eff.org
Barry Steinhardt, president
E-mail: Barrys@eff.org

Eli Lilly
Lilly Corporate Center
Indianapolis, IN 46285
Web site: http://www.lilly.com
Randall L. Tobias, CEO
Pharmaceuticals

HRH Queen Elizabeth II
Buckingham Palace
London SW1
England
Queen of Great Britain

Elliot, Chris
151 El Camino Dr.
Beverly Hills, CA 90212
Actor

Elliott, David James
9560 Wilshire Blvd., #516
Beverly Hills, CA 90212
Actor

Ellis, Daryl and Don
PO Box 120186
Nashville, TN 37212
Country music duo

El Paso Natural Gas
1001 Louisiana St.
Houston, TX 77002
Web site: http://www.epng.com
William A. Wise, CEO
Pipelines

Elvira (Cassandra Peterson)
15030 Ventura Blvd., #1-710
Sherman Oaks, CA 91403
Web site: http://www.elvira.com
Television personality

Ely, Joe
c/o Campfire Nightmares
7101 Hwy. 71W., Ste. A9
Austin, TX 78735
Country singer

EMC
35 Parkwood Dr.
Hopkinton, MA 01748
Web site: http://www.emc.com
Michael C. Ruettgers, CEO
Computer peripherals

Emerson Electric
8000 W. Florissant Ave.
St. Louis, MO 63136
Web site: .http://
    www.emersonelectric.com
Charles F. Knight, CEO
Electronics, electrical equipment

Emilio
719 W. Vestal, Ste. E
San Antonio, TX 78221
Country singer

Emery, Ralph
PO Box 140688
Nashville, TN 37214
Nashville Network talk show host

Empower America
1776 I St., #890
Washington, DC 20006
Web site: http://
www.empower.org/
E-mail: flueta@erols.com
Josette Shiner, president
*Combination of public policy
institute and grass-roots political
organization that promotes
progressive conservative policies*

Endometriosis Alliance, The
PO Box 326
Cooper Station
New York, NY 10276
Web site: http://
www.monmouth.com/
-mkatzman/healing/
endo.htm
*A mutual self-help, nonprofit
organization providing accurate,
current, and independent
information about endometriosis*

Endometriosis Association, The
8585 N. 76th Pl.
Milwaukee, WI 53223
Web site: http://
www.EndometriosisAssn.org/
E-mail:
endo@endometriosisassn.org
*Nonprofit organization that
provides support to women and
girls, educates the public and
medical community, and
conducts and promotes research
related to endometriosis*

Energizer Battery
Checkerboard Sq.
St. Louis, MO 63164
Patrick Muhkay, president

Energizer Bunny, The
Checkerboard Sq.
St. Louis, MO 63164

Energy Conservation Coalition
6930 Carroll Ave., #600
Tokoma Park, MD 20912
E-mail: eaf@igc.apc.org
*A department of environmental
action*

Engelhard
101 Wood Ave.
Iselin, NJ 08830
Web site: http://
www.engelhard.com
Orin R. Smith, CEO
Chemicals

Engels, Marty
11365 Ventura Blvd., #100
Studio City, CA 91604
Comedian

Ty England Fan Club
PO Box 120964
Nashville, TN 37212
Web site: www.tyengland.com
Country singer

Bill Engvall Fan Club
PO Box 60388
Colorado Springs, CO 80906
Web site: www.wbr.com/
nashville.bengvall/
Country singer

Enron
1400 Smith St.
Houston, TX 77002
Web site: http://
www.enron.com
Kenneth L. Lay, CEO
Pipelines

Entergy
639 Loyola Ave.
New Orleans, LA 70113
Web site: http://
www.entergy.com
Edwin A. Lupberger, CEO
Gas and electric utilities

Environment Defense Fund
1875 Connecticut Ave. NW
Washington, DC 20009
Web site: http://www.edf.org/
E-mail: www.edf.org
Fred Krupp, executive director
Representing 300,000 members,
  combines science, economics, and
  law to find economically
  sustainable solutions to
  environmental problems

**Environmental Health Center—
  Dallas**
8345 Walnut Hill Ln., Ste. 220
Dallas, TX 75231
Web site: http://www.ehcd.com/
E-mail: inform@ehcd.com
Carolyn Gorman, Patient
  Education director
Diagnosis and treatment for
  individuals with allergy and
  environment-related illnesses

Environmental Law Institute
1616 P St. NW, #200
Washington, DC 20036
Web site: http://www.eli.org/
J. William Futrell, president
Working to advance environmental
  protection by improving law,
  policy, and management

**Environment and Wildlife
  Protection**
1725 DeSales St. NW, #500
Washington, DC 20036
E-mail:
  dccmc.mhs.compuserve.com

E-Rotic
Postfach
47628 Straehlen
Germany
Music group

Estee Lauder
767 5th Ave.
New York, NY 10153
Leonard A. Lauder, CEO
Soaps, cosmetics

Estevez, Emilio
PO Box 4041
Malibu, CA 90264
Actor
Birthday: 5/12/62

Eszterhas, Joe
8942 Wilshire Blvd.
Beverly Hills, CA 90211
Screenwriter

Etheridge, Melissa
PO Box 884563
San Francisco, CA 94188
Singer

**Ethics and Public Policy
  Center**
1015 15th St. NW, #900
Washington, DC 20005
Web site: http://www.eppc.org/
E-mail: ethics@eppc.org
Elliott Abrams, president
Studies the interconnections
  between religious faith, political
  practice, and social values

Eubanks, Bob
11365 Ventura Blvd., #100
Studio City, CA 91604
TV game show host
Birthday: 1/8/38

Eubanks, Kevin
c/o "The Tonight Show"
NBC Entertainment
3000 W. Alameda Ave.
Burbank, CA 91527
Bandleader

**Euthanasia Research &
Guidance Organization
(ERGO!)**
24829 Norris Ln.
Junction City, OR 97448
Web site: http://
www.FinalExit.org
E-mail: ergo@efn.org
Derek Humphry, president
*Organization of people who believe
in the right to die*

Evangeline
Lafayette Square Station
PO Box 2700
New Orleans, LA 70176
Country music group

Evangelista, Linda
c/o Elite Model Management
111 E. 22nd St., 2nd Fl.
New York, NY 10010
Supermodel

Evans, Dale
15650 Senneca Rd.
Victorville, CA 92392
Queen of the Cowboys
Birthday: 10/31/12

Everett, Jim
c/o New Orleans Saints
901 Papworth Ave.
Metairie, LA 70005
Football player

Everly Brothers
c/o Judy Newby
PO Box 120725
Nashville, TN 37212
Singers

Ewing, Skip
PO Box 17254
Nashville, TN 37217
Country singer

Exxon International Oil
5959 Las Colinas Blvd.
Irving, TX 75039
Lee R. Raymond, CEO
Web site: http://
www.exxon.com
Petroleum refining

F

A letter is a cozy quilt, hand-stitched with the thread of friendship.

—FRAN BULLINGTON

Fabares, Shelly (Michelle Marie Fabares)
PO Box 6010-909
Sherman Oaks, CA 91413
Actress
Birthday: 1/19/42

FAIR (Fairness & Accuracy in Reporting)
130 W. 25th St.
New York, NY 10001
Web site: http://www.fair.org/fair/
E-mail: fair@fair.org
Jeff Cohen, executive director
National media watch group

Fairchild, Barbara
695 Scaffold Cane Rd., #B
Berea, KY 40403
Country singer

Fairchild, Morgan (Patsy McClenny)
PO Box 57593
Sherman Oaks, CA 91403
Actress
Birthday: 2/30/50

Faithless
c/o Intercord
Aixheimer Str. 26
70619 Stuttgart
Germany
Music group

Faith No More
5550 Wilshire Blvd., #202
Los Angeles, CA 90036
Music group

Falk, Peter
1004 N. Roxbury Dr.
Beverly Hills, CA 90210
Actor
Birthday: 9/26/27

Families and Work Institute
330 7 Ave., 14th Fl.
New York, NY 10001
Web site: http://www.familiesandworkinst.org/
E-mail: afarber@familiesandwork.org
Ellen Galinsky, president
Nonprofit organization that addresses the changing nature of work and family life

Families USA Foundation

1334 G St. NW, #300
Washington, DC 20005
Web site: http://
www.familiesusa.org/
E-mail: info@familiesusa.org
Ronald F. Pollack, vice
president and executive
director
National nonprofit, nonpartisan organization dedicated to the achievement of high-quality, affordable health and long-term care for all Americans

Family Violence Prevention Fund

383 Rhode Island St., #304
San Francisco, CA 94103
Web site: http://
www.igc.apc.org/fund/
E-mail: fund@igc.apc.org
Esta Soler, executive director
National nonprofit organization that focuses on domestic violence education, prevention, and public policy reform

Fannie Mae

3900 Wisconsin Ave. NW
Washington, DC 20016
Web site: http://
www.fanniemae.com
E-mail:
webmaster@fanniemae.com
James A. Johnson, CEO
World's largest diversified financial company and the nation's largest source of home mortgage funds

Farentino, Debra

c/o 3 Arts Entertainment
9460 Wilshire Blvd., #700
Beverly Hills, CA 90212
Actress

Fargo, Donna

PO Box 233
Crescent, GA 31304
Country singer
Birthday: 11/10/45

Farm Journal

1325 G St. NW, Ste. 200
Washington, DC 20005
Web site: http://
www.farmjournal.com
Amber Spafford, editorial staff
member
E-mail: AESpaf@aol.com
Charlene Fink, machinery and
crop production editor
E-mail: clfinck@aol.com
Founded in Philadelphia in 1877, boasts 660,000 subscribers nationwide, making it the largest circulation farm magazine

Farmland Industries

3315 N. Farmland Trffcwy.
Kansas City, MO 64116
Harry D. Cleberg, CEO
Food producer

Farrakhan, Rev. Louis

734 W. 79th St.
Chicago, IL 60620
Spokesman for the Nation of Islam

Farrell, Mike

MSC 826 PO Box 6010
Sherman Oaks, CA 91413-6010
or
14011 Ventura Blvd.
Sherman Oaks, CA 91423
Actor
Birthday: 2/6/39

Farrell, Terry

c/o Don Buchwald and
Associates
9229 Sunset Blvd., #710
Los Angeles, CA 90069
Actress
Birthday: 11/19/63

Faustino, David
1806 N. Maple St.
Burbank, CA 91505
Actor
Birthday: 3/7/74

Favre, Brett
c/o Green Bay Packers
PO Box 10628
Green Bay, WI 54307
Football player

Al Fayed, Mohammed
4 Rte. Du Champ
    D'Entrainment WVI
Paris
France

FDX
2005 Corporate Ave.
Memphis, TN 38132
Web site: http://
    www.fdxcorp.com
Frederick W. Smith, CEO
Mail, package, freight delivery

F.E.A.R. Foundation
PO Box 15421
Washington, DC 20003
Web site: http://www.fear.org/
E-mail: powerhit@fli.net
Robert Bauman, member of
    board of directors
*Forfeiture Endangers American
    Rights is a national nonprofit
    organization dedicated to reform
    of federal and state asset
    forfeiture laws to restore due
    process and protect the property
    rights of innocent citizens.*

**Federal Bureau of
    Investigation (FBI)**
Press Office
10th & Pennsylvania Ave. NW,
    #7222
Washington, DC 20535
Web site: http://www.fbi.gov
Louis J. Freeh, director

**Federal Election Commission
    (FEC)**
999 E St. NW
Washington, DC 20463
Web site: http://www.fec.gov/
E-mail: webmaster@fec.gov
Joan D. Aikens, chairman
*Administers and enforces the
    Federal Election Campaign Act
    (FECA)*

Federal Home Loan Mortgage
8200 Jones Branch Dr.
McLean, VA 22102
Web site: http://
    www.freddiemac.com
Leland C. Brendsel, CEO
Diversified financials

Federated Department Stores
7 W. 7th St.
Cincinnati, OH 45202
Web site: http://
    www.federated-fds.com
James M. Zimmerman, CEO
*General merchandisers—Macy's,
    Bloomingdale's, Aeropostal,
    Charter Club, Burdines,
    Lazarus, The Bon Marché,
    Stern's*

**Federation for American
    Immigration Reform**
1666 Connecticut Ave. NW,
    #400
Washington, DC 20009
Web site: http://www.fairus.org/
E-mail: fair@fairus.org
John Tanton, chairman of
    board of directors
*National, membership-based,
    educational organization, with
    70,000 members across the
    country, working to help the
    American public convince
    Congress that our nation's
    immigration laws must be
    reformed*

Feldman, Corey
1017½ Westwood Blvd.
Los Angeles, CA 90025
Actor
Birthday: 3/16/71

Feldon, Barbara
14 E. 74th. St.
New York, NY 10021
Actress
Birthday: 3/12/41

Fender, Freddie
PO Box 530
Bel Aire, OH 43906
Country singer
Birthday: 6/4/37

Ferguson, Tom
PO Box 50249
Austin, TX 78763
Web site: www.healthy.net/
   selfcare
E-mail: doctom@doctom.com.
Author of Health Online
   Addision-Wesley *and editor*
   and publisher of The
   Ferguson Report: The
   Newsletter of Consumer
   Health Informatics and
   Online Health.

Ferraro, Chris
c/o Pittsburgh Penguins
Civic Arena
66 Mario Lemieux Pl.
Pittsburgh, PA 15219
Hockey player

Ferrigno, Lou
PO Box 1671
Santa Monica, CA 90402
Actor, bodybuilder
Birthday: 11/9/51

Field, Sally
PO Box 492417
Los Angeles, CA 90049
Actress
Birthday: 11/6/46

Fierstein, Harvey
232 N. Canon Dr.
Beverly Hills, CA 90210
Actor

Fiorentino, Linda
c/o C.A.A.
9830 Wilshire Blvd.
Beverly Hills, CA 90212
Actress
Birthday: 3/9/30

First Chicago NBD Corp.
1 First National Plaza
Chicago, IL 60670
Web site: http://
   www.fcnbd.com
Verne G. Istock, CEO
Commercial bank

First Data
401 Hackensack Ave.
Hackensack, NJ 07601
Web site: http://
   www.firstdatacorp.com
Henry C. Duques, CEO
Computer and data services

FirstEnergy
76 S. Main St.
Akron, OH 44308
Web site: http://
   www.firstenergycorp.com
Willard R. Holland, CEO
Gas and electric utilities

First Union Corp.
1 First Union Ctr.
Charlotte, NC 28288
Web site: http://
   www.firstunion.com
Edward E. Crutchfield, CEO
Commercial bank

Fishel, Danielle
c/o "Boy Meets World"
ABC-TV
2040 Ave. of the Stars
Los Angeles, CA 90064
Actress

Fisichella, Giancarlo
c/o Jordan Formula One Ltd.
Silverstone Circuit
Towcester
Northhamptonshire NN12 8TN
England
Professional Formula-1 driver

Fixx, The
6255 Sunset Blvd., 2nd Fl.
Los Angeles, CA 90028
Music group

Flack, Roberta
1 W. 72nd St.
New York, NY 10022
Singer
Birthday: 2/10/39

Flaming Lips, The
PO Box 75995
Oklahoma City, OK 73141
Music group

Fleet Financial Group
1 Federal St.
Boston, MA 02110
Web site: http://www.fleet.com
Terrence Murray, CEO
Commercial bank

Fleetwood Enterprises
3125 Myers St.
Riverside, CA 92503
Web site: http://
www.fleetwood.com.
Glenn F. Kummer, CEO
Engineering, construction

Fleetwood Mac
9107 Wilshire Blvd., #300
Beverly Hills, CA 90210
Music group

Fleming
6301 Waterford Blvd.
Oklahoma City, OK 73126
Web site: http://
www.fleming.com
Robert E. Stauth
Wholesalers, food products

Fleming, Peggy
c/o Studio Fan Mail
1122 S. Robertson Blvd., Ste.
15
Los Angeles, CA 90035
Actress, ice skater
Birthday: 7/27/48

Fletcher, Louise
1520 Camden Ave., #105
Los Angeles, CA 90025
Actress

Flockhart, Calista
c/o "Ally McBeal"
Ren Mar Studios
846 N. Cahuenga Blvd.
Bldg. A, 2nd Fl.
Hollywood, CA 90038
Actress

Florida Progress
1 Progress Plaza
St. Petersburg, FL 33701
Web site: http://www.fpc.com
Richard Korpan, CEO
Gas and electric utilities

Fluor
3353 Michelson Dr.
Irvine, CA 92698
Web site: http://www.fluor.com
Peter Fluor, CEO
Engineering, construction

FMC
200 E. Randolph Dr.
Chicago, IL 60601
Web site: http://www.fmc.com
Robert N. Burt, CEO
Chemicals

Fogelberg, Dan
PO Box 2399
Pagosa Springs, CO 81147
Singer
Birthday: 8/31/51

Fogerty, John
PO Box 375
Granada Hills, CA 91364
Singer, songwriter

Foley, David
c/o NBC
3000 W. Alameda Ave.
Burbank, CA 91523
Actor

Fonda, Bridget
9560 Wilshire Blvd., #516
Beverly Hills, CA 90212
Actress, Jane Fonda's niece
Birthday: 1/27/64

Fonda, Jane
1050 Techwood Dr. NW
Atlanta, GA 30318
Actress
Birthday: 12/21/37

Food for Less
1100 W. Artesia Blvd.
Compton, CA 90220
George G. Golleher, CEO
Food and drug stores

**Food Research and Action
Center**
1875 Connecticut Ave. NW,
#540
Washington, DC 20009
Web site: http://www.frac.org/
E-mail: webmaster@frac.org
Carol Tucker Foreman, chair
of Board of Directors
*Working to improve public policies
to eradicate hunger and
undernutrition in the U.S.*

Foo Fighters
c/o Capitol Records
1750 N. Vine St.
Los Angeles, CA 90028
Music group

Forbes, Steve
60 5th Ave.
New York, NY 10011
Magazine publisher

Force, John
c/o John Force Racing
23253 East LaPalma Ave.
Yorba Linda, CA 92687
Race car driver

Ford, Chris
c/o Milwaukee Bucks
1001 N. 4th St.
Milwaukee, WI 53203
Basketball player

Ford, Faith
7920 Sunset Blvd., #350
Los Angeles, CA 90046
Actress
Birthday: 9/14/64

Ford, Gerald R. and Betty
PO Box 927
Rancho Mirage, CA 92270
Former President and First Lady
Birthday: Gerald R. Ford
7/14/13
*Betty Ford asks for a $5 check
made out to The Betty Ford
Center*

Ford, Patricia
c/o Playmate Promotions
9242 Beverly Blvd.
Beverly Hills, CA 90210
Model

Ford, Whitey
38 Schoolhouse Ln.
Lake Success, NY 10020
Former baseball player

Ford Foundation
320 E. 43rd St.
New York, NY 10017
Web site: http://
www.fordfound.org
*Grant organization that supports
activities that strengthen
democratic values, reduce
poverty and injustice, promote
international cooperation, and
advance human achievement*

Any Ford Model
[Model's Name]
c/o Ford Model Mgmt.
344 E. 59th St.
New York, NY 10022
Address to write to Ford models

Ford Motor Company
P.O. Box 1899
Dearborn, MI 48121-1899
Web site: http://www.ford.com
Alexander J. Trotman, CEO
Motor vehicles and parts

Forester Sisters
1516 16th Ave. S.
Nashville, TN 37212
Country music group

Fort James Corp
120 Tredegar St.
Richmond, VA 23219
Web site: http://
www.fortjames.com
Miles L. Marsh, CEO
Forest and paper products

Fortune Brands
1700 E. Putnam Ave.
Old Greenwich, CT 06870
Web site: http://
www.fortunebrands.com
Thomas C. Hays, CEO
Metal products

Foster, Jodie
10900 Wilshire Blvd., #511
Los Angeles, CA 90024
or
c/o Egg Pictures
7920 Sunset Blvd., #1429
Los Angeles, CA 90024
Actress, director
Birthday: 11/19/62

Foster, Radney
c/o Fitzgerald Hartley
1212 16th Ave. S.
Nashville, TN 37212
Country singer

Foster Wheeler
Perryville Corporate Park
Clinton, NJ 08809
Web site: http://www.fwc.com
Richard J. Swift, CEO
Engineering, construction

**Foundation for Biomedical
Research**
818 Connecticut Ave. NW,
303
Washington, DC 20006
Web site: http://
www.fbresearch.org/
E-mail: info@fbresearch.org
Frankie Trull, president
*Nonprofit organization that focuses
on the proper use of animals in
medical research*

Foundation Health Systems
21600 Oxnard St.
Woodland Hills, CA 91367
Web site: http://www.fhs.com
Malik M. Hasan, CEO
Health care

Fox, Michael J.
Lottery Hill Farm
South Woodstock, VT 05071
Actor
Birthday: 6/9/61

Fox Brothers
6116 Sullivan Trail
Nazareth, PA 18064
Country music group

Foxworthy, Jeff
8380 Melrose Ave., #310
Los Angeles, CA 90069
Comedian, actor

Foxx, Jamie
15445 Ventura Blvd., #790
Sherman Oaks, CA 91403
Actor

FPL Group
700 Universe Blvd.
Juno Beach, FL 33408
Web site: http://
  www.fplgroup.com
James L. Broadhead, CEO
Gas and electric utilities

Francis, Cleve
PO Box 15258
Alexandria, VA 22309
Country singer

Francis, Ron
c/o Pittsburgh Penguins
66 Mario Lemieux Pl.
Pittsburgh, PA 15219
Hockey player

Fraser, Brendan
c/o William Morris Agency
151 S. El Camino Dr.
Beverly Hills, CA 90212
Actor

Fred Meyer
3800 S.E. 22nd Ave.
Portland, OR 97202
Web site: http://
  www.fredmeyer.com
Robert G. Miller, CEO
Food and drug stores

Freedom Forum
1101 Wilson Blvd.
Arlington, VA 22209
Web site: http://
  www.freedomforum.org/
E-mail:
  news@freedomforum.org
Charles L. Overby, chairman
  and CEO
*Nonpartisan, international
  foundation dedicated to free
  press, free speech, and free spirit
  for all people. Its mission is to
  help the public and the news
  media understand one another
  better*

**Freedom Forum Media Studies
Center**
580 Madison Ave., 42nd Fl.
New York, NY 10022
Web site: http://
  www.freedomforum.org/
  whoweare/media.asp
E-mail:
  mfitzsi@mediastudies.org
Allen H. Neuharth, founder
*Nation's premier media think tank
  devoted to improving
  understanding of media issues
  by the press and the public*

Fregosi, Jim
c/o Phillies
PO Box 7575
Philadelphia, PA 19101
Baseball player

Frentzen, Heinz-Harald
c/o Williams GP Engineering
  Ltd.
Grove
Wantage
Oxfordshire OX12 ODQ
England
Professional Formula-1 driver

Fricke, Janie
PO Box 798
Lancaster, TX 75146
Country singer

"Friends"
c/o Warner Bros.
4000 Warner Blvd.
Burbank, CA 91522
TV series

**Friends Committee on
National Legislation**
245 2nd St. NE
Washington, DC 20002
Web site: http://www.clark.net/
pub/fcnl/
E-mail: fcnl@fcnl.org
*Nationwide network of thousands
of Quakers, bringing the
testimonies of Friends to bear on
a wide range of national
legislation regarding peace and
social justice issues*

Friends of the Earth
218 D St. SE, 2nd Fl.
Washington, DC 20003
Web site: http://www.foe.co.uk/
E-mail: webmaster@foe.co.uk
Charles Secrett, executive
director
*Largest international network of
environmental groups in the
world, represented in 52
countries*

Frizzell, David
c/o Christina Frazer
PO Box 120964
Nashville, TN 37212
Country singer

Fuel Cells 2000
Web site: http://
www.fuelcells.org/
E-mail:
webmaster@fuelcells.org
Robert R. Rose, executive
director
*Private, nonprofit, educational
organization providing
information to policy makers, the
media, and the public and
supporting the early use of fuel
cells through pilot projects and
government purchases*

Fuhrman, Mark
PO Box 141
Sandpoint, ID 83864
*Police witness in O. J. Simpson
trial*

Fujita, Yoshio
6-21-7 Renkojl
Tama-shi 206
Japan
Astronomer

**Fully Informed Jury
Association (FIJA)**
PO Box 59
Helmville, MT 59843

Fund for Animals
850 Sligo Ave., #300
Silver Spring, MD 20910
Web site: http://envirolink.org/
arrs/fund/
E-mail: fund4animals@fund.org
*Active anti-hunting organization
in the United States*

A letter sings of love and hope,
still warm from the hug of an envelope.

—VICKI RENTZ

G, Kenny
Turner Management Group
3500 W. Olive Ave., #900
Burbank, CA 91505
Musician
Birthday: 6/5/56

Gagne, Greg
c/o Los Angeles Dodgers
1000 Elysian Park Ave.
Los Angeles, CA 90012
Baseball player

Gallagher, Danny
49 Crouch Hill, Finsbury Park
London N4
England
Healer

Galloway, Joey
c/o Seattle Seahawks
11220 NE 53rd St.
Kirkland, WA 98033
Football player

Game Show Network
550 Madison Ave.
Culver City, CA 90232
Michael Fleming, president
Cable television network
E-mail: michaeL
    fleming@spe.sony.com

Gannett
1100 Wilson Blvd.
Arlington, VA 22234
Web site: http://
    www.gannett.com
John J. Curley, CEO
Publishing, printing

Gantner, Jim
c/o Milwaukee Brewers
Milwaukee County Stadium
Milwaukee, WI 53214
Baseball player

Gantin, Bernardin Cardinal
Piazza S. Calisto 16
00153 Roma
Italy
Cardinal

Gap
1 Harrison St.
San Francisco, CA 94105
Web site: http://www.gap.com
Millard S. Drexler, CEO
Clothing retailer

Garcia, Andy
c/o Paradigm
10100 Santa Monica Blvd.,
    25th Fl.
Los Angeles, CA 90067
Actor

Garr, Teri
9200 Sunset Blvd., #428
Los Angeles, CA 90069
or
9150 Wilshire Blvd., #350
Beverly Hills, CA 90212-3427
Actress
Birthday: 12/11/45

Garrison, David
9229 Sunset Blvd., #710
Los Angeles, CA 90069
Actor

Gates, Bill
1 Microsoft Way
Redmond, WA 98052
Founder of Microsoft

Gateway
610 Gateway Dr.
North Sioux City, SD 57049
Web site: http://www.gw2k.com
Ted Waitt, CEO
Computers, office equipment

Gatlin Brothers
PO Box 153452
Irving, TX 75015-3452
Country music group

Gayle, Crystal
51 Music Sq. E.
Nashville, TN 37203
Country singer
Birthday: 1/9/51

Gaynor, Gloria
c/o Cliffside Music
PO Box 374
Fairview, NJ 07010
Singer
Birthday: 9/7/48

Geary, Tony
c/o "General Hospital"
ABC-TV
4151 Prospect Ave.
Los Angeles, CA 90027
Soap opera star

Geffen, David
PO Box 8520
Universal City, CA 91608
President, Geffen Records

Geldof, Bob
c/o Juke Productions
3300 Harrow Rd.
London W9 2HP
England
Musician

Gellar, Sarah Michelle
c/o "Buffy the Vampire
   Slayer"
The Warner Brothers
   Television Network
4000 Warner Blvd.
Burbank, CA 91522
Actress

GenAmerica Corporation
700 Market St.
St. Louis, MO 63101
Richard A. Liddy, CEO
Life and health insurance (stock)

General Dynamics
3190 Fairview Park Dr.
Falls Church, VA 22042
Web site: http://www.gdeb.com/
   pr/corp_info
Nicholas D. Chabraja, CEO
Aerospace

General Electric
3135 Easton Turnpike
Fairfield, CT 06431
Web site: http://www.ge.com
John F. Welch, Jr., CEO
Electrical equipment company

General Mills
1 General Mills Blvd.
Minneapolis, MN 55426
Web site: http://
   www.generalmills.com
Stephen W. Sanger, CEO
Food producer

General Motors
PO Box 431301
Detroit, MI 48243-7301
John F. Smith, Jr., CEO
Web site: http://www.gm.com
Auto and truck manufacturer

General Re
695 E. Main St.
Stamford, CT 06904
Web site: http://
www.genre.com
Ronald E. Ferguson, CEO
P & C insurance (stock)

Genuine Parts
2999 Circle 75 Pkwy.
Atlanta, GA 30339
Web site: http://
www.genpt.com
Larry L. Prince, CEO
Wholesalers, automobile parts

Georgia-Pacific
133 Peachtree St. NE
Atlanta, GA 30303
Web site: http://www.gp.com
A. D. Correll, CEO
Forest and paper products

GeRue, Gene "Bumpy"
HC78, Box 1105
Zanoni, MO 65784
Home page: http://
www.ruralize.com
E-mail:
genegerue@ruralize.com
Author of the book How to Find
Your Ideal Country Home,
Ruralize Your Dream

Giant Food
6300 Sheriff Rd.
Landover, MD 20785
Pete L. Manos, CEO
Food and drug stores

Gibson, Don
PO Box 50474
Nashville, TN 37205
Country singer

Gibson, Mel
4000 Warner Blvd., #P3-17
Burbank, CA 91522
Actor
Birthday: 1/7/56

Gibson Miller Band
c/o Sherry Halton
PO Box 120964
Nashville, TN 37212
Country music group

Gifford, Kathie Lee
625 Madison Ave., #1200
New York, NY 10022
TV host
Birthday: 8/16/53

Gilbert, Melissa
PO Box 57593
Sherman Oaks, CA 91403
Actress
Birthday: 5/8/64

Gill, Vince
PO Box 1407
White House, TN 37188
Country singer
Birthday: 4/12/57

Gillette
Prudential Tower Building
Boston, MA 02199
Alfred M. Zeien, CEO
Metal products

Gilley, Mickey
PO Box 1242
Pasadena, TX 77501
Country singer
Birthday: 3/9/36

Gilliam, Terry
The Old Hall
South Grove
Highgate
London N6
England
Comedian, actor, director
Birthday: 1/22/40

Gilmore, Jimmie Dale
c/o Main Grand Stand
  Promotions
122 Longwood Ave.
Austin, TX 78734
Country singer

Gimble, Johnny
PO Box 347
Dripping Springs, TX 78620
Country singer

Ginsberg, Ruth Bader
1 First St. NE
Washington, DC 20543
Supreme Court justice

Golden, William Lee
RR 2 Saundersville Rd.
Hendersonville, TN 37075
Country singer

Goldens, The
PO Box 1795
Hendersonville, TN 37077
Country music group

Golden West Financial Corp.
1901 Harrison St.
Oakland, CA 94612
H. M. Sandler, CEO
Savings institution

Goldsboro, Bobby
PO Box 158569
Nashville, TN 37215
Country singer

Gonzalez, Juan
c/o Texas Rangers
1000 Ballpark Way
Arlington, TX 76011
Baseball player

**Goodbye, A Choice-in-Dying
  Society**
PO Box 39149, Point Grey
  RPO
Vancouver, BC V6R 4P1
Canada
Charles and Doris Clapham,
  executives
*Organization of people who believe
  in the right to die*

Gooding, Cuba, Jr.
5750 Wilshire Blvd., #580
Los Angeles, CA 90036
Actor

Goodrich, Gail
c/o Basketball Hall of Fame
1150 W. Columbus Ave.
Springfield, MA 01101
Basketball player

Goodyear Tire & Rubber
1144 E. Market St.
Akron, OH 44316
Web site: http://
  www.goodyear.com
Samir G. Gibara, CEO
Rubber and plastic products

Gorbachev, Mikhail
49 Leningradsky prospekt 209
Moscow
Russia
Former head of the Soviet Union
Birthday: 3/2/31

Gordeeva, Ekaterina
c/o Intl. Skating Ctr.
1375 Hopmeadow St.
Simsbury, CT 06070
Figure skater

Gore, Al
Admiral House
34th & Massachusetts
Washington, DC 20005
E-mail: vice.president@
  whitehouse.gov
Vice President of the United States
Birthday: 3/31/48

Gore, Tipper
Admiral House
34th & Massachusetts
Washington, DC 20005
Wife of Vice Pres. Al Gore

Gorshin, Frank
c/o Gor Publications
PO Box 17731
West Haven, CT 06516
or
11365 Ventura Blvd., #100
Studio City, CA 91604
Actor
Birthday: 4/5/34

Gosdin, Vern
2509 W. Marquette Ave.
Tampa, FL 33614
Country singer

Gottfried, Gilbert
1350 Ave. of the Americas
New York, NY 10019
Comedian

Gotti, John
#182661-053
USP Marion
PO Box 1000
Marion, IL 62958
*Convicted of murdering Paul
    Castellano, alleged boss of the
    Gambino Family, and his
    driver, Thomas Bilotti;
    nicknamed the Teflon Don*
Birthday: 10/27/40

GPU
300 Madison Ave.
Morristown, NJ 07962
Web site: http://www.gpu.com
Fred D. Hafer, CEO
Gas and electric utilities

Graham, The Rev. Billy
PO Box 779
Minneapolis, MN 55440
Evangelist
Birthday: 11/7/18

Grant, Amy
2910 Poston Ave.
Nashville, TN 37203
Singer
Birthday: 11/25/60

Gray, Linda
PO Box 5064
Sherman Oaks, CA 91403
Actress
Birthday: 9/12/41

Graybar Electric
34 N. Meramec Ave.
St. Louis, MO 63105
Carl L. Hall, CEO
Wholesaler

Gray Panther Project Fund
2025 Pennsylvania Ave. NW,
    #821
Washington, DC 20006
*A national organization of
    intergenerational activists
    dedicated to social change*

Great Plains
PO Box 2411
Murfreesboro, TN 37133
Country music group

Green Bay Packers, Inc.
1265 Lombardi Ave.
Green Bay, WI 54304
Robert E. Harlan, president
    and CEO
Ron Wolf, EVP and general
    manager
*A publically owned nonprofit
    corporation—unlike any other
    football team*

Greenpeace
1436 U St. NW
Washington, DC 20009
Web site: http://
    www.greenpeaceusa.org/
E-mail:
    info@wdc.greenpeace.org
Lynn Thorp, campaigns
    director, Greenpeace USA
Worldwide environmental group

The Greens (Green Party USA)
PO Box 1134
Lawrence, MA 01842
Web site: http://
www.envirolink.org/greens/
usa/contax.html
E-mail: gpusa@igc.apc.org
Tom Sevigne, cochair
E-mail: capeconn@snet.net
Environmental political party

Greenwood, Lee
1311 Elm Hill Pike
Nashville, TN 37214
Country singer

Gregg, Ricky Lynn
PO Box 8924
Bossier City, LA 71113
Country singer

Gregory, Clinton
PO Box 707
Hermitage, TN 37076
Country singer

Grey, Joel
1325 Ave. of the Americas
New York, NY 10019
Actor
Birthday: 4/11/32

Griese, Bob
c/o Pro Football Hall of Fame
2121 George Halas Dr. NW
Canton, OH 44708
Former football player

Griffey, Ken, Jr.
PO Box 4100
Seattle, WA 98104
Baseball player

Griffith, Andy
PO Box 1968
Manteo, NC 27954
Actor
Birthday: 6/2/26

Griffith, Nanci
PO Box 128037
Nashville, TN 37212
Singer

Grimes, Dorothy
128 Roberts Rd.
Aston, PA 19014
Healer

Grisham, John
PO Box 1780
Oxford, MS 38655
Author

Grizzard, Lewis
2951 Piedmont Rd. NE, #100
Atlanta, GA 30305
Country singer

Groening, Matt
10201 West Pico Blvd.
Los Angeles, CA 90035
*Creator and developer of "The
Simpsons"*
Birthday: 2/15/54

GTE
1 Stamford Forum
Stamford, CT 06904
Web site: http://www.gte.com
Charles R. Lee, CEO
Telecommunications

**Guardian Life Insurance Co.
of America**
201 Park Ave. S.
New York, NY 10003
Joseph D. Sargent, CEO
*Life and health insurance
(mutual)*

Guerrero, Roberto
c/o Pagan Racing
298A Gasoline Alley
Indianapolis, IN 46222
Auto racing driver

Guest, Christopher
PO Box 2358
Running Springs, CA 92382
Actor

Gumbel, Bryant
524 W. 57th St.
New York, NY 10019
TV show host
Birthday: 9/29/48

Gumbel, Greg
524 W. 57th St.
New York, NY 10019
TV show host

Guthrie, Arlo
The Farm
Washington, MA 01223
Singer, songwriter
Birthday: 7/10/47

Guy, Jasmine
21243 Ventura Blvd., #101
Woodland Hills, CA 91364
Actress, dancer
Birthday: 3/10/64

Gwynn, Tony
c/o San Diego Padres
PO Box 2000
San Diego, CA 92112
Baseball player

News from home is best carried in a letter, and so much can be written on a little piece of paper. Inside the envelope can be sunshine or dark dismal days.

—HANS CHRISTIAN ANDERSEN

Haas, Lukas
10683 Santa Monica Blvd.
Los Angeles, CA 90025
Actor
Birthday: 4/16/76

Haggard, Merle
3009 East St.
Sevierville, TN 37862
Country singer

Haim, Corey
316 N. Alfred St.
Los Angeles, CA 90046
Actor
Birthday: 12/23/72

Häkkinen, Mika
c/o McLaren Intl. Ltd.
Woking Business Park
Albert Dr.
Woking
Surrey GU21 5JS
England
Professional Formula-1 driver
Birthday: 9/28/68

Halal, William E.
Dept. of Management Science
School of Business and Public
    Management
George Washington University
2115 G Street NW, Monroe
    Hall 401-D
Washington, DC 20052
E-mail:
    halal@gwis2.circ.gwu.edu
Professor of management

Hale, Alan Spencer
5476 St. Paul Rd.
Morristown, TN 37813
Country singer

Hale, Barbara
15301 Ventura Blvd., #345
Sherman Oaks, CA 91403
Actress
Birthday: 2/18/21

Hall, Monty
11365 Ventura Blvd., #100
Studio City, CA 91604
TV game show host
Birthday: 8/25/24

Hall, Tom T.
PO Box 12146
Franklin, TN 37065
Country singer

Halliburton
3600 Lincoln Plaza
Dallas, TX 75201
Web site: http://
  www.halliburton.com
Richard B. Cheney, CEO
Engineering, construction

Hamill, Mark
PO Box 1051
Santa Monica, CA 90406
Actor
Birthday: 9/25/51

Hamilton, Scott
1 Erieview Plaza
Cleveland, OH 44114
Figure skater, sports commentator

Hamilton, George, IV
c/o Blade Agency
PO Box 1556
Gainesville, FL 32602
Country singer

Handgun Control, Inc.
1225 Eye Street NW, Ste. 1100
Washington, DC 20005
Web site: http://
  www.handguncontrol.org/
Sarah Brady, chairman
Gun control organization

Hanna, Bill
3400 Cahuenga Blvd.
Hollywood, CA 90068
Animation executive

Hannaford Bros.
145 Pleasant Hill Rd.
Scarborough, ME 04074
Web site: http://
  www.hannaford.com
Hugh G. Farrington, CEO
Food and drug stores

Hannigan, Alyson
c/o "Buffy the Vampire
  Slayer"
4000 Warner Blvd.
Bldg. #34R
Burbank, CA 91522
Actress

HRH Prince Hans Adam
Schloss Vaduz
Liechtenstein
Prince of Liechtenstein

Hanson Brothers
Hitz List
PO Box 703136
Tulsa, OK 74140
Web site: http://
  www.hansononline.com
E-mail: hansonfans@
  hansononline.com
*Pop group, brothers Isaac, Zac,
  and Taylor*

Harcourt General
27 Boylston St.
Chestnut Hill, MA 02167
Richard A. Smith, CEO
General merchandisers

Hardaway, Anfernee
c/o Orlando Magic
One Magic Pl.
Orlando, FL 32801
Basketball player

Harding, Tonya
121 Morrison St. SW, #1100
Portland, OR 97204
Figure skater
Birthday: 11/12/70

Hargitay, Mariska
924 Westwood Blvd., #900
Los Angeles, CA 90024
Actress

Harling, Keith
PO Box 1304
Goodlettsville, TN 37070
E-mail:
    fanclub@keithharling.com
Country music singer

Harmon, Angie
c/o The Baywatch Prod. Co.
5433 Beethoven St.
Los Angeles, CA 90066
Actress

Harnischfeger Industries
3600 South Lake Dr.
St. Francis, WI 53235
Web site: http://
    www.harnischfeger.com
Jeffrey T. Grade, CEO
Industrial and farm equipment

Harper, Tess
8484 Wilshire Blvd., #500
Beverly Hills, CA 90211
Actress
Birthday: 11/30/51

Harper, Valerie
616 N. Maple Dr.
Beverly Hills, CA 90210
Actress
Birthday: 8/22/40

Harris
1025 W. NASA Blvd.
Melbourne, FL 32919
Web site: http://
    www.harris.com
Phillip W. Farmer, CEO
Electronics, electrical equipment

Harris, Del
c/o Great Western Forum
PO Box 10
Inglewood, CA 90306
L.A. Lakers head coach
Birthday: 6/18/37

Harris, Emmylou
PO Box 99497
Louisville, KY 40299
Singer
Birthday: 4/2/48

Harris, Neal Patrick
11350 Ventura Blvd., #206
Studio City, CA 91604
Actor
Birthday: 6/15/73

Harrison, A. J.
c/o Romaha Records
PO Box 823
Snellville, GA 30078
Web site: http://
www.aj-harrison.com/
Singer, actor

HRH Prince Harry
Highgrove House
Gloucestershire
England
Son of Prince Charles

Freddie Hart & the Heartbeats
c/o Tessier March Talent, Inc.
505 Canton Pass
Madison, TN 37115
Country music group

Hart, Mary
150 S. El Camino Dr., #303
Beverly Hills, CA 90212
*Cohost of Entertainment
    Tonight*
Birthday: 11/8/51

Hartford Financial Services
Hartford Plaza
Hartford, CT 06115
Web site: http://
    www.thehartford.com
Ramani Ayer, CEO
P & C insurance (stock)

Hasbro
1027 Newport Ave.
Pawtucket, RI 02862
Web site: http://
www.hasbro.com
Alan G. Hassenfeld, CEO
Toys, sporting goods

Hatcher, Teri
10100 Santa Monica Blvd.,
#410
Los Angeles, CA 90067
Actress

Haven, Annette
PO Box 1244
Sausalito, CA 94966
Porn star

Hawking, Stephen
DAMTP
Silver St.
Cambridge CB3 9EW
England
E-mail: S.W. Hawking
@damtp.cam.ac.uk
Birthday: 1/8/42
*Perhaps best known for his 1974
discovery that black holes emit
radiation; author of* A Brief
History of Time *and* Black
Holes and Baby Universes
and Other Essays

Hawn, Goldie
500 S. Buena Vista St., #1D6
Burbank, CA 91505
Actress
Birthday: 11/2/45

Hayes, Isaac
PO Box 674891
Marietta, GA 30067
Singer
Birthday: 8/20/42

Hayes, Wade
PO Box 128546
Nashville, TN 37212
Country singer

**Health Care Finance
Administration**
7500 Security Blvd.
Baltimore, MD 21244
Web site: http://www.hcfa.gov/
E-mail: Question@hcfa.gov
Nancy-Ann Min DeParle,
administrator
*Federal agency that administers the
Medicare, Medicaid, and Child
Health Insurance programs*

**Health Insurance Association
of America**
555 13th St. NW, #600E
Washington, DC 20004
Web site: http://www.hiaa.org/
E-mail: webmaster@hiaa.org
Charles N. Kahn, COO and
president
*National trade association whose
more than 250 members are
insurers and managed care
companies that serve tens of
millions of Americans*

HealthSouth
1 HealthSouth Pkwy.
Birmingham, AL 35243
Web site: http://
www.healthsouth.com
Richard M. Scrushy, CEO
Health care

Heft, Bob
PO Box 131
Napoleon, OH 43545
Designed the 50-star U.S. flag

Helms, Bobby
c/o Tessier March Talent, Inc.
505 Canton Pass
Madison, TN 37115
Country singer

Hemlock Society USA
PO Box 101810
Denver, CO 80250
Web site: http://
    www.hemlock.org/hemlock/
E-mail: hemlock@privatei.com
John Westover, president
A right-to-die organization

Henderson, Florence
9000 Sunset Blvd., #1200
Los Angeles, CA 90069
Actress

Henderson, Tareva
PO Box 17303
Nashville, TN 37217
Country singer

Hendricks, Ted
c/o Pro Football Hall of Fame
2121 George Halas Dr. NW
Canton, OH 44708
Former football player

**Official "Hercules: The
    Legendary Journeys" Fan
    Club**
c/o Creation Entertainment
664A W. Broadway
Glendale, CA 91204

Ty Herndon & Friends
c/o Leigh Ritsema
PO 120658
Nashville, TN 37212
Country music group

Hershey, Barbara
c/o CAA
9830 Wilshire Blvd.
Beverly Hills, CA 90212
Actress
Birthday: 2/5/48

Hershey Foods
100 Crystal A Dr.
Hershey, PA 17033
Web site: http://hersheys.com
Kenneth L. Wolfe, CEO
Food producer, chocolate maker

Herzigova, Eva
20 W. 20th St., #600
New York, NY 10011
Supermodel

Hewlett Packard
3000 Hanover St.
Palo Alto, CA 94304
Web site: http://www.hp.com
Lewis E. Platt, CEO
Computers, office equipment

H. F. Amhanson
4900 Rivergrade Rd.
Irwindale, CA 91706
Web site: http://
    www.homesavings.com/
    home.shtml
Charles Rinehart, CEO
Savings institution

High Frontier, Inc.
2800 Shirlington Rd., #405A
Arlington, VA 22206
Web site: http://
    www.highfrontier.org/
Henry F. Cooper, chairman
*Mission is to ensure the nation is
    protected against ballistic missile
    attack*

Highway 101
PO Box 120875
Nashville, TN 37212
Country music group

Hill, Faith
PO Box 24266
Nashville, TN 37202
Web site: http://www.faith-
    hill.com/faith.html
Country singer

Hill, Kim
c/o Blanton Harrell
2910 Poston Ave.
Nashville, TN 37203
Country singer

Hilton Hotels
9336 Civic Center Dr.
Beverly Hills, CA 90210
Web site: http://
www.hilton.com
Stephen Bollenbach, CEO
Hotels, casinos, resorts

Hines, Gregory
377 W. 11th St., #PH-4
New York, NY 10014
Dancer, actor
Birthday: 2/14/46

**Hispanic Policy Development
Project**
36 E. 22nd St., 9th Fl.
New York, NY 10010

H. J. Heinz
600 Grant St.
Pittsburgh, PA 15219
Anthony J. F. O'Reilly, CEO
Food producer

**H. John Heinz III Center for
Science, Economics and the
Environment**
1001 Pennsylvania Ave. NW,
Ste. 735 S.
Washington, DC 20004
Web site: http://
www.heinzctr.org/
E-mail: info@heinzctr.org
John Sawhill, chairman of
board of trustees
*Nonprofit organization devoted to
collaborative research on
environmental problems, its
mission is to create and
disseminate nonpartisan policy
options for solving
environmental problems*

Hobbs, Becky
PO Box 121974
Nashville, TN 37212
Country singer

Holden, Rebecca
PO Box 23504
Nashville, TN 37202
Country singer

Hollywood Reporter
5055 Wilshire Blvd., 6th Fl.
Los Angeles, CA 90036
Web site: http://
www.hollywoodreporter.com/
David Hunter, film reviewer
Newspaper for producers

Holmes, Larry
101 Larry Holmes Dr. #500
Easton, PA 18042
Boxer
Birthday: 11/3/49

Home Depot
2455 Paces Ferry Rd. NW
Atlanta, GA 30339
Web site: http://
www.homedepot.com
Arthur Blank, CEO
Specialist retailers, hardware

Honeywell
2701 4th Ave. S
Minneapolis, MN 55408
Web site: http://
www.honeywell.com
Michael R. Bonsignore, CEO
Scientific, photo, control equipment

Hooters, Heather
536 Romance Rd., #90
Portage, MI 49002
Porn star

Hoover Institution
Stanford University
Palo Alto, CA 94305
Web site: http://
   www.hoover.org/
Herbert Hoover III, chairman
*Public policy research center
   devoted to advanced study in
   domestic public policy and
   international affairs*

Hopper, Dennis
c/o Creative Artists Agency
9830 Wilshire Blvd.
Beverly Hills, CA 90212
Actor, director

Hormel Foods
1 Hormel Pl.
Austin, MN 55912
Web site: http://
   www.hormel.com
Joel W. Johnson, CEO
Food maker

Household Financial
2700 Sanders Rd.
Prospect Heights, IL 60070
Web site: http://
   www.household.com
William F. Aldinger III, CEO
Diversified financials

Houston International
1111 Louisiana
Houston, TX 77210
Web site: http://
   www.houind.com
Don D. Jordan, CEO
Gas and electric utilities

Howard, Jan
Grand Ole Opry
2804 Opryland Dr.
Nashville, TN 37214
Country singer

Howard, Jayne
PO Box 95
Upperco, MD 21155
Author

Howard, Ron
c/o Creative Artists Agency
9830 Wilshire Blvd.
Beverly Hills, CA 90212
Director
Birthday: 3/1/54

Huddleston, David
3518 Cahuenga Blvd. W., #216
Los Angeles, CA 90068
Actor

Hudson Institute
PO Box 26919
5395 Emerson Way
Indianapolis, IN 46226
Web site: http://
   www.hudson.org/
E-mail: claraw@hii.hudson.org
Teresa Rhodes, director
*Private, not-for-profit research
   organization founded in 1961
   by the late Herman Kahn;
   analyzes and makes
   recommendations about public
   policy for business and
   government executives and for
   the public at large*

Hulce, Tom
175 5th Ave., #2409
New York, NY 10010
Actor
Birthday: 12/6/53

Humana
500 W. Main St.
Louisville, KY 40201
Web site: http://
   www.humana.com
Gregory H. Wolf, CEO
Health care

Human Events
422 1st St. SE
Washington, DC 20003
A weekly conservative newspaper

Human Rights Campaign
1101 14th St. NW, #200
Washington, DC 20005
Web site: http://
   www.hrcusa.org/
E-mail: hrc@hrc.org
Elizabeth Birch, executive
   director
E-mail: eb@hrc.org
Largest full-time lobbying team in
   the nation devoted to issues of
   fairness for lesbian and gay
   Americans

Humperdinck, Engelbert
10100 Sunset Blvd.
Los Angeles, CA 90077
Singer
Birthday: 5/2/36

Hunt, Dave
PO Box 7019
Bend, OR 97708
Religious author

Hunt, Linda
c/o J. Michael Bloom
233 Park Ave. S., #1000
New York, NY 10003
Actress
Birthday: 4/2/45

Hunter, Bobbie
PO Box 33116
Northglenn, CO 81226
Porn star

Hunter, Holly
19528 Ventura Blvd., #343
Tarzana, CA 91356
Actress

Hunter, Rachel
23 Beverly Park
Beverly Hills, CA 90210
Supermodel

Hunter, Tommy
c/o RCA Records
1 Music Cir. N.
Nashville, TN 37203
Country singer

Husky, Ferlin
38 Music Sq. E.
Nashville, TN 37203
Country singer

Hutton, Sylvia
PO Box 158467
Nashville, TN 37215
Country singer

Hyland, Brian
c/o Stone Buffalo
PO Box 101
Silver Lakes, CA 92342
Musician

Hynde, Chrissie
30 Ives St.
London SW3 2ND
England
Singer
Birthday: 9/7/50

I

Persons do not become a society by living in physical proximity, any more than a man ceases to be socially influenced by being so many feet or miles removed from others. A letter may institute a more intimate association between human beings separated thousands of miles from each other than exists between dwellers under the same roof.

—JOHN DEWEY

IBP
IBP Ave.
Dakota City, NE 68731
Web site: http://
  www.ibpinc.com
Robert L. Peterson, CEO
Food producer

Ice-T
2287 Sunset Plaza Dr.
Los Angeles, CA 90069
Rapper, actor
Birthday: 2/16/58

Idol, Billy
8209 Melrose Ave.
Los Angeles, CA 90046
Singer

Ikon Office Solutions
70 Valley Stream Pkwy.
Valley Forge, PA 19482
Web site: http://www.ikon.com
John E. Stuart, CEO
Wholesalers

Illinois Tool Works
3600 W. Lake Ave.
Glenview, IL 60025
Web site: http://
  www.itwinc.com
W. James Farrell, CEO
Metal products

Iman
111 E. 22nd St., #200
New York, NY 10010
Singer, model, wife of David Bowie
Birthday: 7/25/55

IMC Global
2100 Sanders Rd.
Northbrook, IL 60062
Web site: http://
  www.imcglobal.com
Robert F. Fowler, Jr., CEO
Chemicals

Inacom
10810 Farnam Dr.
Omaha, NE 68154
Web site: http://
  www.inacom.com
Bill L. Fairfield, CEO
*Wholesalers—information and
  telecommunications*

Independent, The
625 Broadway, 9th Fl.
New York, NY 10012
*Magazine for independent
  filmmakers*

**Information Infrastructure
  Project**
Science, Technology & Public
  Policy Program
John F. Kennedy School of
  Government
Harvard University
79 John F. Kennedy St.
Cambridge, MA 02138

Ingels, Marty
Suite One Productions
8127 Melrose Ave., #1
Los Angeles, CA 90046
Actor

Ingersoll-Rand
200 Chestnut Ridge Rd.
Woodcliff Lake, NJ 07675
Web site: http://
  www.ingersoll-rand.com
James E. Perrella, CEO
Industrial and farm equipment

Ingle, John
c/o "General Hospital"
ABC-TV
4151 Prospect Ave.
Los Angeles, CA 90027
Soap opera star

Ingram Micro
1600 E. St. Andrew Pl.
Santa Ana, CA 92705
Web site: http://
  www.ingrammicro.com
Jerre L. Stead, CEO
*Wholesalers–computer technology
  products and service*

Inland Steel Industries
30 W. Monroe St.
Chicago, IL 60603
Web site: http://
  www.inland.com
Robert J. Darnall, CEO
Metals

**Institute for Awakening
  Technology**
695 5th St.
Lake Oswego, OR 97034
A public interest group

**Institute for Contemporary
  Studies**
720 Market St., 4th Fl.
San Francisco, CA 94102
Web site: http://
  www.self.govern.inter.net/
  ICA/Welcome.html
E-mail:
  suzannevan@earthlink.net
Robert B. Hawkins, Jr.,
  president and CEO
*Nonprofit, nonpartisan policy
  research institute promoting self-
  governance and entrepreneurial
  ways of life*

**Institute for Food and
  Development Policy**
398 60th St.
Oakland, CA 94618
Web site: http://
  www.foodfirst.org/
E-mail: foodfirst@igc.apc.org
Jude Kaye, president
*Purpose is to eliminate the
  injustices that cause hunger*

**Institute for International
  Economics**
11 DuPont Cir. NW, #620
Washington, DC 20036
Web site: http://www.iie.com/
E-mail: bcoulton@iie.com
C. Fred Bergsten, director
*Private, nonprofit, nonpartisan
  research institution devoted to
  the study of international
  economic policy*

Institute for Policy Studies
1601 Connecticut Ave. NW
Washington, DC 20009
Web site: http://www.ips-dc.org/
E-mail: ncecd@igc.apc.org
Contact: Peter Zimite
*Nonprofit, nonpartisan research
and public education
organization dedicated to
educating the public on the need
and the means for an order
transfer of military resources to
civilian use*

**Institute for Women's Policy
Research**
1400 20th St. NW, #104
Washington, DC 20036
Web site: http://www.iwpr.org/
Margaret Simms, board chair
*Independent, nonprofit, scientific
research organization established
in 1987 to rectify the limited
availability of policy: relevant
research on women's lives and
to inform and stimulate debate
on issues of critical importance
for women*

**Institute of Criminal Law and
Procedure**
Georgetown University Law
Center
600 New Jersey Ave. NW
Washington, DC 20001

Intel
2200 Mission College Blvd.
Santa Clara, CA 95052-8119
Web site: www.intel.com
Andrew S. Grove, CEO
*Computer peripherals and chip
maker*

**International Business
Machines**
Old Orchard Rd.
Armonk, NY 10504
Web site: http://www.ibm.com
Louis V. Gerstner, CEO
Maker of computer systems

**International Ghost Hunters
Society**
56875 Columbia River Hwy.
Warren, OR 97053
Web site: http://
www.ghostweb.com/
E-mail:
ghostweb@ghostweb.com
Dave Oester and Rev. Sharon
Gill, ghost hunters
*Worldwide paranormal research
organization dedicated to the
study of ghosts and poltergeists
phenomena known as the spirits
of the dead*

International Paper
2 Manhattanville Rd.
Purchase, NY 10577
Web site: http://
www.ipaper.com
John T. Dillon, CEO
Forest and paper products

**International Society for
Technology in Education
(ISTE)**
480 Charnelton St.
Eugene, OR 97401
Web site: http://www.iste.org/
E-mail: Email: cust_
svc@ccmail.uoregen.edu
Lynne Schrum, president
*Largest teacher-based, nonprofit
organization in the field of
educational technology. Its
mission is to help K–12
classroom teachers and
administrators share effective
methods for enhancing student
learning through the use of new
classroom technologies.*

International Women's Health Coalition
24 E. 21st St.
New York, NY 10010
Web site: http://www.iwhc.org/
E-mail: info@iwhc.org
Adrienne Germain, president
Nonprofit organization that works with individuals and groups in Africa, Asia, and Latin America to promote women's reproductive and sexual health and rights

Interpublic group
1271 6th Ave.
New York, NY 10020
Web site: http://www.interpublic.com
Philip H. Geier, Jr., CEO
Advertising, marketing

Interstate Bakeries
12 E. Armour Blvd.
Kansas City, MO 64111
Charles A. Sullivan, CEO
Food producers

Investigative Reporters and Editors (IRE)
UMC School of Journalism/ 26A
University of Missouri
Columbia, MO 65211
Web site: http://www.ire.org
E-mail: jourie@muccmail.missouri.edu
Rosemary Armao, executive director
E-mail: r2croak@aol.com
Grass-roots nonprofit organization dedicated to improving the quality of investigative reporting within the field of journalism

Ireland, Kathy
Sterling/Winters Company
1900 Ave. of the Stars, #1640
Los Angeles, CA 90067
or
PO Box 5353
Santa Barbara, CA 93130
Model, actress

Iron Maiden
Post Office 10
London SW19 3TW
England
Music group

Ito, Lance A.
Department 127
Criminal Courts Building
210 W. Temple St.
Los Angeles, CA 90012
Judge who presided over the O. J. Simpson trial

ITT
1330 6th Ave.
New York, NY 10019
Rand V. Araskog, CEO
Hotels, casinos, resorts

ITT Industries
4 W. Red Oak Ln.
White Plains, NY 10604
Web site: http://www.ittind.com
D. Travis Engen, CEO
Motor vehicles and parts

Ivey, Judith
c/o Bressler/Kelly/Kipperman
15760 Ventura Blvd., #1730
Encino, CA 91436
Actress
Birthday: 9/4/51

Izaak Walton League of America
1401 Wilson Blvd., Level B
Arlington, VA 22209
Web site: http://www.iwla.org/
E-mail: general@iwla.org
Jim Mosher, conservation
director
One of the oldest conservation organization in the United States

J

Whatever happens to us in our lives, we find questions recurring that we would gladly discuss with some friend. Yet it is hard to find just the friend we should talk to. Often it is easier to *write* to someone whom we do not expect to ever see.

—ELEANOR ROOSEVELT

Jackson, Alan
PO Box 121945
Nashville, TN 37212
Country singer
Birthday: 10/17/?

Jackson, Glenda
59 Frith St.
London W1
England
Actress
Birthday: 5/9/36

Jackson, Janet
14755 Ventura Blvd., #1–710
Sherman Oaks, CA 91403
Singer

Jackson, Jeremy
c/o Mary Grady Agency
4444 Lankershim Blvd., #207
N. Hollywood, CA 91602
Actor
Birthday: 10/16/80

Jackson, Jonathan
1825 N. Pass Ave.
Burbank, CA 91505
Actor

Jackson, Kate
PO Box 57593
Sherman Oaks, CA 91403
Actress

Jackson, Michael
Neverland Ranch
Los Olivos, CA 93441
Singer
Birthday: 8/29/58

Jackson, Stonewall
PO Box 463
McMinnville, TN 37110
Country singer

James, Art
11365 Ventura Blvd., #100
Studio City, CA 91604
TV host

James, Brian
PO Box 1207
Pineville, WV 24874
Country singer

James, Dalton
c/o I.C.M.
8942 Wilshire Blvd.
Beverly Hills, CA 90211
Actor
Birthday: 3/19/71

James, Sonny
818 18th Ave. S.
Nashville, TN 37212
Country singer

Japanese American Citizens League (JACL)
1765 Sutter St.
San Francisco, CA 94065
Web site: http://www.jacl.org/
E-mail: jacl@jacl.org
Helen Kawagoe, national president
E-mail: president@jacl.org
Founded in 1929 to fight discrimination against people of Japanese ancestry; the largest and one of the oldest Asian American organizations in the United States

J. C. Penney
6501 Legacy Dr.
Plano, TX 75024
Web site: http:// www.jcpenney.com
James E. Oesterreicher, CEO
General merchandisers

Jean, Norma
1300 Division St.
Nashville, TN 37203
Country singer

Jefferson Smurfit
8182 Maryland Ave.
St. Louis, MO 63105
Web site: http://www.smurfit.ie
Richard W. Graham, CEO
Forest and paper products

Jenner, Bruce
PO Box 11137
Beverly Hills, CA 90213
Olympic track & field medalist
Birthday: 10/28/49

Jennings, Peter
7 W. 66th St.
New York, NY 10023
News anchor
Birthday: 7/29/38

Jennings, Waylon
1117 17th Ave. S.
Nashville, TN 37203
Country singer
Birthday: 6/15/37

Jeter, Derek
c/o New York Yankees
Yankee Stadium
161 St. & River Ave.
Bronx, NY 10451
Baseball player

Jewell
PO Box 33494
San Diego, CA 92163
Singer

Jewish Defense League
PO Box 480370
Los Angeles, CA 90048
Web site: http://www.jdl.org
E-mail: jdljdl@aol.com
Irv Rubin, national chairman
Organization that sees the need for a movement that is dedicated specifically to Jewish problems and that allocates its time, resources, energies, and funds to Jews

Jews for the Preservation of Firearms Ownership
2874 S. Wentworth Ave.
Milwaukee, WI 53207
Web site: http://www.jpfo.org/
E-mail: Against-Genocide @JPFO.org
Aaron Zelman, executive director
Membership in this organization is open to all law-abiding firearms owners who believe that ownership of firearms is a civil right—not a privilege, as a driver's license is

Jim & Jesse
8574 Tram Rd.
Tallahassee, FL 32311
Country duo

**Joan Shorenstein Barone
Center on Press, Politics,
and Public Policy**
John F. Kennedy School of
Government
Harvard University
79 JFK St.
Cambridge, MA 02138
Web site: http://
ksgwww.harvard.edu/
~presspol/home.htm

John, Elton
Woodside
Crump Hill Rd.
Old Windsor
Berkshire
England
Singer

John Birch Society, Inc., The
PO Box 8040
Appleton, WI 54913
Web site: http://www.jbs.org/
E-mail: jbs@jbs.org
Thomas R. Eddlem, research
director
E-mail: teddlem@jbs.org
*Devoted to the free market system,
competitive capitalism, and
private enterprise*

**John D. and Catherine T.
MacArthur Foundation**
140 S. Dearborn St., Ste. 100
Chicago, IL 60603
Web site: http://
www.macfdn.org/
E-mail: 4answers@macfdn.org
Adele Simmons, president
*Gives "genius grants"—no strings
money awarded to people with
exceptional creative ability*

**John Hancock Mutual Life
Insurance Company**
John Hancock Pl.
Boston, MA 02117
Stephen L. Brown, CEO
*Life and health insurance
(mutual)*

**John Simon Guggenheim
Memorial Foundation**
90 Park Ave.
New York, NY 10016
Web site: http://www.gf.org
E-mail: fellowships@gf.org
Joseph A. Rice, chairman of
the board
*Grant foundation for arts and
sciences and the humanities,
except for performers (they will
fund a choreographer, but not a
dancer)*

Johnson, Beverly
c/o Beverly Glen Enterprises
250 W. 40th St., 4th Fl.
New York, NY 10018
Model

Johnson, Davey
c/o Baltimore Orioles
333 W. Camden St.
Baltimore, MD 21201
Baseball player

Johnson, Don
3400 Riverside Dr., #100
Burbank, CA 91505
Actor
Birthday: 12/15/49

Johnson, Earvin "Magic"
9100 Wilshire Blvd., #1060 W.
Tower
Beverly Hills, CA 90212
Former basketball player

Johnson, Jimmy
Pro Player Stadium
2269 N.W. 199th St.
Miami, FL 33056
Miami Dolphins head coach
Birthday: 7/16/43

Johnson, Keyshawn
c/o New York Jets
1000 Fulton Ave.
Hempstead, NY 11550
Football player

Johnson, Lady Bird
c/o LBJ Presidential Library
2313 Red River St.
Austin, TX 78705
Former First Lady

Johnson, Michael
818 18th Ave. S., 3rd. Fl.
Nashville, TN 37211
Country singer

Johnson & Johnson
1 J&J Plaza
New Brunswick, NJ 08933
Web site: http://www.jnj.com
Ralph S. Larsen, CEO
Pharmaceuticals

Johnson Controls
5757 N. Green Bay Ave.
Milwaukee, WI 53209
Web site: http://www.jci.com
James H. Keyes, CEO
Motor vehicles and parts

**Joint Center for Political and
  Economic Studies**
1090 Vermont Ave. NW, #1100
Washington, DC 20005
Web site: http://
  www.jointctr.org/
Eddie N. Williams, president
*Nonprofit institution conducting
  research on political, economic,
  and social policy issues of
  concern to African Americans*

Jones, David Lynn
c/o Mercury
901 18th Ave. S.
Nashville, TN 37203
Country singer

Jones, Davy
PO Box 400
Beavertown, PA 17813
Musician, member of the Monkees

Jones, George
Rt. 3, Box 150
Murphy, NC 28906
Country singer

Jones, James Earl
PO Box 610
Pawling, NY 12564
Actor

Jones, Jenny
454 N. Columbus Dr., 4th Fl.
Chicago, IL 60611
Web site: http://
  www.jennyjones.com
Talk show host

Jones, Parnelli
PO Box W
Torrance, CA 90507
Auto racing driver

Jones, Quincy
Quincy Jones/David Salzman
  Entertainment
3800 Barham Blvd., #503
Los Angeles, CA 90068
Composer, musician

Jones, Randy
c/o San Diego Padres
PO Box 2000
San Diego, CA 92112
Baseball player

Jones, Shirley
Suite One Productions
8127 Melrose Ave., #1
Los Angeles, CA 90046
or
11365 Ventura Blvd., #100
Studio City, CA 91604
Actress

Michael Jordan
c/o Chicago Bulls
1901 West Madison St.
Chicago, IL 60612

Jordanaires, The
PO Box 15914
Nashville, TN 37215
Singing group

**Joseph & Edna Josephson
Institute of Ethics**
4640 Admiralty Way, #1001
Marina del Rey, CA 90292
Web site: http://
www.josephsoninstitute.org/
E-mail: ji@jiethics.org
Frances Hesselbein, chair of
board of governors
*Public-benefit, nonpartisan,
nonprofit membership
organization founded by
Michael Josephson in honor of
his parents to improve the
ethical quality of society by
advocating principled reasoning
and ethical decision making*

Scott Joss Fan Club
PO Box 6208
Santa Rosa, CA 95406
Country musician

J. P. Morgan
60 Wall St.
New York, NY 10260
Web site: http://
www.jpmorgan.com
Douglas A. Warner III, CEO
Commercial banks

Juan Carlos, King
Palacio de la Carcuela
Madrid
Spain
King of Spain

Judd, Ashley
PO Box 682068
Nashville, TN 37217
Actress

Judd, Naomi
PO Box 682068
Nashville, TN 37217
Country singer

Judd, Wynonna
PO Box 682068
Nashville, TN 37217
E-mail: fanclub@wynonna.com
Country singer

Jurgenson, Sonny
c/o Pro Football Hall of Fame
2121 George Halas Dr. NW
Canton, OH 44708
Former football player

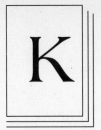

K

As long as there are postmen, life will have zest.

—WILLIAM JAMES

Kadrey, Richard
E-mail: kadrey@well.sf.ca.us
Science fiction novelist

Kaelin, Brian "Kato"
8383 Wilshire Blvd., #954
Beverly Hills, CA 90211
O. J. Simpson's houseguest

Kahn, Chaka
PO Box 16680
Beverly Hills, CA 90209
Singer
Birthday: 3/23/53

Kanarek, Lisa
600 Preston
Forest Center #120
Dallas, TX 75230
Author

Kane, Carol
8106 Santa Monica Blvd.,
 #1426
W. Hollywood, CA 90046
Actress
Birthday: 6/18/52

Karolyi, Bela
RR #12
Box 140
Huntsville, TX 77340
Gymnastics coach

Karras, Alex
Georgian Bay Productions
3815 W. Olive Ave., #202
Burbank, CA 91505
Actor
Birthday: 7/15/35

Kasem, Casey
11365 Ventura Blvd., #100
Studio City, CA 91604
Radio and TV host

Katayama, Ukyo
c/o Minardi Team S.p.A
Via Spellanzani 21
48018 Faenza/RA
Italy
Professional Formula-1 driver

Katzenberg, Jeffrey
100 Universal City Plaza #10
Universal City, CA 91608
Cofounder of Dreamworks

Kauffman, Bruce
E-mail:
 72520.1674@compuserve.com
Author, journalist

Kawasaki, Guy
E-mail:
 76703.3031@compuserve.com
Mac guru

Kay, Alan
E-mail:
    kay2@applelink.apple.com
*Codeveloper (father of the Apple
    Macintosh)*

Kazan, Elia
174 E. 95th St.
New York, NY 10128
Director, producer
Birthday: 9/7/09

Keaton, Michael
11901 Santa Monica, #547
Los Angeles, CA 90025
Actor
Birthday: 9/9/51

Keel, Howard
c/o Clifford Productions
394 Red River Rd.
Palm Desert, CA 9221
Actor
Birthday: 4/13/17

Keel, John A.
PO Box 351
Murray Hill Station
New York, NY 10016
UFO researcher

Keeshan, Bob
40 W. 57th St., #1600
New York, NY 10019
Captain Kangaroo
Birthday: 6/27/27

Kehoe, Brendan
E-mail:brendan@cygnus.com
Author, journalist

Keillor, Garrison
E-mail:
    gkeillor@madmax.mpr.org
Radio host

Keith, Toby
PO Box 8739
Rockford, IL 61126
Country singer

Keller, Marthe
5 rue Saint Dominique
75007 Paris
France
Actress
Birthday: 2/28/45

Kelley, DeForest
415 N. Cannon Dr., #121
Beverly Hills, CA 90212
Actor
Birthday: 1/20/20

Kellner, Mark
E-mail: kellner@psilink.com
Writer

Kellogg
1 Kellogg Sq.
Battle Creek, MI 49016
Web site: http://
    www.kelloggs.com
Arnold G. Langbo, CEO
Food producer

Kelly Services
999 W. Big Beaver Rd.
Troy, MI 48084
Web site: http://
    www.kellyservices.com
Terence E. Adderley, CEO
Temporary services

Kendalls, The
1109 17th Ave. S.
Nashville, TN 37212
Singing group

Kennedy, Jamie
c/o Brillstein-Grey Enterprises
9150 Wilshire Blvd., #350
Beverly Hills, CA 90212
Actor

Kennedy, Ray
PO Box 158309
Nashville, TN 37215
Country singer

Kennedy, Tom
11365 Ventura Blvd., #100
Studio City, CA 91604
*TV game show host, Jack Narz's
brother*
Birthday: 2/26/27

Kentucky Headhunters
301 Ridgecrest Dr.
Goodlettsville, TN 37072
Musical group

Kenzle, Leila
c/o "Mad About You"
9336 Washington Blvd.
Culver City, CA 90232
Actress

Kercheval, Ken
c/o David Westberg
1724 N. Vista St.
Los Angeles, CA 90046
Actor
Birthday: 7/15/35

Kerns, Joanna
PO Box 49216
Los Angeles, CA 90049
Actress
Birthday: 2/12/53

Kershaw, Doug
PO Box 24762
San Jose, CA 95154
Cajun singer and musician

Kershaw, Sammy
PO Box 121739
Nashville, TN 37212
Country singer

Ketchum, Hal
PO Box 12025
Nashville, TN 37212
Country singer

Kevorkian, Dr. Jack
4870 Lockhart St.
W. Bloomfield, MI 48323
Suicide assistance doctor

Key, Jimmy
c/o Baltimore Orioles
333 West Camden St.
Baltimore, MD 21201
Baseball player

KeyCorp
127 Public Sq.
Cleveland, OH 44114
Web site: http://
   www.keybank.com
Robert W. Gillespie, CEO
Commercial bank

Kidd, Jason
c/o Phoenix Suns
PO Box 1369
Phoenix, AZ 85001
Basketball player

Kidder, Margot
Pine Creek Rd.
Livingstone, MT 59047
Actress
Birthday: 10/17/48

Killebrew, Harmon
PO Box 14550
Scottsdale, AZ 85267
Former baseball player

Kilmer, Val
PO Box 362
Tesuque, NM 87574
Actor

Kimberly-Clark
351 Phelps Dr.
Irving, TX 75038
Web site: http://www.
kimberly-clark.com
Wayne R. Sanders, CEO
Forest and paper products

Kimes, Royal Wade
PO Box 128038
Nashville, TN 37212
Country singer

King, Don
c/o Don King Enterprises
871 W. Oakland Park Ave.
Fort Lauderdale, FL 33311
Impressario
Birthday: 8/20/31

King, Pee Wee
c/o CMA
1 Music Cir. S.
Nashville, TN 37203
Country singer

Kinnear, Greg
3000 W. Alameda Ave., #2908
Burbank, CA 91523
Actor

Kinski, Nastassja
c/o William Morris Agency
151 El Camino Dr.
Beverly Hills, CA 90212
Actress, model

Kirkland, Sally
c/o William Morris Agency
151 El Camino Dr.
Beverly Hills, CA 90212
Actress
Birthday: 10/31/44

Kirsebom, Vendela
151 El Camino Dr.
Beverly Hills, CA 90212
Actress

Klasky, Arlene
1258 N. Highland Ave.
Hollywood, CA 90038
Web site: http://
   www.klaskycsupo.com
Creator of "Rugrats"

Klemperer, Werner
44 W. 62nd St., 10th Fl.
New York, NY 10023
Actor
Birthday: 3/29/19

Klum, Heidi
c/o Elite Model Management
111 E. 22nd St.
New York, NY 10010
Model

Kmart
3100 W. Big Beaver Rd.
Troy, MI 48084
Web site: http://
   www.kmart.com
Floyd Hall, CEO
General merchandisers

Knight-Ridder
1 Herald Plaza
Miami, FL 33132
Web site: http://www.kri.com
P. Anthony Ridder, CEO
Publishing, printing

Kodjoe, Boris
c/o Ford Model Agency
344 E. 59th St.
New York, NY 10022
Model

Kohl's
N. 56 W. 17000 Ridgewood Dr.
Menomonee Falls, WI 53051
Web site: http://nt1.irin.com/
   irin/Detail.CFM/kss
William S. Kellogg, CEO
General merchandisers

Koontz, Dean
PO Box 9529
Newport Beach, CA 92658
Author

Krauss, Alison
PO Box 121711
Nashville, TN 37212
Singer

Kreskin
44 N. 2nd St.
Easton, PA 18042
Mentalist

Kristofferson, Kris
PO Box 2147
Malibu, CA 90265
or
313 Lakeshore Dr.
Marietta, GA 30067
Songwriter, actor

Kroger
1014 Vine St.
Cincinnati, OH 45202
Web site: http://
   www.kroger.com
Joseph A. Pichler, CEO
Food and drug stores

Kstsulas, Andreas
c/o Innovative Artists
1999 Ave. of the Stars, #2850
Los Angeles, CA 90067
*Plays Commander Tomalak on
   "Star Trek: The Next
   Generation"*

Kurtz, Swoozie
320 Central Park W.
New York, NY 10025
Actress
Birthday: 9/6/44

People in the flesh are a lot more complicated than they appear on paper, which is both one of the attractions and one of the shortcomings of carrying on a prolonged correspondence.

—SHANA ALEXANDER

Labelle, Patti
PO Box 30335
Philadelphia, PA 19103
Singer
Birthday: 10/4/44

Labonte, Terry
PO Box 4617
Archdale, NC 28263
Race car driver
Birthday: 11/16/56

Terry Labonte Fan Club
PO Box 843
Trinity, NC 27370

Ladd, Cheryl
PO Box 1329
Santa Ynez, CA 93460
Actress
Birthday: 7/2/51

Ladd, Diane
Diane Ladd Productions, Inc.
PO Box 17111
Beverly Hills, CA 90209-3111
*Actress, Laura Dern is her
   daughter.*
Birthday: 11/29/32

Lagerfeld, Karl
c/o Chanel
29 rue Cambon
75001 Paris
France
Fashion designer

Lahti, Christine
500 25th St.
Santa Monica, CA 90402
Actress
Birthday: 4/5/50

Lake, Ricki
410 5th Ave., 7th Fl.
New York, NY 10016
Actress, talk show host
Birthday: 9/21/68

Lakin, Christine
Step by Step Fan Mail
2040 Ave. of the Stars
Los Angeles, CA 90067
Actress
Birthday: 1/25/79

Lamas, Lorenzo
3727 W. Magnolia Blvd.,
   Ste. 807
Burbank, CA 91505
Actor
Birthday: 1/20/58

Lambert, Christopher
9560 Wilshire Blvd., #500
Beverly Hills, CA 90212-2400
Actor
Birthday: 3/29/57

Landcaster, Sarah
c/o "Saved by the Bell: The
    New Class"
NBC-TV
3000 W. Alameda Ave.
Burbank, CA 91523
Actress

Landers, Ann
435 N. Michigan Ave.
Chicago, IL 60611
Advice columnist

Landers, Audrey
c/o Queen Bee Prod./
    Huggabag Prod.
3112 Nicka Dr.
Los Angeles, CA 90077
Actress
Birthday: 7/18/59

Landers, Judy
c/o Media Artists Group
8383 Wilshire Blvd., #954
Beverly Hills, CA 90211
Actress
Birthday: 10/7/61

Lando, Joe
c/o William Morris Agency
151 S. El Camino Dr.
Beverly Hills, CA 90212
Actor
Birthday: 12/9/61

Landry, Tom
8411 Preston Rd., Ste. 720-LB3
Dallas, TX 75225
or
c/o Football Hall of Fame
2121 George Halas Dr. NW
Canton, OH 44708
Former football player

Lane, Cristy
LS Records
120 Hickory St.
Nashville, TN 37115
Country singer

Lane, Diane
1901 Ave. of the Stars, #1245
Los Angeles, CA 90067
Actress
Birthday: 1/22/63

Lane, Nathan
PO Box 1249
White River Junction, VT
    05001
or
c/o St. James Theater
246 W. 44th St.
New York, NY 10036
Actor

lang, k. d.
75 Rockefeller Plaza
New York, NY 10019
or
c/o Burnstead Productions
PO Box 33800
Station D
Vancouver, BC V6J 5C7
Canada
Singer
Birthday: 11/2/61

Lange, Jessica
% CAA
9830 Wilshire Blvd.
Beverly Hills, CA 90212
Actress
Birthday: 4/20/49

Lange, Ted
18653 Ventura Blvd., #131-B
Tarzana, CA 91356
Actor

Langella, Frank
1999 Ave. of the Stars, Ste.
    2850
Los Angeles, CA 90067
Actor
Birthday: 1/1/40

Langenkamp, Heather
9229 Sunset Blvd., #311
Los Angeles, CA 90069
Actress

Lansbury, Angela
100 Universal City Plaza,
  Bldg. 426
Universal City, CA 91608
Actress

LaPaglia, Anthony
8942 Wilshire Blvd.
Beverly Hills, CA 90211
Actor

Larson, Gary
4900 Main St., #900
Kansas City, MO 62114
Cartoonist

La Salle, Eriq
c/o "ER"
4000 Warner Blvd.
Burbank, CA 91522
Actor

Lasorda, Tommy
c/o L.A. Dodgers
1000 Elysian Park Blvd.
Los Angeles, CA 90012
Former manager of the Dodgers

Laughlin, Tom
PO Box 25355
Los Angeles, CA 90025
Actor, director

Lauper, Cyndi
2211 Broadway, #10F
New York, NY 10024
Singer, songwriter
Birthday: 6/20/53

Lauren, Ralph
1107 5th Ave.
New York, NY 10128
Fashion designer
Birthday: 10/14/39

Laurie, Hugh
c/o William Morris Agency
151 El Camino Dr.
Beverly Hills, CA 90212
Actor

Lavin, Linda
PO Box 2847
Wilmington, NC 28402
Actress

Lawless, Lucy
Creation Entertainment
411 N. Central Ave., #300
Glendale, CA 91203
Actress

Lucy Lawless Fan Club
65 Edwin Rd.
Waltham, MA 02154

Lawrence, Martin
c/o U.T.A.
9560 Wilshire Blvd., #516
Beverly Hills, CA 91212
or
PO Box 7304, Ste. 440
N. Hollywood, CA 91603
Actor

Lawrence, Sharon
PO Box 462048
Los Angeles, CA 90046
Actress

Lawrence, Tracy
9 Music Sq., Ste. 110
Nashville, TN 37203
Country singer

Lawson, Dennis
21 Golden Sq.
London W1R 3PA
England
Actor

League of Conservation Voters
1707 L St. NW, #550
Washington, DC 20036
Web site: http://www.lcv.org
Deb Callahan, president
*Works to create a Congress more
responsive to your
environmental concerns*

**League of United Latin
American Citizens (LULAC)**
1600 E. Desert Inn Rd., #207
Las Vegas, NV 89109
Web site: http://www.lulac.org/
E-mail: LNESCNat@aol.com
Belen Robles, national
president
E-mail: LULACExec@aol.com
*Works to bring about positive
social and economic changes for
Hispanic Americans*

**League of Women Voters of
the United States**
1730 M St. NW
Washington, DC 20036
Web site: http://www.lwv.org/
Becky Cain, president
*Multi-issue organization whose
mission is to encourage the
informed and active
participation of citizens in
government*

Leakey, Dr. Richard
PO Box 24926
Nairobi
Kenya
Paleontologist

Lear
21557 Telegraph Rd.
Southfield, MI 48086
Web site: http://www.lear.com
Kenneth L. Way, CEO
Motor vehicles and parts

Leary, Dennis
9560 Wilshire Blvd., #516
Beverly Hills, CA 90212
Actor

Le Blanc, Matt
11766 Wilshire Blvd., #1470
Los Angeles, CA 90025
Actor

Le Brock, Kelly
PO Box 57593
Sherman Oaks, CA 91403
Actress

LeDoux, Chris
PO Box 253
Sumner, IA 50674
Country singer

Lee, Brenda
c/o Pat O'Leary
PO Box 2700
Murfreesboro, TN 37133
Singer

Lee, Christopher
21 Golden Sq.
London W12 3PA
England
Actor

Lee, Johnny
PO Box 368
Old Hickory, TN 37138
Country singer

Lee, Pamela Anderson
151 El Camino Dr.
Beverly Hills, CA 90212
Actress
Birthday: 7/1/67

Lee, Spike
40 Acres and a Mule Filmworks
124 DeKalb Ave., 2nd Fl.
Brooklyn, NY 11217
Director

Lee, Stan
c/o Marvel Films
1440 S. Sepulveda, Ste. 114
Los Angeles, CA 90025
Publisher of Spider Man

Leggett & Platt
1 Leggett Rd.
Carthage, MO 64836
Web site: http://
  www.regionalstock.com/
  leg.html
Harry M. Cornell, Jr., CEO
Furniture

Lehman Brothers Holdings
3 World Financial Ctr.
New York, NY 10285
Web site: http://
  www.lehman.com
Richard S. Fuld, Jr.,
Securities

**Hudson Leick Official Fan
  Club**
PO Box 775
Fair Oaks, CA 95628
Web site: http://
  www.hudsonleickfan.com
Actress

Leisure, David
8428-C Melrose Pl.
Los Angeles, CA 90046
Actor
Birthday: 11/16/50

Lemmon, Jack
c/o Jalem Productions, Inc.
141 El Camino Dr., Ste. 201
Beverly Hills, CA 90212
Actor
Birthday: 2/8/25

Lennox, Annie
35–37 Park Gate Rd., Unit 2
Ransome's Docks
London SW11 4NP
England
Singer
Birthday: 12/25/54

Leno, Jay
PO Box 7885
Burbank, CA 91510
Host of "The Tonight Show"
Birthday: 4/20/50

Leonard, Robert Sean
PO Box 454
Sea Isle City, NJ 08243
Actor
Birthday: 2/28/69

Leoni, Téa
2300 W. Victory Blvd., #384
Burbank, CA 91506
or
3500 W. Olive, #1400
Burbank, CA 91505
*Actress, married to David
  Duchovny*

Leto, Jared
1999 Ave. of the Stars,
  Ste. 2850
Los Angeles, CA 90067
Actor

Letterman, David
1697 Broadway
New York, NY 10019
Host of "Late Night"

Levine, Michael
5750 Wilshire Blvd., #555
Los Angeles, CA 90036
E-mail: levinepr@earthlink.net
Media expert, author of The
  Address Book

Lewinsky, Monica
10100 Santa Monica Blvd., 8th
  Fl.
Los Angeles, CA 90067
E-mail; mslewinsky@aol.com
Former White House intern

Lewis, Al
PO Box 277
New York, NY 10044
Actor, played Grandpa on "The Munsters"

Lewis, Carl
PO Box 571990
Houston, TX 77082
Olympic competitor in track & field

Lewis, Gary
PO Box 53664
Indianapolis, IN 46253
Musician

Lewis, Huey
PO Box 819
Mill Valley, CA 94942
Singer
Birthday: 7/5/50

Lewis, Jerry
3160 W. Sahara Ave., #816
Las Vegas, NV 89102
Actor, comedian
Birthday: 3/17/26

Lewis, Jerry Lee
PO Box 3864
Memphis, TN 38173
Singer

LG&E
220 W. Main St.
Louisville, KY 40232
Web site: http://www.lgeenergy.com
Roger W. Hale, CEO
Gas and electric utilities

Libertarian Party
2600 Virginia Ave. NW, #100
Washington, DC 20037
Web site: http://www.lp.org/
Steve Dasbach, chair
E-mail: 76060.3222@compuserve.com
Karen Allard, vice chair
E-mail: 102160.1007@compuserve.com
Holds that all individuals have the right to exercise sole dominion over their own lives, and the right to live in whatever manner they choose, so long as they do not forcibly interfere with the equal right of others to live in whatever manner they choose

Liberty Mutual Insurance Group
175 Berkeley St.
Boston, MA 02117
Gary L. Countryman, CEO
P & C insurance (mutual)

Liddy, G. Gordon
PO Box 3649
Washington, DC 20007
Web site: http://www.rtis.com/liddy/
E-mail: potent357@aol.com
Watergate conspirator, talk show host

Lien, Jennifer
9200 Sunset Blvd., #625
Los Angeles, CA 90069
Actor, plays Kes on "Star Trek: Voyager"

Limbaugh, Rush
366 Madison Ave., #700
New York, NY 10017
E-mail: 70277.2502@compuserve.com
Talk show host

Limited
3 Limited Pkwy.
Columbus, OH 43230
Web site: http://
www.limited.com
Leslie H. Wexner, CEO
Specialist retailers

Lincoln National
200 E. Berry St.
Fort Wayne, IN 46802
Web site: http://www.lnc.com
Ian M. Rolland, CEO
Life and health insurance (stock)

Linden, Hal
8730 Sunset Blvd., #470
Los Angeles, CA 90069
Actor
Birthday: 3/20/31

Lindenberg, Udo
c/o Management
Alte Dorfstr. 74
21444 Vierhöfen
Germany
Singer

Lindsey, George
1025 16th Ave., #300
Nashville, TN 37212
Country singer

Liotta, Ray
955 S. Carrillo Dr., #300
Los Angeles, CA 90048
Actor
Birthday: 12/18/55

Lipnicki, Jonathan
c/o Brillstein-Greg Enterprises
9150 Wilshire Blvd., #350
Beverly Hills, CA 90212
Actor
Birthday: 10/22/90

Little Richard (Richard Wayne Penniman)
8401 Sunset Blvd.
Los Angeles, CA 90069
Singer
Birthday: 12/5/32

Little Texas
PO Box 1797
Granbury, TX 76048
Music group

Litton Industries
21240 Burbank Blvd.
Woodland Hills, CA 91367
Web site: http://
www.littoncorp.com
John M. Leonis, CEO
Electronics, electrical equipment

Livingston, Ron
c/o Gold/Marshak &
Associates
3500 W. Olive Ave., #1400
Burbank, CA 91505
Actor

LL Cool J
c/o Rush Management
298 Elizabeth St.
New York, NY 10012
Rap artist

Lloyd, Christopher
PO Box 491246
Los Angeles, CA 90049
Actor

Lloyd, Kathleen
10100 Santa Monica Blvd.,
#2500
Los Angeles, CA 90067
Actress

Locke, Sondra
PO Box 69865
Los Angeles, CA 90069
Actress
Birthday: 5/28/47

Lockhart, June
PO Box 3207
Santa Monica, CA 90403
Actress

Lockheed Martin
6801 Rockledge Dr.
Bethesda, MD 20817
Web site: http://www.lmco.com
Vance D. Coffman, CEO
Aerospace

Locklear, Heather
8033 Sunset Blvd., #4048
Los Angeles, CA 90046
or
c/o William Morris Agency
151 El Camino Dr.
Beverly Hills, CA 90212
Actress
Birthday: 9/25/61

Loeb, Lisa
PO Box 910
Village Station
New York, NY 10014
Actress

Loews
667 Madison Ave.
New York, NY 10021
L.A. Tisch, CEO
P & C insurance (stock)

Lollobrigida, Gina
Via Appia Antica 223
00179 Roma
Italy
Actress
Birthday: 7/4/27

London, Jason
151 El Camino Dr.
Beverly Hills, CA 90212
Actor

Lonestar
PO Box 128467
Nashville, TN 37212
Musical group

Long, Kathy
1800 Ave. of the Stars, Ste. 400
Los Angeles, CA 90067
*Actress and former kickboxing
    champion*

Long, Shelley
15237 Sunset Blvd.
Pacific Palisades, CA 90272
or
9830 Wilshire Blvd.
Beverly Hills, CA 90212
Actress
Birthday: 8/23/49

**Long Island Lighting Co./
    Keyspan Energy**
175 Old Country Rd.
Hicksville, NY 11801
Web site: http://www.lilco.com
William J. Catacosinos, CEO
Gas and electric utilities

Longs Drug Stores
141 N. Civic Dr.
Walnut Creek, CA 94596
Web site: http://www.longs.com
Steve Roath, CEO
Food and drug stores

Lopez, Jennifer
9560 Wilshire Blvd., #500
Beverly Hills, CA 90212
Actress

Lopez, Mario
4526 Wilshire Blvd.
Los Angeles, CA 90010
Actor
Birthday: 10/10/73

Lord, Rebecca
16161 Ventura Blvd., #374
Encino, CA 91436
Actress

Lords, Traci (Norman Kuzma)
9150 Wilshire Blvd., #175
Beverly Hills, CA 90212
Actress
Birthday: 5/7/68

Loren, Sophia (Sophia Scicolone)
c/o Cineart
36 rue de Ponthieu
75008 Paris
France
Actress
Birthday: 9/20/34

Louganis, Greg
PO Box 4130
Malibu, CA 90264
Olympic diver

Louis-Dreyfus, Julia
c/o U.T.A.
9560 Wilshire Blvd., #516
Beverly Hills, CA 90212
Actress

Louvin, Charlie
PO Box 140324
Nashville, TN 37214
Country singer

Love, Courtney
33401 N.E. 78th St.
Carnation, WA 98014
Singer, songwriter

Loveless, Patty
PO Box 1423
White House, TN 37188
Country singer

Lovett, Lyle
General Delivery
Klein, TX 77391
or
4155 E. Jewell Ave., #412
Denver, CO 80222
Singer

Lowe, Rob
c/o U.T.A.
9560 Wilshire Blvd., #500
Beverly Hills, CA 90212
Actor
Birthday: 3/17/64

Lowell, Carey
8942 Wilshire Blvd.
Beverly Hills, CA 90211
Actress

Lowe's
State Hwy. 268 E.
North Wilkesboro, NC 28659
Web site: http://www.lowes.com
Robert L. Tillman, CEO
Specialist retailers

Low Income Housing Information Service
1012 14th St., #1200
Washington, DC 20005
Web site: http://www.nlihc.org/index.htm
E-mail: info@nlihc.org
Helen Dunlap, president
The only national organization dedicated solely to ending America's affordable housing crisis

LTV
200 Public Sq.
Cleveland, OH 44114
Web site: http://www.ltvsteel.com
David H. Hoag, CEO
Metal producer

Lucas, George
3270 Kerner Blvd.
Box #2009
San Rafael, CA 94912
Director, producer
Birthday: 5/14/44

Lucci, Susan
PO Box 621
Quogue, NY 11959
Soap opera star
Birthday: 12/23/45

Lucent Technologies
600 Mountain Ave.
Murray Hill, NJ 07974-0636
Web site: http://
www.lucent.com
Richard A. McGinn, CEO
Electronics, electrical equipment

Luchsinger, Susie
PO Box 990
Atoka, OK 74525
Country singer

**LULAC National Education
Service Center (League of
United Latin American
Citizens)**
117 S.E. End Ave.
Pomona, CA 91766
Frank Dominguez, coordinator
*Organization encouraging women
in science and engineering*

Lumbly, Carl
c/o Innovative Artists
1999 Ave. of the Stars, #2850
Los Angeles, CA 90067
Actor

Lundgren, Dolph
9056 Santa Monica Blvd.,
Ste. 100
Hollywood, CA 90069
Actor
Birthday: 10/18/59

Lundy, Jessica
924 20th St., #1
Santa Monica, CA 90403
Actress

Lütgenhorst, David
c/o Agentur Goosmann
Fichtenstr. 33
85774 Unterföhring
Germany
Actor

Lutheran Brotherhood
625 4th Ave. S.
Minneapolis, MN 55415

Lynch, David
PO Box 93624
Los Angeles, CA 90093
Director

Lynley, Carol
c/o Pierce & Shelly
612 Lighthouse Ave., #275
Pacific Grove, CA 93951
E-mail: carolynley@aol.com
Actress
Birthday: 2/13/42

Lynn, Amber
12400 Ventura Blvd., #329
Studio City, CA 91604
Actress

Lynn, Loretta
PO Box 40328
Nashville, TN 37204
Country singer

Lynne, Shelby
PO Box 190
Monroeville, AL 36461
Country singer

Lyondell Petrochemical
1221 McKinney Ave.
Houston, TX 77010
Web site: http://
www.lyondell.com
Dan F. Smith, CEO
Chemicals

Excuse me for not answering your letter sooner, but I've been so busy not answering letters that I couldn't get around to yours in time.

—GROUCHO MARX

MacAnally, Mac
c/o T. K. Kimbrell
TKO Management
4205 Hillsboro Rd., Ste. 208
Nashville, TN 37215
Country singer

MacDowell, Andie
c/o ICM
8942 Wilshire Blvd.
Beverly Hills, CA 90211
Actress
Birthday: 5/4/58

Macnee, Patrick
PO Box 1685
Palm Springs, CA 92263
Actor
Birthday: 2/6/22

MacNichol, Peter
c/o Gallin-Morey Associates
345 N. Maple Dr., #300
Beverly Hills, CA 90210
Actor

MacPherson, Elle
107 Greene St.
New York, NY 10012
Actress

Macy, William H.
c/o Writers & Artists Agency
924 Westwood Blvd., #900
Los Angeles, CA 90024
Actor

Madden, John
1 W. 72nd St.
New York, NY 10023
Director
Birthday: 4/10/36

Madonna
c/o Fred De Mann Mgmt.
8000 Beverly Blvd.
Los Angeles, CA 90048
*Singer/actress; the name of her
    daughter is Lourdes (born
    1996)*
Birthday: 8/16/58

"MAD TV"
c/o Ren Mar Studios
846 N. Cahuenga Blvd.
Los Angeles, CA 90028
Television show

Mae, Vanessa
c/o EMJ Records
43 Brook Green
London W6 7EF
England
Singer
Birthday: 10/27/78

Magnussenn, Jan
c/o Stewart Grand Prix Ltd.
16 Tanners Dr.
Blakelands
Milton Keynes MK14 5BW
or
c/o Team AMG Mercedes
Daimlerstr. 1
71563 Affalterbach
Germany
Professional Formula-1 driver
Birthday: 7/4/73

Maher, Bill
120 E. 23rd St.
New York, NY 10010
or
c/o "Politically Incorrect"
CBS Television City
7800 Beverly Blvd.
Los Angeles, CA 90036
*Actor, host of "Politically
Incorrect"*

Majorino, Tina
c/o Paradigm Talent Agency
10100 Santa Monica Blvd.
Los Angeles, CA 90067
Actress

Makkena, Wendy
c/o Marsha McManus
2372 Veteran Ave., Ste. 102
Los Angeles, CA 90064
Actress

• **Malkovich, John**
PO Box 1171
Weston, CT 06883
Actor
Birthday: 12/9/53

Mandela, Nelson
51 Plain St.
Johannesburg 2001
South Africa
President of South Africa

Mandrell, Barbara
PO Box 620
Hendersonville, TN 37077
Singer

Irlene Mandrell Friend's Club
544 Nashville Pike, Ste. 244
Gallatin, TN 37066
Singer

Mandrell, Louise
713 W. Main
Hendersonville, TN 37075
or
PO Box 800
Hendersonville, TN 37077
Singer

Manetti, Larry
c/o Epstein/Wyckoff
280 S. Beverly Dr., #400
Beverly Hills, CA 90212
Actor

Manhattan Institute
52 Vanderbilt Ave.
New York, NY 10017
Web site: http://
www.manhattan-institute.org/
E-mail: barreiro@
manhattan-institute.org
Lawrence Mone, president
*Encourages public policies at all
levels of government which will
allow individuals the greatest
scope for achieving their
potential*

Mann, Michael
13746 Sunset Blvd.
Pacific Palisades, CA 90272
Director

Manoff, Dinah
21244 Ventura Blvd., #101
Woodland Hills, CA 91364
Actress
Birthday: 1/25/58

Manpower
5301 N. Ironwood Rd.
Milwaukee, WI 53217
Web site: http://
  www.manpower.com
Mitchell S. Fromstein, CEO
Temporary help

**Manpower Demonstration
  Research Corporation**
16 E. 34th St., 19th Fl.
New York, NY 10016
Web site: http://www.mdrc.org/
  E-mail:
  information@mdrc.org
Richard Murnane, chair,
  Committee on Education
  Studies
*Nonprofit, nonpartisan research
  organization that develops and
  evaluates innovative approaches
  to moving people from welfare to
  work, building a stronger work
  force through training,
  revitalizing low-income
  communities, and improving
  education for at-risk youth*

Manson, Charles
#B33920
Pelican Bay Prison
Box 7000
Crescent City, CA 95531-7000
Convicted serial killer, cult leader
Birthday: 11/11/34

Manson, Marilyn
83 Riverside Dr.
New York, NY 10024
Musician

Mantegna, Joe
c/o Peter Strain
1500 Broadway, #2001
New York, NY 10036
Actor

Mantooth, Randolph
300 W. 55th St., #9-C
New York, NY 10019
Actor
Birthday: 9/19/44

Mapco
1800 S. Baltimore Ave.
Tulsa, OK 74119
Web site: http://
  www.mapcoinc.com
James E. Barnes, CEO
Petroleum refining

Maradona, Diego
c/o FC Boca Juniors
Brandsen 805
1161 Capital Federal
Argentina
Professional soccer player
Birthday: 10/30/60

March, Barbara
c/o Judy Schoen Associates
606 N. Larchmont Blvd., #309
Los Angeles, CA 90004
*Plays Lursa on "Star Trek: The
  Next Generation" and "Star
  Trek: Deep Space Nine"*

March, Jane
5 Jubilee Pl., #100
London SW3 3TD
England
Actress

Marcy Brothers
PO Box 2502
Oroville, CA 95965
Musical group

HRH Princess Margaret
Kensington Palace
London N5
England
Birthday: 8/21/30
Queen Elizabeth's sister

Margulies, Julianna
8942 Wilshire Blvd.
Beverly Hills, CA 90211
Actress

Marriott International
10400 Fernwood Rd.
Bethesda, MD 20817
Web site: http://
   www.marriott.com
J. Willard Marriott, Jr., CEO
Hotels, casinos, resorts

Marrs, Texe
1708 Patterson Rd.
Austin, TX 78733
Religious author

Marshall, Peter
11365 Ventura Blvd., #100
Studio City, CA 91604
TV game show host
Birthday: 3/20/27

Marsh and McLennan
1166 6th Ave.
New York, NY 10036
Web site: http://
   www.marshmac.com
A.J.C. Smith, CEO
Diversified financials

Martin, Pamela Sue
c/o Pierce & Shelly
612 Lighthouse Ave., #275
Pacific Grove, CA 93951
E-mail:
   PAMSUEMART@aol.com
Actress
Birthday: 1/5/54

Martin, Ricky
8439 Sunset Blvd., #405
Los Angeles, CA 90069
Singer
Birthday: 12/24/71

Martin, Steve
PO Box 929
Beverly Hills, CA 90213
or
c/o I.C.M.
8942 Wilshire Blvd.
Beverly Hills, CA 90211
Actor, comedian

Martindale, Wink
11365 Ventura Blvd., #100
Studio City, CA 91604
TV game show host
Birthday: 12/4/34

Masco
21001 Van Born Rd.
Taylor, MI 48180
Web site: http://
   www.masco.com
Richard A. Manoogian, CEO
Metal products

Maske, Henry
c/o Sauerland Promotion
Hochstadentstr. 1–3
50674 Köln
Germany
or
c/o WLT Sport Int.
Römerstr. 108
54293 Trier
Germany
Former professional boxer
Birthday: 1/6/64

Mason, Marsha
RR #2
Box 269 #305
Santa Fe, NM 87505
Actress
Birthday: 4/3/42

Massachusetts Mutual Insurance Company
1295 State St.
Springfield, MA 01111
Thomas B. Wheeler, CEO
Life and health insurance (mutual)

Masterson, Mary Stuart
c/o Constellation
PO Box 1249
White River Junction, VT 05001
Actress

Mastrantonio, Mary Elizabeth
c/o Hofflund-Tolone
9465 Wilshire Blvd., #620
Beverly Hills, CA 90212
Actress
Birthday: 11/17/58

Matheson, Tim
9171 Wilshire Blvd., #406
Beverly Hills, CA 90210
Actor
Birthday: 12/31/48

Mathis, Johnny
c/o Peter Levison Communications
1762 Westwood, Ste. 210
Los Angeles, CA 90024
Singer
Birthday: 9/30/35

Matlin, Marlee
12304 Santa Monica Blvd., Ste. 119
Los Angeles, CA 90025
Actress
Birthday: 8/24/65

Matthau, Walter
1999 Ave. of the Stars, #2100
Los Angeles, CA 90067
Actor
Birthday: 10/1/20

Mattel
333 Continental Blvd.
El Segundo, CA 90245
Web site: http://www.barbie.com
Jill E. Barad, CEO
Toys, sporting goods

Mattingly, Don
RR #5
Box 74
Evansville, IN 47711
Former baseball player

Mature, Victor
PO Box 706
Rancho Santa Fe, CA 92067
Actor
Birthday: 1/29/16

Mavericks, The
PO Box 22586
Nashville, TN 37202
Musical group

Maxxam
5847 San Felipe
Houston, TX 77057
Charles E. Hurwitz, CEO
Metals

May Department Stores
611 Olive St.
St. Louis, MO 63101
Web site: http://www.maycompany.com
David C. Farrell, CEO
General merchandisers

Mayhew, Peter
c/o Star Wars Fan Club
PO Box 111000
Aurora, CO 80042
Actor
Played Chewbacca in Star Wars

Mays, Willie
3333 Henry Hudson Pkwy.
New York, NY 10463
Retired baseball player
Birthday: 5/6/31

Maytag
403 W. 4th St. N.
Newton, IA 50208
Web site: http://
www.maytagcorp.com
Leonard A. Hadley, CEO
Electronics, electrical equipment

MBNA
Wilmington, DE 19884
Web site: http://
www.mbnainternational.com
Alfred Lerner, CEO
Commercial bank

McAllister, Dawson
PO Box 8123
Irving, TX 75016
Christian talk show host

McBride, Martina
PO Box 291627
Nashville, TN 37229
Country singer

McBride & the Ride
PO Box 17617
Nashville, TN 37217
Music group

McCarters Fan Club
PO Box 41455
Nashville, TN 37204
Music group's fan club

McCarthy, Andrew
c/o I.C.M
8942 Wilshire Blvd.
Beverly Hills, CA 90211
Actor
Birthday: 11/29/62

McCarthy, Jenny
c/o MTV
1515 Broadway
New York, NY 10036
Actress
Birthday: 11/2/72

McCartney, Paul
1 Soho Sq.
London W1
England
Former Beatle

McClain, Charly
c/o American Concert &
Touring
1200 Division St.
Nashville, TN 37203
Country singer

McClanahan, Rue
9454 Wilshire Blvd., #405
Beverly Hills, CA 90212
Actress
Birthday: 2/21/34

**Delbert McClinton
International**
47 Music Sq. E.
Nashville, TN 37203
Country singer's fan club

McConaughey, Matthew
PO Box 1145
Malibu, CA 90265
Actor
Birthday: 11/4/69

McCord, Kent
15301 Ventura Blvd., #345
Sherman Oaks, CA 91403
Actor

McCormack, Mary
c/o The Gersh Agency
PO Box 5617
Beverly Hills, CA 90209
Actress

McCormick, Carolyn
15760 Ventura Blvd., #1730
Encino, CA 91436
Actress

Maureen McCormick Fan Club
22817 Pera Rd.
Woodland Hills, CA 91364
*Played Marsha on "The Brady
Bunch"*

McCoy, Charlie
c/o Hee Haw
2806 Opryland Dr.
Nashville, TN 37214
Country musician

McCoy, Neal
PO Box 662
Poteau, OK 74953
Country singer

McCullough, Julie
c/o Pierce & Shelly
612 Lighthouse Ave., #275
Pacific Grove, CA 93951
E-mail: JulieMcCul@aol.com
Actress

McDaniel, Mel
PO Box 2285
Hendersonville, TN 37077
Country singer

McDermott, Dylan
2700 Neilson Way, #1133
Santa Monica, CA 90405
Actor

McDonald, Christopher
8033 Sunset Blvd., #4011
Los Angeles, CA 90046
Actor

McDonald's
McDonald's Plaza
Oak Brook, IL 60523
Web site: http://
   www.mcdonalds.com
Michael R. Quinlan, CEO
Restaurant chain

McDonnell, Mary
PO Box 6010-540
Sherman Oaks, CA 91413
Actress

McDormand, Frances
333 West End Ave., Ste. 12-C
New York, NY 10023
Actress

McDowell, Malcolm
c/o I.C.M.
Oxford House
76 Oxford St.
London WIN 0AX
England
Actor
Birthday: 6/19/43

McDowell, Ronnie
PO Box 186
Russellville, AL 35653
Country singer

McEntire, Reba
PO Box 121996
Nashville, TN 37212
or
40 Music Sq. W.
Nashville, TN 37203
Country singer
Birthday: 3/28/55

McEuen, John
6044 Deal Ave.
Nashville, TN 37209
Country singer

McFadden, Gates
c/o Innovative Artists
1999 Ave. of the Stars, #2850
Los Angeles, CA 90067
Actress
*Played Dr. Beverly Crusher on
   "Star Trek: The Next
   Generation"*
Birthday: 8/28/49

McGinley, Ted
1925 Century Park E., Ste.
   2320
Los Angeles, CA 90067
Actor
Birthday: 5/30/58

McGraw, Ali
c/o Provident Financial Mgmt.
10345 W. Olympic Blvd., #200
Los Angeles, CA 90064
Actress
Birthday: 4/1/38

McGraw, Tim
PO Box 22939
Nashville, TN 37202
Country singer

McGraw-Hill
1221 6th Ave.
New York, NY 10020
Web site: http://
   www.mcgraw-hill.com
Harold McGraw III, CEO
Publishing, printing

McGregor, Ewan
2 Goodwin's Ct.
London, WC2N 4LL
England
Actor
Birthday: 3/31/71

MCI Communications
1801 Penn. Ave. NW
Washington, DC 20006
Web site: http://www.mci.com
Gerald H. Taylor, CEO
Telecommunications

McKeon, Nancy
PO Box 6778
Burbank, CA 91510
Actress
Birthday: 4/4/66

McKesson
1 Post St.
San Francisco, CA 94104
Web site: http://
   www.mckesson.com
Mark A. Pulido, CEO
Wholesalers

McLean, Don
PO Box 102
Castine, ME 04421
Singer, songwriter
Birthday: 10/2/45

McNeil, Robert Duncan
c/o Susan Smith Assoc.
121 N. San Vincente Blvd.
Beverly Hills, CA 92011
Actor
Plays Lt. Tom Paris on "Star Trek: Voyager"

McNichol, Kristy
c/o W.M.A.
151 El. Camino Dr.
Beverly Hills, CA 90212
Actress
Birthday: 9/9/62

McPherson, Elle
40 E. 60th St.
New York, NY 10022
Model

McRaney, Gerald
329 N. Wetherly Dr., #101
Beverly Hills, CA 90211
Actor, married to Delta Burke
Birthday: 8/19/48

Mead
Courthouse Plaza N. E.
Dayton, OH 45463
Web site: http://
   www.mead.com
Jerome F. Tatar, CEO
Forest and paper products

Meadows, Jayne
15201-B Burbank Blvd.
Van Nuys, CA 91411
Actress

Meara, Anne
c/o Innovative Artists
1999 Ave. of the Stars, #2850
Los Angeles, CA 90067
Comedian, actress, married to Jerry Stiller

Meatloaf (Marvin Lee Aday)
PO Box 68
Stockport
Cheshire SK3 0JY
England
Singer
Birthday: 9/27/51

Media Access Project
2000 M St. NW, #400
Washington, DC 20036
*Public interest law firm,
concentrating on
telecommunications issues*

Media Research Center
113 S. West St., #200
Alexandria, VA 22314

Mediascope
12711 Ventura Blvd., #280
Studio City, CA 91604
Web site: http://
www.mediascope.org/
mediascope/index.htm
E-mail: facts@mediascope.org
*National, nonprofit public policy
organization founded in 1992
to promote constructive
depictions of health and social
issues in the media, particularly
as they relate to children and
adolescents*

Media Studies Center
580 Madison Ave., 42nd Fl.
New York, NY 10022
Web site: http://
www.freedomforum.org/
whoweare/media.asp
E-mail:
sowens@mediastudies.org
Michael I. Sovern, chairman
*Seeks to promote media
professionalism, foster greater
public understanding of how the
media work, strengthen
journalism practice and*

*education, and examine the
effects of mass communication
and communication technology
on society*

**Medical Research
Modernization Committee**
PO Box 2751
New York, NY 10163
Web site: http://
www.mrmcmed.org/
E-mail: mrmcmed@aol.com
Stephen R. Kaufman, cochair
*Works to modernize medical
research and promote human
health: concludes that animal
experiments take desperately
needed money but rarely
contribute to human health*

MedPartners
3000 Galleria Tower, Ste. 1000
Birmingham, AL 35244
Web site: http://
www.medpartners.com
Mac Crawford, CEO
Health care

Mellencamp, John
Rt. 1, Box 361
Nashville, IN 47448
Rock singer, songwriter, guitarist
Birthday: 10/7/51

Mellon Bank Corporation
1 Mellon Bank Ctr.
Pittsburgh, PA 15258
Web site: http://
www.mellon.com
Frank V. Cahouet, CEO
Commercial bank

Ken Mellons Fan Club
PO Box 158732
Nashville, TN 37215
Country music fan club

"Melrose Place"
c/o Spelling Television
5700 Wilshire Blvd.
Beverly Hills, CA 90036
TV series

Members of Mayday
c/o Low Spirit Recordings
Giesebrechtstr. 16
10629 Berlin
Germany
Music group

Menendez, Erik
#1878449
CSP-Sac
Box 290066
Represa, CA 95671
Convicted of killing his parents

Menendez, Lyle
#1887106
California Correctional
   Institute
Box 1031
Tehachapi, CA 93581
Convicted of killing his parents

Mensy, Tim
PO Box 128007
Nashville, TN 37212
Country singer

Mercantile Stores
9450 Seward Rd.
Fairfield, OH 45246
Web site: http://
   www.mercstores.com
David L. Nichols, CEO
General merchandisers

Merchant, Natalie
c/o Creative Artists Agency
9830 Wilshire Blvd.
Beverly Hills, CA 90212
Singer, songwriter
Birthday: 10/26/63

Merck
1 Merck Dr.
Whitehouse Station, NJ 08889
Web site: http://
   www.merck.com
Raymond V. Gilmartin, CEO
Pharmaceuticals

Merisel
200 Continental Blvd.
El Segundo, CA 90245
Web site: http://
   www.merisel.com
Dwight Steffensen, CEO
Computer wholesalers

Meriwether, Lee
PO Box 260402
Encino, CA 91326
Actress, former Miss America
Birthday: 5/27/35

Merrill Lynch
250 Vesey St.
New York, NY 10281
Web site: http://www.ml.com
David H. Komansky, CEO
Securities

Metallica
729 7th Ave., #1400
New York, NY 10019
Heavy metal group

Metropolitan Life Insurance
1 Madison Ave.
New York, NY 10010
Harry P. Kamen, CEO
*Life and health insurance
   (stock)*

**Mexican American Legal
   Defense and Education Fund
   (MALDEF)**
733 15th St. NW, #920
Washington, DC 20005
Web site: http://
   www.MALDEF.org/
E-mail: info@maldef.org
Al Kauffman, attorney

National nonprofit organization whose mission is to protect and promote the civil rights of the more than 29 million Latinos living in the United States

Meyer, Dina
c/o UTA
9560 Wilshire Blvd.
Beverly Hills, CA 90212
Actress

Mickey Mouse
500 S. Buena Vista St.
Burbank, CA 92521
Web site: http://
   www.disney.com/
Cartoon character ("Steamboat Willie," first Mickey Mouse cartoon, released 11/18/28)

MicroAge
2400 S. MicroAge Way
Tempe, AZ 85282
Web site: http://
   www.microage.com
Jeffrey D. McKeever, CEO
Wholesaler

Micron Technology
8000 S. Federal Way
Boise, ID 83707
Web site: http://
   www.micron.com
Steven R. Appleton, CEO
Electronics, electrical equipment

Microsoft
1 Microsoft Way
Redmond, WA 98052
Web site: http://
   www.microsoft.com
William H. Gates, CEO
Computer software

Midler, Bette
c/o All Girl Productions
100 Universal City Plaza
Bldg. 507, #4C
Universal City, CA 91608
Actress, singer
Birthday: 12/1/45

Mighty Morphin Power Rangers
26020-A Avenue Hall
Valencia, CA 91355
TV heroes

Mike & the Mechanics
c/o Hit & Run Music
25 Ives St.
London SW3 2ND
England
Music group

Milano, Alyssa
151 El Camino Dr.
Beverly Hills, CA 90212
Actress
Birthday: 12/19/73

Miles, Vera
Box 1704
Big Bear Lake, CA 92315
Actress
Birthday: 8/23/30

Millennium Chemicals
230 Half Mile Rd.
Red Bank, NJ 07701
William M. Landuyt, CEO
Chemicals

Miller, Bill
c/o Sherry Halton
1223 17th Ave. S.
Nashville, TN 37212
Singer

Miller, Dennis
7800 Beverly Blvd.
Los Angeles, CA 90036
TV host, comedian, actor
Birthday: 10/5/43

Miller, Penelope Ann
c/o Kincaid Mgmt.
43-B Navy St.
Venice, CA 90291
Actress
Birthday: 1/13/64

Mills, Sir John
Hill House
Denham Village
Buckinghamshire
England
Actor
Birthday: 2/22/08

Milsap, Ronnie
PO Box 40325
Nashville, TN 37204
Country singer

Minghella, Anthony
c/o Miramax Film Corp.
375 Greenwich St., 4th Fl.
New York, NY 10013
Film director

Minnelli, Liza
150 E. 69th St., #21-G
New York, NY 10021
or
PO Box 790039
Middle Village, NY 11379
*Actress, singer, Judy Garland's
   oldest daughter*
Birthday: 3/12/46

**Minnesota Mining &
   Manufacturing (3M)**
3M Center
St. Paul, MN 55144
Web site: http://
   www.mmm.com
Livio D. DeSimone, CEO
*Scientific, photo, control
   equipment, Scotch tape*

Mitchell, Dennis
c/o U.S. Olympic Committee
1750 E. Boulder St.
Colorado Springs, CO 80909
Olympic sprinter

Mitchell, Waddie
PO Box 268
Elko, NV 89801
Cowboy poet

Mobil
3225 Gallows Rd.
Fairfax, VA 22037
Web site: http://
   www.mobil.com
Lucio A. Noto, CEO
Petroleum refining

Moceanu, Dominique
c/o Gymnastics Federation
201 S. Capitol Ave.
Indianapolis, IN 46255
Olympic gymnast

Modine, Matthew
9696 Culver Blvd., #203
Culver City, CA 90232
Actor
Birthday: 3/22/59

Moll, Richard
270 N. Cannon Dr.
Beverly Hills, CA 90210
Actor
Birthday: 1/13/43

Molly & the Heymakers
PO Box 1160
Hayward, WI 54843
Music group

Monkees, The
8369A Sausalito Ave.
West Hills, CA 91304
Music group

Monsanto
800 N. Lindbergh Blvd.
St. Louis, MO 63167
Web site: http://
   www.monsanto.com
Robert B. Shapiro, CEO
Chemicals

Montana, Joe
PO Box 7342
Menlo Park, CA 94026
Football quarterback

Montana, Patsy
3728 Highway 411
Madisonville, TN 37354
Country singer

Montanans for Property Rights
PO Box 130399
Coram, MT 59913
Web site: http://
    members.spree.com/mfpr/
E-mail: mfpr7@yahoo.com
Russell Crowder, member of
    board of directors
*Defends the rights of Montana
    property owners*

Montgomery, George
PO Box 2187
Rancho Mirage, CA 92270
Actor

Montgomery, John Michael
PO Box 639
Danville, KY 40423
Country singer

Moore, Demi
c/o Rufglen Films
1453 3rd. St., #420
Santa Monica, CA 90401
E-mail: DemiM2@aol.com
Actress
Birthday: 11/11/62

Moore, Dudley
73 Market St.
Venice, CA 90291
Actor
Birthday: 4/19/35

Moore, Mary Tyler
510 E. 86th St., #21A
New York, NY 10028
or
c/o William Morris Agency
1325 Ave. of the Americas
New York, NY 10019
Actress
Birthday: 12/29/36

Moore, Roger
Chalet Le Fenil
3783 Grund bei Gstaad
Switzerland
or
2–4 Noel St.
London W1V 3RB
England
Actor
Birthday: 10/14/27

Moran, Erin
PO Box 3261
Quartz Hill, CA 93586
Actress
Birthday: 10/18/61

**Moreno, Rita (Rosita Dolores
    Alverio)**
9000 Sunset Blvd., #1200
Los Angeles, CA 90069
Actress
Birthday: 12/11/31

Morgan, Lorrie
c/o Neal O'Neal
PO Box 78
Spencer, TN 38585
Country singer

**Morgan Stanley Dean Witter
    Discover**
1585 Broadway
New York, NY 10036
Web site: http://
    www.deanwitterdiscover.com
Philip J. Purcell, CEO
Securities

Morissette, Alanis
75 Rockefeller Plaza, #2100
New York, NY 10019
Singer, songwriter

Morita, Pat
PO Box 491278
Los Angeles, CA 90049
Actor
Birthday: 6/28/30

Morris, Gary
607 W. Church Dr.
Sugar Land, TX 77478
Singer, songwriter

Morrison, Van
12304 Santa Monica Blvd.,
  #300
Los Angeles, CA 90025
Singer, songwriter
Birthday: 8/31/45

Mortensen, Viggo
c/o CAA
9830 Wilshire Blvd.
Beverly Hills, CA 90212
Actor

Morton International
100 N. Riverside Plaza
Chicago, IL 60606
Web site: http://
  www.mortonintl.com
S. Jay Stewart, CEO
Chemicals

Moses, Rick
c/o The Calder Agency
19919 Redwing St.
Woodland Hills, CA 91364
Actor
Birthday: 9/5//52

Moss, Kate
205 W. 39th St., #1200
New York, NY 10018
Model
Birthday: 1/16/74

Motorola
1303 E. Algonquin Rd.
Schaumburg, IL 60196
Web site: http://www.mot.com
Christopher B. Galvin, CEO
Electronics, electrical equipment

Mowrey, Dude
PO Box 24491
Nashville, TN 37202
Country musician

MTV
1515 Broadway
New York, NY 10036
Web site: http://www.mtv.com/
E-mail: MTVNEWS@MTV.COM
Cable TV network

Mueller-Stahl, Armin
c/o ZBF-Agentur
Ordensmeisterstr. 15
12099 Berlin
Germany
Actor
Birthday: 12/17/30

Muldaur, Diana
10100 Santa Monica Blvd.,
  #2490
Los Angeles, CA 90067
Actress
Birthday: 8/19/38

Mulgrew, Kate
c/o "Star Trek: Voyager"
Paramount Pictures
5555 Melrose Ave.
Los Angeles, CA 90038
Actress
Birthday: 4/29/45

Mulroney, Dermot
1180 S. Beverly Dr., #618
Los Angeles, CA 90035
Actor
Birthday: 10/31/63

Murphey, David Lee
PO Box 24333
Nashville, TN 37202
Country singer

Murphey, Michael Martin
PO Box 777
Taos, NM 87571
Country & cowboy singer

Murphy, Eddie
PO Box 1028
Englewood Cliffs, NJ 07632
or
c/o International Creative
   Mgmt.
8942 Wilshire Blvd.
Beverly Hills, CA 90211
or
152 W. 57th St. Ste. 4700
New York, NY 10019
Actor, comedian
Birthday: 4/3/61

Murray, Anne
4950 Yonge St., #2400
Toronto, ON M2N 6K1
Canada
Singer

Murray, Bill
RFD #1, Box 573
Palisades, NY 10964
Actor

Muster, Thomas
c/o AMJ Pro Mgmt.
Steinfeldstr. 17
2351 Wiener Neudorf
Austria
Tennis player
Birthday: 10/2/67

Mutual of Omaha Insurance
Mutual of Omaha Plaza
Omaha, NE 68175
John William Weekly, CEO
*Life and health insurance
   (mutual)*

Myers, Mike
9150 Wilshire Blvd., #350
Beverly Hills, CA 90212
Actor
Birthday: 5/25/63

A writer lives in awe of words for they can be cruel or kind, and they can change their meanings right in front of you. They pick up flavors and odors like butter in a refrigerator.

—ANONYMOUS

NAACP (National Association for the Advancement of Colored People)
1025 Vermont Ave. NW, Ste. 1120
Washington, DC 20005
Kweisi Mfume, president and CEO
Web site: http://www.naacp.org/
Primary objective is to ensure the political, educational, social, and economic equality of minority group citizens of the United States

Nabors, Jim
PO Box 10364
Honolulu, HI 96816
Actor, singer
Birthday: 6/11/33

Nakano, Shinji
c/o Prost Grand Prix
Technopole de la Nièvre
58470 Magny Cours
France
Professional Formula-1 driver

Nana
c/o Booya Music
Marlowring 3
22525 Hamburg
Germany
Singer
Birthday: 10/5/71

Nannini, Alessandro
c/o Team Alfa Corse
Via Enrico Fermi 7
20019 Settimo Milianese
Italy
Race car driver
Birthday: 7/7/59

Narz, Jack
11365 Ventura Blvd., #100
Studio City, CA 91604
TV game show host, Tom Kennedy's brother
Birthday: 11/13/22

Nash, Graham
14930 Ventura Blvd., #205
Sherman Oaks, CA 91403
Rock musician

Nash Finch
7600 France Ave. S.
Edina, MN 55435
Alfred N. Flaten, Jr., CEO
Wholesalers

National Abortion Federation
1436 U St. NW, #103
Washington, DC 20003
Web site: http://www.prochoice.org/
Association of providers of abortion services in the United States and Canada

National Abortion Reproductive Rights Action League
1156 15th St. NW, #700
Washington, DC 20009
Web site: http://www.naral.org/
E-mail: naral@newmedium.com
Kate Michelman, president
Promotes reproductive freedom and dignity for women and their families

National Academy of Science
2101 Constitution Ave. NW
Washington, DC 20418
Web site: http://www.nas.edu/
E-mail: wwwfdbk@nas.edu
Dan Quinn, media relations officer
Private, nonprofit society of scholars engaged in scientific and engineering research, dedicated to the furtherance of science and technology and to their use for the general welfare

National Alliance for the Mentally Ill
200 N. Glebe Rd., #1015
Arlington, VA 22203
Web site: http://www.nami.org/
E-mail: namiofc@aol.com
Sue Davis, secretary of board of directors
Organization working with and for persons with mental illnesses and their families

National Association of Home Builders
1201 15th St. NW
Washington, DC 20005
Web site: http://www.nahb.com/
E-mail: info@nahb.com
Don Martin, president
The voice of America's housing industry

National Association of Manufacturers
1331 Pennsylvania Ave. NW, #1500
Washington, DC 20004
Web site: http://www.nam.org/
E-mail: manufacturing@nam.org
Earnest W. Deavenport, Jr., chairman of the board
Founded in 1895 to advance a progrowth, promanufacturing policy agenda

National Association of Professional Pet Sitters
1200 G St. NW, Ste. 760
Washington, DC 20005
Web site: http:// www.petsitters.org/about.htm
Promotes the concept of in-home pet care, to support the professionals engaged in at-home pet care, promote the welfare of animals, and improve and expand the industry of pet sitting

National Association of Realtors
700 11th St. NW
Washington, DC 20001
Web site: http:// nar.realtor.com/
E-mail: infocentral@realtors.org
R. Layne Morrill, president
Members are residential and commercial REALTORS ® who are brokers, salespeople, property managers, appraisers, counselors, and others engaged in all aspects of the real estate industry

National Audubon Society
666 Pennsylvania Ave. SE, #200
Washington, DC 20003
Web site: http://
www.audubon.org/
E-mail: jbianchi@audubon.org
Oakes Ames, board member
Ruth O. Russell, board
member
*Seeks to conserve and restore
natural ecosystems, focusing on
birds and other wildlife, for the
benefit of humanity and the
earth's biological diversity*

**National Caucus and Center
on Black Aged Inc.**
1424 K St. NW, #500
Washington, DC 20005
Web site: http://www.
ncba-blackaged.org/
E-mail: ncba@aol.com
*National nonprofit organization
dedicated to improving the
quality of life for African
Americans and low-income
elderly*

**National Center for Law and
Deafness**
800 Florida Ave. NE
Washington, DC 20002

**National Center for State
Courts**
300 Newport Ave.
Williamsburg, VA 23185
E-mail: nchest@ncsc.dni.us

**National Center on Institutions
and Alternatives (NCIA)**
635 Slater Ln., #G100
Alexandria, VA 22314
E-mail: ncia@lgc.apc.org

National City Corp.
1900 E. 9th St.
Cleveland, OH 44114
Web site: http://
www.national-city.com
David A. Daberko, CEO
Commercial bank

**National Organization for the
Reform of Marijuana Laws
(NORML)**
1001 Connecticut Ave. NW,
#1010
Washington, DC 20036
Website:http://www.norml.org/
E-mail: natlnorml@aol.com
Allen St. Pierre, executive
director NORML
Foundation
*Since its founding in 1970,
NORML has been the principal
national advocate for legalizing
marijuana*

**National Organization for
Women (NOW)**
1000 16th St. NW, #700
Washington, DC 20036
Web site: http://now.org/now
E-mail: now@now.org
Patricia Ireland, president
*Dedicated to making legal,
political, social, and economic
change in our society in order to
achieve its goal, which is to
eliminate sexism*

**National Rainbow Coalition,
Inc.**
PO Box 27385
Washington, DC 20005
Web site: http://
www.tripod.com/jobs_career/
goodworks/jobs/708.html
Angela Davis, director
*Multiracial, multiissue national
organization founded by Rev.
Jesse L. Jackson*

National Republican Congressional Campaign Committee
32 1st St. SE
Washington, DC 20003
Web site: www.nrcc.org
John Linder, chairman
Political committee devoted to increasing the 228-member Republican majority in the U.S. House of Representatives

National Taxpayer's Union
108 N. Alfred St.
Alexandria, VA 22314
Web site: http://www.ntu.org/
E-mail:ntu@townhall.com
Rete Sepp, media relations
E-mail: pressguy@ntu.org
The largest grassroots taxpayer organization, with more than 300,000 members across all 50 states

National Trust for Historic Preservation
1785 Massachusetts Ave. NW
Washington, DC 20036
Web site: http://www.nthp.org
Richard Moe, president
Dedicated to showing how preservation can play an important role in strengthening a sense of community and improving the quality of life

National Urban League
500 E. 62nd St.
New York, NY 10021
Web site: http://www.nul.org/
E-mail: info@nul.org
Jonathan S. Linen, chairman
The premier social service and civil rights organization in America

National Wildlife Federation
8925 Leesburg Pike
Vienna, VA 22184
Tom Lustig, counsel
Web site: http://www.nwf.org/
Focuses its efforts on five core issue areas (Endangered Habitat, Water Quality, Land Stewardship, Wetlands, and Sustainable Communities), and pursues a range of educational projects and activist, advocacy, and litigation initiatives, within these core areas

NationsBank Corp.
100 N. Tryon St.
Charlotte, NC 28255
Web site: http://www.nationsbank.com
Hugh L. McColl, Jr., CEO
Commercial bank

Nationwide Insurance Enterprise
1 Nationwide Plaza
Columbus, OH 43215
Dimon R. McFerson, CEO
P & C insurance (stock)

Native American Rights Fund
1506 Broadway
Boulder, CO 80302
Web site: http://www.narf.org/
E-mail: pereira@narf.org
John E. Echohawk, a Pawnee, executive director
Nonprofit legal organization dedicated to the preservation of the rights and culture of Native Americans

Naughton, David
3500 W. Olive Ave., #1400
Burbank, CA 91505
Actor
Birthday: 2/13/51

Navistar International
455 N. Cityfront Plaza Dr.
Chicago, IL 60611
Web site: http://
   www.navistar.com
John R. Horne, CEO
Motor vehicles and parts

Navratilova, Martina
c/o WTA Tour
1266 E. Main St., #4
Stamford, CT 06902
Former professional tennis player
Birthday: 10/18/56

NCR
1700 S. Patterson Blvd.
Dayton, OH 45479
Web site: http://www.ncr.com
Lars Nyberg, CEO
Computers, office equipment

Neal, Patricia
PO Box 1043
Edgartown, MA 02539
Actress
Birthday: 1/20/26

Nealon, Kevin
9363 Wilshire Blvd., #212
Beverly Hills, CA 90210
Actor

Needham, Tracey
"J.A.G."
c/o Badgley and Connor
9229 Sunset Blvd., #311
Los Angeles, CA 90069
Actress

Neeson, Liam
150 S. Rodeo Dr., #220
Beverly Hills, CA 90212
Actor
Birthday: 6/7/52

Neil, Sam
PO Box 153
Noble Park
Victoria 3174
Australia
Actor
Birthday: 9/14/47

Nelligan, Kate
40 W. 57th St.
New York, NY 10019
Actress
Birthday: 3/16/51

Nelson, Willie
PO Box 7104
Lancaster, PA 17604
or
Rt #1
Briarcliff TT
Spicewood, TX 78669
Singer, songwriter
Birthday: 4/30/33

Nesmith, Michael
2828 Donald Douglas Lane,
   Ste. 15
Santa Monica, CA 90405
*Singer, producer, actor on "The
   Monkees"*
Birthday: 12/30/42

Neville, Aaron
Box 750187
New Orleans, LA 70175
Singer
Birthday: 1/24/41

Nevins, Jason
c/o Sony Music/Epic
Stephanstr. 15
60313 Frankfurt
Germany
Member of Run-D.M.C.

New Century Energies
1225 17th St.
Denver, CO 80202
Web site: http://www.psco.com/
   nce/index.htm
Bill D. Helton, CEO
Gas and electric utilities

New Edition
PO Box 77505
San Francisco, CA 94107
Music group

Newell
29 E. Stephenson St.
Freeport, IL 61032
Web site: http://
    www.newellco.com
John J. McDonough, CEO
Metal products

New Israel Fund
1625 K St. NW, Ste. 500
Washington, DC 20006
Web site: http://www.nif.org/
E-mail: info@nif.org
Frank Fisher, president
*Organization for pluralism &
    religious freedom in Israel*

Newman, Barry
N. Oakhurst Dr., #115
Beverly Hills, CA 90210
Birthday: 11/7/38
Actor

Newman, Jimmy C.
2804 Opryland Dr.
Nashville, TN 37214
Country singer

Newman, Paul
1120 5th Ave., #1C
New York, NY 10128
*Actor, married to Joanne
    Woodward*
Birthday: 1/26/25

Newman, Randy
21241 Ventura Blvd., #241
Woodland Hills, CA 91364
Singer
Birthday: 11/28/43

Newmar, Julie
11365 Ventura Blvd., #100
Studio City, CA 91604
Actress

Newton, Juice
PO Box 293323
Lewisville, TX 75029
Singer

Newton-John, Olivia
PO Box 2710
Malibu, CA 90265
Singer, actress
Birthday: 9/26/47

New York Life Insurance
51 Madison Ave.
New York, NY 10010
Seymour G. Sternberg, CEO
*Life and health insurance
    (mutual)*

New York Times
229 W. 43rd St.
New York, NY 10036
Web site: http://
    www.nytimes.com
Russell T. Lewis, CEO
Publishing, printing

NGC
1000 Louisiana St.
Houston, TX 77002
Web site: http://
    www.ngccorp.com
C. L. Watson, CEO
Pipelines

Niagara Mohawk Power
300 Erie Blvd. W.
Syracuse, NY 13202
Web site: http://www.nimo.com
William E. Davis, CEO
Gas and electric utilities

Nichols, Nichelle
22647 Ventura Blvd.
Woodland Hills, CA 91364
Actress, Lt. Uhura of "Star Trek"

Nicholson, Jack
15760 Ventura Blvd., #1730
Encino, CA 91436
Actor
Birthday: 4/22/37

Nicklaus, Jack
11760 U.S. Hwy. #1–6
N. Palm Beach, FL 33408
Professional golfer
Birthday: 1/21/40

Nicks, Stevie
PO Box 7855
Alhambra, CA 91802
Member of Fleetwood Mac

Nicollier, Claude
c/o NASA
Johnson Space Center
Dept. CB
Houston, TX 77058
Astronaut

Nielsen, Brigitte
PO Box 57593
Sherman Oaks, CA 91403
Actress
Birthday: 7/15/63

Nielsen, Leslie
c/o Bresler Kelly Kipperman
15760 Ventura Blvd., Ste. 1730
Encino, CA 91436
Actor
Birthday: 2/11/26

Nike
1 Bowerman Dr.
Beaverton, OR 97005
Web site: http://info.nike.com
Phil Knight, CEO
Sportswear company

Nimoy, Leonard
2300 W. Victory Blvd., #C-384
Burbank, CA 91506
Actor, director
Birthday: 3/26/31

Nine Inch Nails
c/o Island Records
22 St. Peter's Sq.
London W6 9NW
England
Music group

Nitty Gritty Dirt Band
111 16th Ave. S.
Nashville, TN 37212
Music group

Nixons, The
c/o Rainmaker Artists
PO Box 720195
Dallas, TX 75372
Music group

No Doubt
ND Friend Club
PO Box 8899
Anaheim, CA 92812
Music group fan club

Nolin, Gena Lee
151 El Camino Dr.
Beverly Hills, CA 90210
Actress, model

Nolte, Nick
c/o Kingsgate Films
6153 Bonsall Dr.
Malibu, CA 90265
Actor
Birthday: 2/8/40

Nomo, Hideo
c/o Los Angeles Dodgers
1000 Elysian Park Ave.
Los Angeles, CA 90012
Pitcher

Nordstrom
1501 5th Ave.
Seattle, WA 98101
Web site: http//
   www.norstrom-pta.com
John Whitacre, CEO
General merchandisers

Norfolk Southern
3 Commercial Pl.
Norfolk, VA 23510
Web site: http//
    www.nscorp.com
David R. Goode, CEO
Railroads

Norris, Chuck (Carlos Ray)
PO Box 872
Navasota, TX 77868
Actor
Birthday: 3/10/40

North, Oliver
RR #1, Box 560
Bluemont, VA 22012
*Former presidential aide and
    senatorial candidate, radio talk
    show host*

Northeast Utilities
107 Selden St.
Berlin, CT 06037
Web site: http://www.nu.com
Michael G. Morris, CEO
Gas and electric utilities

Northern States Power
414 Nicollet Mall
Minneapolis, MN 55401
Website:http//www.nspco.com/
    index.html
James J. Howard, CEO
Gas and electric utilities

Northrop Grumman
1840 Century Park E.
Los Angeles, CA 90067
Web site: http://
    www.northgrum.com
Kent Kresa, CEO
Aerospace

Northwest Airlines
5101 Northwest Dr.
St. Paul, MN 55111
Web site: http://www.nwa.com
John H. Dasburg, CEO
Airline

**Northwestern Mutual Life
    Insurance**
720 E. Wisconsin Ave.
Milwaukee, WI 53202
James D. Ericson, CEO
*Life and health insurance
    (mutual)*

Norville, Deborah
PO Box 426
Mill Neck, NY 11765
TV hostess

Norwest Corp.
6th & Marquette
Minneapolis, MN 55479
Web site: http://
    www.norwest.com
Richard M. Kovacevich, CEO
Commercial bank

Norwood, Daron
PO Box 674659
Nashville, TN 37203
Country singer

Novak, Kim (Marilyn Novak)
Rte. 3, Box 524
Carmel Highlands, CA 93921
Actress
Birthday: 2/13/33

Novello, Don
PO Box 245
Fairfax, CA 94930
*Comedian known as Father Guido
    Sarducci*
Birthday: 1/1/43

N'Sync
c/o Wright Stuff Mgmt.
7380 St. Lake Rd., #350
Orlando, FL 32819
Music group

Nuclear Energy Institute
1776 I St. NW, #400
Washington, DC 20006
Web site: http://www.nei.org/
E-mail: media@nei.org
Scott Peterson, media relations
*The nuclear energy industry's
Washington-based policy
organization*

**Nuclear Information and
Resource Service**
1424 16th St. NW, #601
Washington, DC 20036
Web site: http://www.nirs.org/
E-mail: NirNet@igc.apc.org
Diane D'Arrigo, director
*Organization concerned with
nuclear power, radioactive
waste, radiation, and
sustainable energy issues*

Nucor
2100 Rexford Rd.
Charlotte, NC 28211
Web site: http://www2.nue.com/
nbs
John D. Correnti, CEO
Metals

Nye, Bill
c/o KCTS TV
401 Mercer St.
Seattle, WA 98109
The Science Guy

The world did not impact upon me until I got to the post office.

—CHRISTOPHER MORLEY

Oak Ridge Boys
329 Rockland Rd.
Hendersonville, TN 37075
Musical group

Oasis
8A Wyndham Pl.
London W1X 1PP
England
Music group

O'Brien, Conan
30 Rockefeller Plaza
New York, NY 10112
Talk show host
Birthday: 4/18/63

O'Brien, Tim
PO Box 4040, Duke Sta.
Durham, NC 27706
Country singer

Occidental Petroleum
10889 Wilshire Blvd.
Los Angeles, CA 90024
Web site: http://www.oxy.com
Ray R. Irani, CEO
Chemicals

O'Connell, Jerry
151 El Camino Dr.
Beverly Hills, CA 90212
Actor
Birthday: 2/17/74

O'Connor, Donald
PO Box 20204
Sedona, AZ 86341
Actor, dancer, director
Birthday: 8/8/25

O'Connor, Renee
c/o Ambrosio/Mortimer and
   Associates
9150 Wilshire Blvd., Ste. 175
Beverly Hills, CA 90212
Actress

**Renee O'Connor Fan Club
   Membership**
PO Box 180435
Austin, TX 78718
E-mail: RocMailer@aol.com

O'Connor, Sinead
c/o EMI Records
43 Brooks Green
London W6 7EF
England
Singer
Birthday: 12/8/67

O'Donnell, Chris
2029 Century Park E., #500
Los Angeles, CA 90067
Actor
Birthday: 1970

O'Donnell, Rosie
c/o ILM
8942 Wilshire Blvd.
Beverly Hills, CA 90211
or
30 Rockefeller Plaza, #800E
New York, NY 10112
Web site: http://
www.rosieo.com
Talk show host, actress
Birthday: 1962

Office Depot
2200 Old Germantown Rd.
Delray Beach, FL 33445
Web site: http://
www.officedepot.com/
David I. Fuente, CEO
Specialist retailers

Office Max
3605 Warrensville Ctr. Rd.
Shaker Heights, OH 44122
Web site: http://
www.officemax.com
Michael Feuer, CEO
Specialist retailers

O'Hara, Maureen
Box 1400
Christiansted
St. Croix, VI 00820
Actress
Birthday: 8/17/20

Olajuwon, Akeem Abdul
10 Greenway Plaza
E. Houston, TX 77046
Basketball player

Oldman, Gary
c/o I.C.M.
Oxford House
76 Oxford St.
London W1N 0AX
England
Actor
Birthday: 3/21/58

Olin, Ken
5855 Topanga Canyon, #410
Woodland Hills, CA 91367
Actor
Birthday: 7/30/54

Olin, Lena
8942 Wilshire Blvd.
Beverly Hills, CA 90211
Actress
Birthday: 3/22/55

Olmos, Edward James
18034 Ventura Blvd., #228
Encino, CA 91316
Actor
Birthday: 2/24/47

Olsen, Ashley
8916 Ashcroft Ave.
Los Angeles, CA 90048
Actress
Birthday: 6/13/86

Olsen, Mary Kate
8916 Ashcroft Ave.
Los Angeles, CA 90048
Actress
Birthday: 6/13/86

Olsten
175 Broad Hollow Rd.
Melville, NY 11747
Web site: http://
www.olsten.com
Frank N. Liguori, CEO
Temporary help

OMC
c/o Polydor Records
PO Box 617
Auckland
New Zealand
Music group

Omnicom
437 Madison Ave.
New York, NY 10022
John D. Wren, CEO
Advertising, marketing

O'Neal, Shaquille
c/o Great Western Forum
PO Box 10
Inglewood, CA 90306
*L.A. Laker center (ht. 7'1",
wt. 315 lbs.)*
Birthday: 3/6/72

O'Neal, Tatum
300 Central Park W., #16-G
New York, NY 10024
Actress
Birthday: 11/5/63

Oracle
500 Oracle Pkwy.
Redwood City, CA 94065
Web site: http://
www.oracle.com
Lawrence J. Ellison, CEO
Computer software

Orlowski, Theresa
c/o VTO Video Verlag
Wohlenbergstr. 4a
30179 Hannover
Germany
Porno queen

Ormond, Julia
c/o CAA
9830 Wilshire Blvd.
Beverly Hills, CA 90212
Actress
Birthday: 1/4/65

Orrall, Robert Ellis
PO Box 121274
Nashville, TN 37212
Country singer

Osborn, Super Dave
10 Universal City Plaza,
Ste. 3100
Universal City, CA 91606
Actor

Osborne Brothers
Grand Ole Opry
2804 Opryland Dr.
Nashville, TN 37214
Music group

Osbourne, Jeffrey
PO Box 3718
Los Angeles, CA 90078
Singer

**Osbourne, Ozzy (John Michael
Osbourne)**
1 Red Pl.
London W1Y 3RE
England
Singer, songwriter
Birthday: 12/3/46

Oslin, K. T.
41 Music Sq. W., #180
Nashville, TN 37203
Singer
Birthday: 5/15/42

**Osmond, Marie (Olive Marie
Osmond)**
PO Box 6000
Provo, UT 84603
or
PO Box 1990
Branson, MO 65616
Singer, actress
Birthday: 10/13/59

Oteri, Cheri
c/o "Saturday Night Live"
NBC-TV
30 Rockefeller Plaza
New York, NY 10112
Comedian

O'Toole, Peter
c/o Veerline Ltd.
8 Baker St.
London WAA 1DA
England
Actor
Birthday: 8/2/32

Overstreet, Paul
PO Box 121976
Nashville, TN 37212
Country singer

Owens, Buck (Alvis Edgar, Jr.)
3223 Sillect Ave.
Bakersfield, CA 93308
Country singer

Owens, Gary
11365 Ventura Blvd., #100
Studio City, CA 91604
Radio and TV personality

Owens & Minor
4800 Cox Rd.
Glen Allen, VA 23060
G. Gilmer Minor III, CEO
Wholesalers

Owens-Corning
1 Owens Corning Pkwy.
Toledo, OH 43659
Web site: http://
  www.owenscorning.com
Glen H. Hiner, CEO
Building materials, glass

Owens-Illinois
1 SeaGate
Toledo, OH 43666
Joseph H. Lemieux, CEO
Building materials, glass

Oxford Health Plans
800 Connecticut Ave.
Norwalk, CT 06854
Web site: http://www.oxhp.com
William M. Sullivan, CEO
Health care

Oz, Frank (Frank Oznovicz)
PO Box 20750
New York, NY 10023
Muppeteer

P

There are no words to express the abyss between isolation and having one ally. It may be conceded to the mathematician that four is twice two. But two is not twice one; two is two thousand times one.

—G. K. CHESTERTON

PACCAR
777 106th Ave. N.E.
Bellevue, WA 98004
Web site: http://
   www.paccar.com
Mark C. Pigott, CEO
Motor vehicles and parts

PacifiCare Health Systems
3120 W. Lake Center Dr.
Santa Ana, CA 92704
Alan R. Hoops, CEO
Health care

Pacific Enterprises
555 W. 5th St.
Los Angeles, CA 90013
Web site: http://
   www.pacent.com
Willis B. Wood, Jr., CEO
Gas and electric utilities

Pacific Life Insurance
700 Newport Center Dr.
Newport Beach, CA 92660
Thomas C. Sutton, CEO
*Life and health insurance
   (mutual)*

PacifiCorp
700 N.E. Multnomah St.
Portland, OR 97232
Web site: http://
   www.pacificorp.com
Frederick W. Buckman, CEO
Gas and electric utilities

**Pacific Research Institute for
   Public Policy**
755 Sansome St., #450
San Francisco, CA 94111
Web site: http://
   www.pacificresearch.org/
E-mail:
   pripp@pacificresearch.org
Jennifer Berkowitz, director of
   public affairs and marketing
*Promotes the principles of
   individual freedom and personal
   responsibility; believes these
   principles are best encouraged
   through policies that emphasize
   a free economy, private
   initiative, and limited
   government*

Pacific Rocket Society
PO Box 241993
Los Angeles, CA 90024
Rod and Randa Milliron
*Organization dedicated to the
   promotion of rocketry, space
   travel, and off-world
   colonization*

**Pacino, Al (Alfredo James
   Pacino)**
301 W. 57th St., #16-C
New York, NY 10017
Actor
Birthday: 4/25/40

Paine Webber Group
1285 6th Ave.
New York, NY 10019
Web site: http://
    www.painewebber.com
Donald B. Marron, CEO
Securities

Palance, Jack
PO Box 6201
Tehachapi, CA 93561
Actor, director
Birthday: 2/18/20

Palin, Michael
68A Delancey St.
London NW1 7RY
England
Actor, writer
Birthday: 5/5/43

Palmer, Arnold
PO Box 52
Youngstown, PA 15696
Golfer

Palmer, Robert
c/o Dera Assoc.
584 Broadway, #1201
New York, NY 10012
Singer, songwriter
Birthday: 1/19/49

Palminteri, Chazz
375 Greenwich St.
New York, NY 10013
Actor
Birthday: 5/15/51

Palomino Road
818 18th Ave. S.
Nashville, TN 37203
Music group

Paltrow, Gwyneth
c/o Creative Artists Agency
9830 Wilshire Blvd.
Beverly Hills, CA 90212
Actress

Panis, Olivier
c/o Prost Grand Prix
Technopole de la Nièvre
58470 Magny Cours
France
Professional Formula-1 driver

Parazynski, Scott
c/o NASA
Johnson Space Center
Astronaut Office/Mail Code
    CB
2101 NASA Road 1
Houston, TX 77058
Astronaut

Parker, Andrea
c/o Susan Smith and Assoc.
121 N. San Vicente Blvd.
Beverly Hills, CA 90211
Actress

Parker, Mary Louise
1350 Ave. of the Americas
New York, NY 10019
Actress
Birthday: 8/2/64

Parker, Ray, Jr.
1755 Broadway
New York, NY 10019
Musician, songwriter

Parker, Sarah Jessica
PO 69646
Los Angeles, CA 90069
Actress
Birthday: 3/25/65

Parker Hannifin
6035 Parkland Blvd.
Cleveland, OH 44124
Web site: http://
    www.parker.com
Duane E. Collins, CEO
Industrial and farm equipment

Parker-Bowles, Camilla
Middlewick House
Nr. Corshm., Wiltshire
England
Prince Charles's friend

Parnell, Lee Roy
PO Box 23451
Nashville, TN 37202
Country singer

Parrish, Julie
PO Box 247
Santa Monica, CA 90406
Actress
Birthday: 10/21/40

Parsons, Karyn
3208 Cahuenga Blvd. W., #16
Los Angeles, CA 90068
Actress

Partnership for the Homeless
305 7th Ave., 13th Fl.
New York, NY 10001
Web site: http://www.
    partnershipforhomeless.org/
E-mail: tpfth@
    partnershipforhomeless.org
*Coordinates shelters and helps
    homeless and formerly homeless
    individuals and families obtain
    housing and other basic needs*

Parton, Dolly
c/o Eunice Eledge
1020 Dollywood Ln.
Pigeon Forge, TN 37863-4101
Country singer, actress
Birthday: 1/19/46

Parton, Stella
PO Box 120295
Nashville, TN 37212
Country singer

"Party of Five"
10201 W. Pico Blvd.
Los Angeles, CA 90035
Television series

Pastorelli, Robert
c/o Shukovsky/English
    Productions
400 Warner Blvd., Room 28
Burbank, CA 91522
Actor

Patkin, Max
2000 Valley Forge Cir., #837
King of Prussia, PA 19406
Actor

**Patric, Jason (Jason Patrick
    Miller)**
c/o Dolores Robinson
    Enterprises
10683 Santa Monica Blvd.
Los Angeles, CA 90025-4807
Actor
Birthday: 6/17/66

Patterson, Floyd
PO Box 336
New Paltz, NY 12561
Former boxer

Patty, Sandi
PO Box 2940
Anderson, IN 46018
Singer of religious music

Pavarotti, Luciano
Via Giardini 941
41040 Saliceto Panaro
Italy
*Opera singer and member of the
    Three Tenors*
Birthday: 10/12/35

Paxton, Bill
c/o William Morris Agency
151 El Camino Dr.
Beverly Hills, CA 90212
Actor
Birthday: 5/17/55

Paycheck, Johnny
1321 Murfreesboro Rd., #600
Nashville, TN 37217
Country singer

Payne, John
Hoogstraat 161
3131 BB Vlaardingen
The Netherlands
Web site: http://
    www.spiritweb.org/Spirit/
    omni.html
Trance channeller

Payton, Walter
300 N. Martingale Rd., #340
Schaumburg, IL 60173
Former football player
Birthday: 6/25/54

Pearce, Guy
c/o I.C.M.
8942 Wilshire Blvd.
Beverly Hills, CA 90211
Actor
Birthday: 10/5/67

Pearl Jam
417 Denny Way, #200
Seattle, WA 98109
Rock group

Pearl River
PO Box 150803
Nashville, TN 37215
Music group

Pearson, Drew
c/o Drew Pearson Marketing
15006 Beltway Dr.
Dallas, TX 75244
Former pro football player

Peck, Gregory
PO Box 837
Beverly Hills, CA 90213
Actor
Birthday: 4/5/16

PECO Energy
2301 Market St.
Philadelphia, PA 19103
Web site: http://www.peco.com
Corbin A. McNeill, Jr., CEO
Gas and electric utilities

Peeples, Nia
PO Box 21833
Waco, TX 76702
Actress

Pei, I. M.
600 Madison Ave.
New York, NY 10022
Architect

Pelé
c/o Minist. Extraordinario de
  Esporte
Praca dos Tres Poderes
70150-900 Brasília D.F.
Brazil
Former soccer player
Birthday: 10/21/40

Penguins, The
708 W. 137th St.
Gardena, CA 90247
Music group

Penn, Robin Wright
c/o Krosnan/Bernstein/
  Thompson
2049 Century Park E., #2500
Los Angeles, CA 90067
Actress, married to Sean Penn
Birthday: 8/8/66

Penn, Sean
2049 Century Park E., #2500
Los Angeles, CA 90067
Actor

Penn & Teller
1325 Ave. of the Americas
New York, NY 10019
Magicians

Penn & Teller Fan Club
MOFO
4132 S. Rainbow Blvd.,
  Ste. 377
Las Vegas, NV 89103

Penn Traffic
1200 State Fair Blvd.
Syracuse, NY 13221
Philip A. Hawkins, CEO
Food and drug stores

Penthouse Pets
277 Park Ave.
New York, NY 10172

People for the American Way
2000 M St. NW, #400
Washington, DC 20036
Web site: http://
    www.thebody.com/pfaw/
    pfawpage.html
E-mail: pfaw@pfaw.org
Founded by a group of civic and
    religious leaders who were
    concerned by the rising tide of
    intolerance against lesbians
    and gays sweeping the nation.
    Produces monthly updates
    of antigay activity around
    the U.S.

People for the Ethical
Treatment of Animals
(PETA)
PO Box 42516
Washington, DC 20015
Web site: http://
www.peta-online.org/
E-mail: peta@norfolk.infi.net
Alex Pacheco, cofounder
Believes that animals are not
    ours to eat, wear, perform
    experiments on, or use for
    entertainment

PepsiCo
700 Anderson Hill Rd.
Purchase, NY 10577
Web site: http://
    www.pepsico.com
Roger A. Enrico, CEO
Beverages

Peres, Shimon
10 Hayarkon St., #3263
Tel Aviv 63571
Israel
Former Prime Minister of Israel

Perfect Stranger
PO Box 330
Carthage, TX 75633
Music group

Perkins, Elizabeth
c/o CAA
9830 Wilshire Blvd.
Beverly Hills, CA 90212
Actress
Birthday: 11/18/60

Perlman, Rhea
PO Box 491246
Los Angeles, CA 90049
Actress
Birthday: 3/31/48

Perlman, Ron
c/o The Gersh Agency
PO Box 5617
Beverly Hills, CA 90210
Actor
Birthday: 4/13/50

Perrine, Valerie
c/o Solie Association
Via Toscana 1
00187 Roma
Italy
Actress
Birthday: 9/3/43

Perry, Luke (Coy Perry III)
8484 Wilshire Blvd., #745
Beverly Hills, CA 90211
Actor
Birthday: 10/11/66

Persuaders, The
225 W. 57th St., #500
New York, NY 10019
Music group

Pesci, Joe
PO Box 6
Lavallette, NJ 08735
Actor
Birthday: 2/9/43

Pestova, Daniela
c/o Elite Model Mgmt.
111 E. 22nd St., #200
New York, NY 10010
Model

Peter Kiewit Sons
1000 Kiewit Plaza
Omaha, NE 68131
Walter Scott, Jr., CEO
Engineering, construction

**Peters, Bernadette (Bernadette
   Lazzara)**
323 W. 80th St.
New York, NY 10024
Actress
Birthday: 2/28/48

Petersen, William L.
c/o ILM
8942 Wilshire Blvd.
Beverly Hills, CA 90211
Actor

Petersen, Wolfgang
c/o C.A.A.
9830 Wilshire Blvd.
Beverly Hills, CA 90212
Director
Birthday: 3/14/41

Pet Shop Boys
c/o EMI Records
20 Manchester Sq.
London W1
England
Music group

Petty, Lori
12301 Wilshire Blvd., #200
Los Angeles, CA 90025
Actress

Petty, Richard
Rt. #4, Box 86
Randleman, NC 27316
Race car driver

Pfizer
235 E. 42nd St.
New York, NY 10017
Web site: http://
   www.pfizer.com
William C. Steere, Jr., CEO
Pharmaceuticals

PG&E
1 Market St.
San Francisco, CA 94105
Web site: http://www.pge.com
Robert D. Glynn, Jr., CEO
Gas and electric utilities

Phair, Liz
611 Broadway, #730
New York, NY 10001
Singer, songwriter
Birthday: 4/17/67

Pharmacia & Upjohn
95 Corporate Dr.
Bridgewater, NJ 08807
Web site: http://
   www.pharmacia.se
Fred Hassan, CEO
Pharmaceuticals

Phelps, Jaycie
Cincinnati Gymnastics
3330 Port Union Rd.
Fairfield, OH 45014
Gymnast

Phelps Dodge
2600 N. Central Ave.
Phoenix, AZ 85004
Web site: http://www.irin.com/
   pd
Douglas C. Yearley, CEO
Metals

Philbin, Regis
7 Lincoln Sq.
New York, NY 10023
Talk show host
Birthday: 8/25/34

Philip Morris Co.
120 Park Ave.
New York, NY 10017-5592
Web site: http://nt1.irin.com/
   irin/Detail.CFM/mo
Geoffrey C. Bible, CEO
Tobacco company

Phillips, Ethan
924 Westwood Blvd., #900
Los Angeles, CA 90024
Actor, plays Neelix on "Star Trek: Voyager"

Phillips, Julianne
1999 Ave. of the Stars, #2850
Los Angeles, CA 90067
Actress, model

Phillips, Lou Diamond (Lou Upchurch)
11766 Wilshire Blvd., #1470
Los Angeles, CA 90025
Actor
Birthday: 2/17/62

Phillips, Stone
157 Columbus Cir., #300
New York, NY 10023
News show host

Phillips Petroleum
Phillips Building
Bartlesville, OK 74004
Web site: http://www.phillips66.com
W. W. Allen, CEO
Petroleum refining

Phoenix Home Life Mutual Insurance
1 American Row
Hartford, CT 06115
Robert W. Fiondella, CEO
Life and health insurance (stock)

Physicians Committee for Responsible Medicine
5100 Wisconsin Ave., #404
Washington, DC 20016
Web site: http://www.pcrm.org/
E-mail: pcrm@pcrm.org
Neal Barnard, president
Nonprofit organization, supported by nearly 5,000 physicians and 100,000 laypersons; promotes preventive medicine through innovative programs, encourages higher standards for ethics and effectiveness in research, and advocates broader access to medical services

Physicians for Social Responsibility
1101 14th St. NW, #700
Washington, DC 20005
Web site: http://www.psr.org/
E-mail: psrnatl@psr.org
Robert K. Musil, executive director
Committed to eliminating weapons of mass destruction, preserving a sustainable environment, and reducing violence and its causes

Picardo, Robert
232 N. Canon Dr.
Beverly Hills, CA 90210
Actor, plays the Doctor on "Star Trek: Voyager"

Pierce, David Hyde
c/o J. Michael Bloom
9255 Sunset Blvd., #710
Los Angeles, CA 90069
Actor

Pietz, Amy
c/o "Caroline in the City"
CBS Entertainment
4024 Radford Ave.
Bungalow 3
Studio City, CA 91604
Actress

Pinella, Lou
PO Box 4100
Seattle, WA 98104
Baseball manager

Pinkard & Bowden
c/o Network, Inc.
1101 18th Ave. S.
Nashville, TN 37212
Musical duo

Pinkett, Jada
c/o United Talent Agency
9560 Wilshire Blvd., #516
Beverly Hills, CA 90212
Actress

Piraro, Dan
c/o "Bizzaro"
1119 N. Edgefield Ave.
Dallas, TX 75208
Cartoonist

Pirates of the Mississippi
PO Box 17617
Nashville, TN 37217
Country music group

Pitino, Rick
Memorial Coliseum
Lexington, KY 40506
Boston Celtics coach

Pitney Bowes
1 Elmcroft Rd.
Stamford, CT 06926
Web site: http://
    www.pitneybowes.com
Michael J. Critelli, CEO
Computers, office equipment

Pitt, Brad
9150 Wilshire Blvd., #350
Beverly Hills, CA 90210
Actor
Birthday: 12/18/64

Pittson
1000 Virginia Center Pkwy.
PO Box 4229
Glen Allen, VA 23058
Michael T. Dan, CEO
Mail, package, freight delivery

**Planned Parenthood
    Federation of America**
1120 Connecticut Ave. NW,
    #461
Washington, DC 20036
Web site: http://
    www.plannedparenthood.org/
E-mail:
    communications@ppfa.org
Gloria Feldt, president
*Offers extensive information on
    all aspects of sexual and
    reproductive health*

Plant, Robert
c/o I.C.M.
Oxford House
76 Oxford St.
London W1N 0AX
England
Singer, songwriter
Birthday: 8/20/48

Plato, Dana
c/o Pierce & Shelly
612 Lighthouse Ave., #275
Pacific Grove, CA 93951
Web site: http://
    www.geocities.com/
    Hollywood/Theater/6288/
E-mail: danaplato1@aol.com
Actress

Platt, Oliver
c/o William Morris Agency
151 El Camino Dr.
Beverly Hills, CA 90212
Actor

Playboy Enterprises Inc.
680 N. Lake Shore Dr.
Chicago, IL 60611
Entertainment company

Any Playboy Playmate
[Playmate's Name]
c/o Playmate Promotions
2112 Broadway
Santa Monica, CA 90404
*Address to write to Playboy
    Playmates*

Pleasant Company
The American Girl Collection
8400 Fairway Pl.
or
PO Box 620190
Middleton, WI 53562
Pleasant Rowland, president
Makers of American Girl dolls

Pleshette, Suzanne
PO Box 1492
Beverly Hills, CA 90210
Actress

Plummer, Amanda
1925 Century Park E., #2320
Los Angeles, CA 90067
Actress
Birthday: 3/23/57

PNC Bank Corp.
249 5th Ave.
Pittsburgh, PA 15222
Web site: http://
   www.pncbank.com
Thomas H. O'Brien, CEO
Commercial bank

Points of Light Foundation
1737 H St. NW
Washington, DC 20006
Web site: http://
   www.pointsoflight.org/
E-mail: volnet@aol.com
Lester M. Alberthal, chairman
   and CEO
*Nonpartisan organization whose
   mission is to engage more people
   more effectively in volunteer
   community service; offers a
   hotline for volunteer opportunity
   information*

Poitier, Sidney
211 E. 70th St.
New York, NY 10021
Actor, writer, producer
Birthday: 2/20/27

Pollack, Kevin
8942 Wilshire Blvd.
Beverly Hills, CA 90211
Actor

Popcorn, Faith
c/o BrainReserve
59 E. 64th St.
New York, NY 10021-7003
Futurist, author of The Popcorn
   Report *and* Clicking

**Population Reference Bureau
Inc.**
1875 Connecticut Ave. NW,
   #520
Washington, DC 20009
Web site: http://www.prb.org/
   prb/
E-mail: popref@prb.org
Contact: Sharon Lee, visiting
   professor
*Dedicated to providing timely and
   objective information on U.S.
   and international population
   trends*

Porizkova, Paulina
c/o Creative Artists Agency
9830 Wilshire Blvd.
Beverly Hills, CA 90212
Model, actress

Portman, Natalie
8942 Wilshire Blvd.
Beverly Hills, CA 90211
Actress

Posh Spice (Victoria Adams)
1790 Broadway, 20th Floor
New York, NY 10019
Girl Group member

Post, Markie
10153½ Riverside Dr., #333
Toluca Lake, CA 90049
Actress
Birthday: 11/4/50

Poston, Tom
1 N. Venice Blvd., Ste. 106
Venice, CA 90291
Actor

Potts, Annie
PO Box 29400
Los Angeles, CA 90027
Actress
Birthday: 10/27/52

Potts, M. C.
PO Box 120161
Nashville, TN 37212
E-mail: mcfanclub@aol.com
Country musician

Powell, Gen. Colin
909 N. Washington St.,
  Ste. 767
Alexandria, VA 22314
Military leader, author
Birthday: 4/5/37

Powers, Stefanie (Jennifer Hart)
PO Box 5087
Sherman Oaks, CA 91403
Actress
Birthday: 11/2/42

PP&L Industries
2 N. 9th St.
Allentown, PA 18101
Web site: http://www.papl.com
William F. Hecht, CEO
Gas and electric utilities

PPG Industries
1 PPG Pl.
Pittsburgh, PA 15272
Web site: http://www.ppg.com
Raymond W. LeBoeuf, CEO
Chemicals

Praxair
39 Old Ridgebury Rd.
Danbury, CT 06810
Web site: http://
  www.praxair.com
H. William Lichtenberger,
  CEO
Chemicals

Presley, Lisa-Marie
1167 Summit Dr.
Beverly Hills, CA 90210
*Daughter of Elvis and Priscilla
  Presley*
Birthday: 2/1/68

Presley, Priscilla
1167 Summit Dr.
Beverly Hills, CA 90210
Actress
Birthday: 5/24/45

Preston, Kelly
15821 Ventura Blvd., #460
Encino, CA 91436
Actress
Birthday: 10/13/62

Pretenders, The
3 E. 54th St. #1400
New York, NY 10022
Rock band

Price, Ray
PO Box 61
Harrisburg, PA 17108
Singer

Pride, Charley
PO Box 670507
Dallas, TX 75367
Country singer

Priestley, Jason
11766 Wilshire Blvd., #1610
Los Angeles, CA 90025
Actor
Birthday: 8/28/69

Principal, Victoria
120 S. Spalding Dr., #205
Beverly Hills, CA 90212
Actress
Birthday: 1/3/50

Principal Finance
711 High St.
Des Moines, IA 50392
David J. Drury, CEO
Life and health insurance (stock)

Procter & Gamble
1 P&G Plaza
Cincinnati, OH 45202
Web site: http://www.pg.com
John E. Pepper, CEO
Soaps, cosmetics

Proffitt's
750 Lakeshore Pkwy.
Birmingham, AL 35211
Web site: http://
  www.proffitts.com
R. Brad Martin, CEO
General merchandisers

Progressive
6300 Wilson Mills Rd.
Mayfield Village, OH 44143
Web site: http://
  www.auto-insurance.com
Peter B. Lewis, CEO
P & C insurance (stock)

Progressive Policy Institute
518 C St. NE
Washington, DC 20002
Web site: http://www.dlcppi.org/
E-mail: info@dlcppi.org
Al From, president
*Works to fashion a public policy
  for the 21st century by adapting
  America's progressive tradition
  of individual liberty, equal
  opportunity, and civic obligation
  to the challenges of the
  Information Age*

Prosky, Robert
306 9th Ave.
Washington, DC 20003
Actor

ProSource
1500 San Remo Ave.
Coral Cables, FL 33146
Thomas C. Highland, CEO
Food services

Provident Companies
1 Fountain Sq.
Chattanooga, TN 37402
J. Harold Chandler, CEO
Life and health insurance (stock)

Prowse, David "Dave"
12 Marshalsea Rd.
London SE1 1HL
England
Actor, played Darth Vader

**Prudential Insurance Company
  of America**
751 Broad St.
Newark, NJ 07102
Arthur F. Ryan, CEO
Life and health insurance (stock)

Prussia, Guido
Guido Prussia Res.
Campo 602
Milano 2
Segrate Milano
Italy
Italian TV journalist

Pruett, Jeanne
7446 Oak Meadow Dr.
Baton Rouge, LA 70818
Country singer

Public Enemy
298 Elizabeth St.
New York, NY 10012
Rap group

**Public Service Enterprise
  Group**
80 Park Plaza
Newark, NJ 07101
Web site: http://www.pseg.com
E. James Ferland, CEO
Gas and electric utilities

Public Service Research Council
527 Maple Ave. E., 3rd Fl.
Vienna, VA 22180
Web site: http://www.psrf.org/
E-mail: info@psrf.org
David Y. Denholm, president
*Studying the impact of unionism
in government on government*

Publix Super Markets
321 S. Kentucky Ave.
Lakeland, FL 33801
Howard M. Jenkins, CEO
Food and drug stores

Puckett, Kirby
c/o Minnesota Twins
501 Chicago Ave. S.
Minneapolis, MN 55415
Former baseball player

Puff Daddy (Sean Combs)
c/o Arista Records
9975 Santa Monica Blvd.
Beverly Hills, CA 90212
Rap artist

Pullman, Bill
c/o CAA
9560 Wilshire Blvd., Ste. 500
Beverly Hills, CA 90212
Actor

Q

Real letter-writing makes writing into a different process because the letter is to somebody—a significant other—and not just a pronouncement to an imaginary world, a generalized other.

—ED POWELL, *The Letter Exchange*

Quaid, Dennis
9665 Wilshire Blvd., #200
Beverly Hills, CA 90212
Actor, Randy's brother
Birthday: 4/9/54

Quaid, Randy
PO Box 17572
Beverly Hills, CA 90209
Actor, Dennis's brother
Birthday: 10/1/50

Quaker
321 N. Clark St.
Chicago, IL 60610
Web site: http://
　www.quakeroats.com
Robert S. Morrison, CEO
Food producer

Quantum
500 McCarthy Blvd.
Milpitas, CA 95035
Web site: http://
　www.quantum.com
Michael A. Brown, CEO
Computer peripherals

Quayle, Dan
c/o Campaign America
1174 N. Pennsylvania Ave., Ste.
　100
Carmel, IN 46032
Former Vice President of the U.S.
Birthday: 2/4/47

Queen Latifah
c/o William Morris Agency
151 El Camino Dr.
Beverly Hills, CA 90212
Actress, singer

Queen Mary Hotel
PO Box 8
1126 Queens Hwy.
Long Beach, CA 90802
Denny Nicholas, director of
　catering
Former cruise ship

Quiet Riot
3208 Cahuenga Blvd. W., #107
Los Angeles, CA 90068
Music group

Quinn, Aidan
500 S. Buena Vista St., #206
Burbank, CA 91521
Actor
Birthday: 3/8/59

Quinn, Anthony
PO Box 479
Bristol, RI 02809
Actor

Quivers, Robin
WXRK-FM
600 Madison Ave.
New York, NY 10022
Radio personality

R

An intention to write never turns into a letter. A letter must happen to one like a surprise, and one may not know where in the day there was room for it to come into being. So it is that my daily intentions have nothing to do with this fulfillment of today.

—RAINER MARIA RILKE, letter to F. von Bülow

Rachins, Alan
9000 Sunset Blvd., #1200
Los Angeles, CA 90069
Actor

**Radio-Television News
  Directors Association
  (RTNDA)**
1000 Connecticut Ave. NW,
  #615
Washington, DC 20036
Web site: http://www.rtnda.org/
  rtnda
E-mail: rtnda@rtnda.org
Barbara Cochran, president
*Represents local and network news
  executives in broadcasting,
  cable, and other electronic media
  in more than 30 countries*

Rae, Cassidy
1801 Ave. of the Stars, #902
Los Angeles, CA 90067
Actress

Rae, Charlotte
10790 Wilshire Blvd., #903
Los Angeles, CA 90024-4448
Actress
Birthday: 4/22/26

**Ted Raimi International Fan
  Club**
PO Box 484
Oshtemo, MI 49077
Actor

Ralston Purina
Checkerboard Sq.
St. Louis, MO 63164
Web site: http://
  www.ralston.com
W. Patrick McGinnis, CEO
Food producer

Rampling, Charlotte
1 av. Emile Augier
78290 Croissy-sur-Seine
France
Actress
Birthday: 2/4/46

Ramsay, Bruce
c/o Brillstein-Grey
  Entertainment
9150 Wilshire Blvd., #350
Beverly Hills, CA 90212
Actor

Rand
1700 Main St.
PO Box 2138
Santa Monica, CA 90407
Web site: http://www.rand.org
E-mail:
  correspondence@rand.org
Paul H. O'Neill, chairman
*Nonprofit institution that helps
  improve policy and decision
  making through research and
  analysis*

Randall, Bobby
PO Box 208
Unicoi, TN 37692
Country singer

● **Randall, Tony (Leonard Rosenberg)**
1 W. 81st St., #6D
New York, NY 10024
Actor, director
Birthday: 2/26/20

Randolph, Boots
798 Lickton Pike
Whites Creeks, TN 37189
Musician

Rapaport, Michael
c/o Innovative Artists
1999 Ave. of the Stars, #2850
Los Angeles, CA 90067
Actor

Rather, Dan
524 W. 57th St.
New York, NY 10019
Anchor corespondent, editor
Birthday: 10/31/31

Ratzenberger, John
7080 Hollywood Blvd., #118
Los Angeles, CA 90028
Actor
Birthday: 4/16/47

Ratzinger, Joseph Cardinal
00120 Vatican City State
Vatican

● **Raven, Eddy**
PO Box 2476
Hendersonville, TN 37077
Country singer

Ray, Jimmy
c/o Sony Music
10 Great Marlborough St.
London W1V 2LP
England
Singer

Rayburn, Gene
11365 Ventura Blvd., #100
Studio City, CA 91604
TV game show host
Birthday: 12/22/17

Raye, Collin
PO Box 530
Reno, NV 89504
Country singer

Raytheon
141 Spring St.
Lexington, MA 02760
Dennis J. Picard, CEO
Electronics, electrical equipment

Read, James
9200 Sunset Blvd., Ste. 315
Los Angeles, CA 90069
Actor
Birthday: 7/3/54

Reader's Digest Association
Reader's Digest Rd.
Pleasantville, NY 10570
Web site: http://
   www.readersdigest.com
George V. Grune, CEO
Publishing, printing

Reagan, Nancy
2121 Ave. of the Stars, 34th Fl.
Los Angeles, CA 90067
Former First Lady, actress
Birthday: 7/6/21

Reagan, Ronald
2121 Ave. of the Stars, 34th Fl.
Los Angeles, CA 90067
Former President of the U.S., actor
Birthday: 2/6/11

Reason Foundation
3415 S. Sepulveda Blvd., #400
Los Angeles, CA 90034
Web site: http://
www.reason.org/
George Passantino, director
E-mail: gpassantino@reason.org
*National research and educational
organization that explores and
promotes the twin values of
rationality and freedom as the
basic underpinnings of a good
society*

Red, Shotgun
PO Box 148135
Nashville, TN 37214
Nashville Network sidekick

Redford, Robert
1101 E. Montana Ave.
Santa Monica, CA 90403
Actor, director, producer
Birthday: 3/8/43

Red Hot Chili Peppers
11116 Aqua Vista, #39
N. Hollywood, CA 91602
Rock band

Rednex
c/o ZYX Music
Benzstraße
Industriegebiet
35797 Merenberg
Germany
Music group

Reebok
100 Technology Center Dr.
Stoughton, MA 02072
Web site: http://
www.reebok.com
Paul B. Fireman, CEO
Apparel

Reed, Jerry
c/o World Class Talent
1522 Demonbruen St.
Nashville, TN 37203
Singer

Reed, Pamela
c/o pmk
955 S. Carrillo Dr., #200
Los Angeles, CA 90048
Actress

Reed, Willis
c/o Basketball Hall of Fame
1150 W. Columbus Ave.
Springfield, MA 01101
Former basketball player

Reef
c/o Sony Music
1 Red Pl.
London W1Y 3RE
England
Music group

Reece, Gabrielle
c/o Elle Magazine
1633 Broadway
New York, NY 10019
Model

Reese, Della
PO Box 2812
Beverly Hills, CA 90210
Actress

Reeve, Christopher
RR #2
Bedford, NY 10506
Actor
Birthday: 9/25/52

Reeves, Del
Grand Ole Opry
2804 Opryland Dr.
Nashville, TN 37214
Country singer

Reeves, Keanu
9460 Wilshire Blvd., #700
Beverly Hills, CA 90212
Actor
Birthday: 9/4/64

Reeves, Ronna
PO Box 80424
Midland, TX 79709
Country singer

Regalbuto, Joe
606 N. Larchmont Blvd., #309
Los Angeles, CA 90004
Actor

Regina Regina Fan Club
PO Box 428
Marshville, NC 28103
Musical group

Reid, Mike
PO Box 218142
Nashville, TN 37203
Country singer

Reilly, Charles Nelson
11365 Ventura Blvd., #100
Studio City, CA 91604
Actor
Birthday: 1/13/31

Reiner, Carl
714 N. Rodeo Dr.
Beverly Hills, CA 90210
Actor, writer, director, Rob's dad
Birthday: 3/20/22

Reiner, Rob
c/o CAA
9830 Wilshire Blvd.
Beverly Hills, CA 90212
Actor, director, producer
Birthday: 3/16/45

Reinhold, Judge
626 Santa Monica Blvd., #113
Santa Monica, CA 90405
Actor
Birthday: 5/21/56

Reiser, Paul
11845 W. Olympic Blvd., #1125
Los Angeles, CA 90064
Actor
Birthday: 3/30/57

Reitman, Ivan
100 Universal City Plaza
Universal City, CA 91608
Director
Birthday: 10/27/46

Reliance Group Holdings
55 E. 52nd St.
New York, NY 10055
Web site: http://rgh.com
Saul P. Steinberg, CEO
P & C insurance (stock)

R.E.M.
PO Box 8032
Athens, GA 30603
or
PO Box 128288
Nashville, TN 37212
Rock band

Remingtons, The
c/o 3 Amigos
25 Paulson Dr.
Burlington, MA 01803
Musical group

Renfro, Brad
PO Box 53454
Knoxville, TN 37950
Actor
Birthday: 7/25/82

**Republican National
   Committee**
310 1st St. SE
Washington, DC 20003
Web site: http://www.rnc.org
E-mail: info@rnc.org
Jim Nicholson, chairman

Republican Industries
110 S.E. 6th St.
Fort Lauderdale, FL 33301
H. Wayne Huizenga, CEO
Specialist retailers

Republic New York Corp.
452 5th Ave.
New York, NY 10018
Web site: http://www.rnb.com
Walter H. Weiner, CEO
Commercial banks

Restless Heart
PO Box 156
Littlestown, PA 17340
Music group

Retton, Mary Lou
1815 Via El Prado, #209
Redondo Beach, CA 90277
Gymnast

Reubens, Paul
PO Box 29373
Los Angeles, CA 90029
Actor who played Pee-wee Herman

Reynolds, Burt
c/o Burt Reynolds Ranch
16133 Jupiter Farms Rd.
Jupiter, FL 33458
Actor
Birthday: 2/11/36

Reynolds, Debbie
305 Convention Center Dr.
Las Vegas, NV 89109
Actress, Carrie Fisher's mom
Birthday: 4/1/32

Reynolds Metals
6601 W. Broad St.
Richmond, VA 23230
Web site: http://www.rmc.com
Jeremiah J. Sheehan, CEO
Metals

Rhys-Davies, John
8033 Sunset Blvd., #29
Los Angeles, CA 90046
Actor

Ricci, Christina
c/o ICM
8942 Wilshire Blvd.
Beverly Hills, CA 90211
Actress

Rich, Katie
8265 Sunset Blvd.
Los Angeles, CA 90046
Actress

Richard, Cliff (Harry Webb)
Portsmouth Rd.
Box 46A
Esher, Surrey KT10 9AA
England
Singer
Birthday: 10/14/40

Richards, Ariana
256 South Robertson Blvd.,
  #8200
Beverly Hills, CA 90211
Actress

Richardson, Joely
c/o I.C.M.
Oxford House
76 Oxford St.
London W1N 0AX
England
Actress

Richardson, Patricia
253 26th St., #A-312
Santa Monica, CA 90402
Actress

Richfood Holdings
8258 Richfood Rd.
Mechanicsville, VA 23116
Web site: http://
  www.richfood.com
John E. Stokely, CEO
Wholesalers

Richie, Lionel
PO Box 9055
Calabasas, CA 91372
Singer

Richter, Jason James
10683 Santa Monica Blvd.
Los Angeles, CA 90025
Actor
Birthday: 1/29/80

Rickles, Don
Premier Artist Services
c/o Eliot Weisman
1401 University Dr., Ste. 305
Coral Springs, FL 33071
Web site: http://
    www.thehockeypuck.com/
Comedian
Birthday: 5/8/26

Rickman, Alan
76 Oxford St.
London W1N 0AX
England
Actor
Birthday: 2/21/46

Riders in the Sky
PO Box 121134
Nashville, TN 37212
Music group

Riley, Jeannie C.
PO Box 680454
Franklin, TN 37068
Country singer

Rimes, LeAnn
6060 N. Central Expwy.,
    Ste. 816
Dallas, TX 75206
or
2945 Fondren
Dallas, TX 75205
Country singer

Ringwald, Molly
9454 Wilshire Blvd., #405
Beverly Hills, CA 90212
Actress
Birthday: 2/28/68

Ripa, Kelly
c/o "All My Children"
320 W. 66 St.
New York, NY 10023
Actress

Ripkin, Cal, Jr.
PO Box 611
Emmittsburg, MD 21721
Baseball player

Ripon Society
501 Capitol Ct. NE, #300
Washington, DC 22000
Web site: http://
    www.riponsociety.com/
Christine Todd Whitman,
    member of Honorary
    Congressional Advisory
    Board
A centrist-oriented Republican
research and public policy
organization that provides an
opportunity to discuss crucial
issues facing our nation

Rite Aid
30 Hunter Ln.
Camp Hill, PA 17011
Web site: http://
    www.riteaid.com
Martin L. Grass, CEO
Food and drug stores

Ritter, John
15030 Ventura Blvd., #806
Sherman Oaks, CA 91403
Actor
Birthday: 9/17/48

Tex Ritter Fan Club
15326 73rd Ave. SE
Snohomish, WA 98290
Sharon L. Sweeting, president
Actor

Rivera, Geraldo
555 W. 57th St., #1100
New York, NY 10019
TV show host
Birthday: 7/4/43

**Rivers, Joan (Joan Alexandra
    Molinsky)**
PO Box 49774
Los Angeles, CA 90049
Comedienne
Birthday: 11/7/37

Rizzuto, Phil
c/o Scooter Company
2482 Ogden Rd.
Union, NJ 07083
Former baseball player

RJR Nabisco
1301 6th Ave.
New York, NY 10019
Web site: http://
www.rjrnabisco.com
Steven F. Goldstone, CEO
Food producer

RMB
c/o Motor Music
Holzdamm 57
20099 Hamburg
Germany
Music group

Robards, Jason
200 W. 57th St., #900
New York, NY 10019
Actor
Birthday: 7/26/32

Robbins, Tim
c/o ICM
40 W. 57th St.
New York, NY 10019
Actor
Birthday: 10/16/58

Roberts, Eric
132 S. Rodeo Dr., #300
Beverly Hills, CA 90212
Actor, Julia's brother
Birthday: 4/18/56

**Roberts, Julia (Julie Fiona
Roberts)**
c/o ICM
8942 Wilshire Blvd.
Beverly Hills, CA 90211
Actress
Birthday: 10/28/67

Roberts, Tanya
3500 W. Olive Ave., #1400
Burbank, CA 91505
Actress

Robinson, Brooks
PO Box 1168
Baltimore, MD 21203
Actor

Robinson, David
c/o San Antonio Spurs
600 E. Market St., Ste. 102
San Antonio, TX 78205
Basketball player

Robinson, Holly
c/o Dolores Robinson
Entertainment
10683 Santa Monica Blvd.
Los Angeles, CA 90025
Actress
Birthday: 9/18/64

Rock, Chris
151 El Camino Dr.
Beverly Hills, CA 90212
Actor

Rockefeller Foundation, The
420 5th Ave.
New York, NY 10018
Web site: www.rockfound.org
Peter C. Goldmark, Jr.,
president
*Grant organization for arts, the
humanities, equal opportunity,
school reform, and international
science-based development*

Rockers, The
PO Box 3859
Stamford, CT 06905
Music group

Rockwell International
600 Anton Blvd.
Costa Mesa, CA 92626
Web site: http://
www.rockwell.com
Don H. Davis, Jr., CEO
Electronics, electrical equipment

Rocky Horror Fan Club
220 W. 19th St.
New York, NY 10011

Rodgers, Jimmie
PO Box 685
Forsyth, MO 65653
Singer

Rodriguez, Chi Chi
1720 Merriman Rd.
PO Box 5118
Akron, OH 4434
Golfer

Rodriguez, Johnny
c/o Evelyn Smart
PO Box 488
Sabinal, TX 78881
Country singer

Rodrique, George
721 Royal St.
New Orleans, LA 70016
*Artist known for "The Blue Dog"
   paintings*

Roe, Tommy
PO Box 26037
Minneapolis, MN 55426
Singer, songwriter

Rogers, Fred
c/o Family Communications
   Inc.
4802 5th Ave.
Pittsburgh, PA 15213
*Children's TV show host,
   Presbyterian minister*
Birthday: 3/20/28

Rogers, Kenny
Box 100 Rte. 1
Colbert, GA 30628
Singer, songwriter
Birthday: 8/21/38

**Kenny Rogers International
   Fan Club**
PO Box 769
Hendersonville, TN 37077

Rogers, Mimi
11693 San Vicente Blvd.,
   Ste. 241
Los Angeles, CA 90049
Actress
Birthday: 1/27/56

Roggin, Fred
3000 W. Alameda Ave.
Burbank, CA 91505
TV show host

Rohm & Haas
100 Independence Mall W.
Philadelphia, PA 19106
Web site: http://
   www.rohmhaas.com
J. Lawrence Wilson, CEO
Chemicals

Rohner, Clayton
8271 Melrose Ave., #110
Los Angeles, CA 90046
Actor

Roker, Al
E-mail: mailbag@roker.com
"Today Show" weatherman

Rolling Stones, The
HK Management
8900 Wilshire Blvd., #200
Beverly Hills, CA 90211
or
PO Box 6152
New York, NY 10128
Rock group

Roman, George
270 N. Canon Dr., #1374
Beverly Hills, CA 90210
Web site: http://
   www.georgeroman.com/
E-mail:
   george@georgeroman.com
Beverly Hills love guru

Roman, LuLu
PO Box 8178
Hermitage, TN 37076
Country singer

Ronald Reagan Presidential Foundation
40 Presidential Dr.
Simi Valley, CA 93065
Web site: http://
  sunsite.unc.edu/lia/
  president/reagan.html
E-mail: library@reagan.nara.gov
Mark A. Hunt, director
The Ronald Reagan Presidential Library

Roper Center for Public Opinion Research
PO Box 440
Storrs, CT 06268
Web site: http://
  www.ropercenter.uconn.edu/
Everett C. Ladd, executive director
The leading nonprofit center for the study of public opinion, maintaining the world's largest archive of public opinion data

Rose, Charlie
356 W. 58th St., 10th Fl.
New York, NY 10019
Television host, journalist

Roseanne (formerly Barr, formerly Arnold)
5664 Cahuenga Blvd., #433
N. Hollywoood, CA 91601
Actress, comedienne
Birthday: 11/3/52

Ross, Diana
PO Box 11059
Glenville Station
Greenwich, CT 06831
Singer, actress
Birthday: 3/26/44

Ross, Marion
20929 Ventura Blvd., #47
Woodland Hills, CA 91364
Actress
Birthday: 10/25/38

Ross, Natanya
1000 Universal Studios Plaza Blvd.
Bldg. 22
Orlando, FL 32819
Actress

Rossellini, Isabella
745 5th Ave., #814
New York, NY 10151
Actress
Birthday: 6/18/42

Rothrock, Cynthia
Rothrock-in
2633 Lincoln Blvd., #103
Santa Monica, CA 90405
Actress

Rourke, Mickey
9150 Wilshire Blvd., #350
Beverly Hills, CA 90212
Actor
Birthday: 7/16/53

Rowland, Rodney
c/o The Booh Shut Agency
11350 Ventura Blvd., #206
Studio City, CA 91604
Actor

Roxette
c/o EMI Svenska AB
Box 1289
17125 Solna
Sweden
Music group

Royal, Billy Joe
PO Box 121862
Nashville, TN 37212
Singer

R. R. Donnelley & Sons
77 W. Wacker Dr.
Chicago, IL 60601
Web site: http://
  www.rrdonnelley.com
William L. Davis, CEO
Publishing, printing

Ruehl, Mercedes
Box 178
Old Chelsea Station
New York, NY 10011
Actress
Birthday: 2/28/48

Ruini, Camillo Cardinal
00120 Vatican City State
Vatican

Run-D.M.C.
160 Varick St.
New York, NY 10013
Music group

RuPaul
6671 Sunset Blvd., #1590
Hollywood, CA 90028
Entertainer

Rush, Geoffrey
c/o Creative Artists Agency
9830 Wilshire Blvd.
Beverly Hills, CA 90212
Actor

Russell, Johnny
PO Drawer 37
Hendersonville, TN 37077
Country singer

Russell, Kurt
1900 Ave. of the Stars, #1240
Los Angeles, CA 90067
Actor
Birthday: 3/17/51

Russell, Nipsey
353 W. 57th St.
New York, NY 10019
Comedian, writer, director
Birthday: 10/13/24

Rutherford, Kelly
PO Box 492266
Los Angeles, CA 90049
Actress

Ryan, Jeri
c/o "Star Trek: Voyager"
Paramount Pictures
5555 Melrose Ave.
Los Angeles, CA 90038
Actress

Ryan, Nolan
PO Box 670
Alvin, TX 77512
Baseball great

Ryan, Tim
PO Box 210615
Nashville, TN 37221
Country singer

Ryder, Winona (Winona Laura Horowitz
10345 W. Olympic Blvd.
Los Angeles, CA 90064
Actress
Birthday: 10/29/71

Ryder Systems
3600 N.W. 82nd Ave.
Miami, FL 33166
Web site: http://www.ryder.com
M. Anthony Burns, CEO
Truck leasing

Rykoff-Sexton
613 Baltimore Dr.
Wilkes-Barre, PA 18702
James L. Miller, CEO
Wholesalers

S

Probably the disembodied abstractness of a letter permits the reader to impute to the writer whatever qualities the reader is already listening for. . . .

—SHANA ALEXANDER, *The Feminine Eye*

Sabatini, Gabriella
1101 Wilson Blvd., Ste. 1800
Arlington, VA 22209
Former professional tennis player

Sabato, Antonio, Jr.
PO Box 12073
Marina del Rey, CA 90295
Actor

Safeco
Safeco Plaza
Seattle, WA 98185
Web site: http://
   www.safeco.com
Roger H. Eigsti, CEO
P & C (stock) insurance

Safeway
5918 Stoneridge Mall Rd.
Pleasanton, CA 94588
Web site: http://
   www.safeway.com
Steven A. Burd, CEO
Food and drug stores

Sagal, Katey
7095 Hollywood Blvd., #792
Hollywood, CA 90028
Actress
Birthday: 1956

Saget, Bob
9150 Wilshire Blvd., #350
Beverly Hills, CA 90212
Actor, TV host
Birthday: 5/17/56

St. Laurent, Yves
5 av. Marceau
75116 Paris
France
Fashion designer
Birthday: 8/1/36

Saint Patrick's Cathedral
460 Madison Ave.
New York, NY 10022
Attn: Msgr. Anthony Dalla Villa

St. Paul Companies
385 Washington St.
St. Paul, MN 55102
Web site: http://
   www.stpaul.com
Douglas W. Leatherdale, CEO
P & C insurance (stock)

Sajak, Pat
10202 W. Washington Blvd.
Culver City, CA 90232
TV game show host
Birthday: 10/26/46

Salo, Mika
c/o Tyrrell Racing
   Organisation Ltd.
Long Reach
Ockham
Woking
Surrey GU23 6PE
England
Professional Formula-1 driver

Salt'n'Pepa
c/o London Records
Chancellor's House
72 Chancellor's Rd.
London W6 9QB
England
Music group

Sambora, Richie
PO Box 827
Hagerstown, MD 21741
Musician, married to Heather
Locklear
Birthday: 7/11/59

Samms, Emma
2934½ N. Beverly Glen Cir.,
  Ste. 417
Los Angeles, CA 90077
Actress
Birthday: 8/28/60

Sandler, Adam
9701 Wilshire Blvd., 10th Fl.
Beverly Hills, CA 90212
Actor, comedian
Birthday: 9/9/66

Santana, Carlos
PO Box 10348
San Rafael, CA 94912
Musician

Sara, Mia
PO Box 5617
Beverly Hills, CA 90210
Actress

Sara Lee
3 First National Plaza
Chicago, IL 60602
Web site: http://
  www.saralee.com
John H. Bryan, CEO
Food producer

**Sarandon, Susan (Susan Abigail
  Tomalin)**
8942 Wilshire Blvd.
Beverly Hills, CA 90211
Actress
Birthday: 10/4/46

Sash
c/o Mighty Records/Polydor
Glockengießerwall 3
20095 Hamburg
Germany
Music group

Savage, Fred
c/o CAA
9830 Wilshire Blvd.
Beverly Hills, CA 90212
Actor
Birthday: 7/9/76

Sawa, Devon
c/o M. Creek
Warner Bros.
4000 Warner Blvd.
Bldg. 76
Burbank, CA 91522
Actor
Birthday: 9/7/78

Sawyer Brown
PO Box 150637
Nashville, TN 37215
Rock band

Saxon, John
PO Box 492480
Los Angeles, CA 90049
Actor, writer
Birthday: 8/5/35

SBC Communications
175 E. Houston
San Antonio, TX 78205
Web site: http://www.sbc.com
Edward E. Whitacre, Jr., CEO
Telecommunications

Scacchi, Greta
c/o Susan Smith and Assoc.
121 N. Vicente Blvd.
Beverly Hills, CA 90211
Actress
Birthday: 2/18/60

Scarabelli, Michele
4720 Vineland Ave., #216
N. Hollywood, CA 91602
Actress

Scary Spice (Melanie Janine Brown)
1790 Broadway, 20th Fl.
New York, NY 10019
Girl group member

Scatman, John
c/o RCA Records
1133 Ave. of the Americas
New York, NY 10036
Singer

Schaech, Jonathan
c/o IFA Talent Agency
8730 Sunset Blvd., #490
Los Angeles, CA 90069
Actor
Birthday: 9/10/69

Scheider, Roy
PO Box 364
Sagaponack, NY 11962
Actor
Birthday: 11/10/35

Schell, Maria
9451 Preitenegg
Austria
Actress
Birthday: 1/15/26

Schering-Plough
1 Giralda Farms
Madison, NJ 07940
Web site: http://
   www.sch-plough.com
Richard Jay Kogan, CEO
Pharmaceuticals

Schiffer, Claudia
5 Union Sq., #500
New York, NY 10003
Supermodel, actress
Birthday: 8/24/71

Schlesinger, John
c/o I.C.M.
Oxford House
76 Oxford St.
London W1N 0AX
England
Director, producer, actor, writer
Birthday: 2/16/26

Schlessinger, Dr. Laura
c/o The New York Times
   Syndication Sales Corp.
122 E. 42nd St.
New York, NY 10168
Advice columnist

Schneider, John
PO Box 2277
Mountain Lake Park, MD
   21550
Singer

Schroder, Rick
9560 Wilshire Blvd., #500
Beverly Hills, CA 90212
Actor
Birthday: 4/13/70

Schulz, Charles
1 Snoopy Pl.
Santa Rosa, CA 95401
Cartoonist
Birthday: 11/26/22

Schumacher, Joel
4000 Warner Blvd.
Bldg. 81, #117
Burbank, CA 91522
Director

Schumacher, Michael
c/o Ferrari S.p.A.
Casella postale 589
41100 Modena
Italy
*Professional Formula-1 driver,
   World Cup winner 1994 and
   1995; Ralf is his brother*
Birthday: 1/3/69

Schumacher, Ralf
c/o Jordan Formula One Ltd.
Silverstone Circuit
Towcester
Northhamptonshire NN12 8TN
Professional Formula-1 driver;
Michael is his brother

Schwartz, Sherwood
The Sherwood Schwartz Co.
1865 Carla Ridge Dr.
Beverly Hills, CA 90210
Creator of "Gilligan's Island"

Schwarzenegger, Arnold
3110 Main St., #300
Santa Monica, CA 90039
Actor, director, bodybuilder
Birthday: 7/30/47

SCI Systems
2101 W. Clinton Ave.
Huntsville, AL 35807
Olin B. King, CEO
Electronics, electrical equipment

Scott, Gini Graham
Creative Communications and
    Research
6114 La Salle Ave., #358
Oakland, CA 94611
E-mail: GiniS@aol.com
Author of over 30 books, host of
the internationally aired radio
show "Changemakers," speaker
and seminar leader, and
director of Changemakers and
Creative Communications and
Research. She specializes in the
area of social issues, criminal
justice, and lifestyles.

Scott, Ridley
c/o CAA
9830 Wilshire Blvd.
Beverly Hills, CA 90212
Director
Birthday: 11/30/37

Scott, Tom Everett
c/o 20th Century Fox
PO Box 900
Beverly Hills, CA 90213
Actor

Scully, Vin
c/o Los Angeles Dodgers
1000 Elysian Park Ave.
Los Angeles, CA 90012
Sportcaster

Seagate Technology
920 Disc Dr.
Scotts Valley, CA 95066
Web site: http://
    www.seagate.com
Alan F. Shugart, CEO
Computer peripherals

Seal
c/o Beethoven Street Mgmt.
56 Beethoven St.
London W10 4LG
England
Singer
Birthday: 2/19/63

Seals, Brady
PO Box 120322
Nashville, TN 37212
Singer

Seals, Dan
PO Box 1770
Hendersonville, TN 37077
Singer

Sears Roebuck
3333 Beverly Rd.
Hoffman Estates, IL 60179
Web site: http://www.sears.com
Arthur C. Martinez, CEO
General merchandisers

Sedaka, Neil
888 7th Ave., #1600
New York, NY 10106
Singer, songwriter
Birthday: 3/13/39

Seinfeld, Jerry
147 S. El Camino Dr., #205
Beverly Hills, CA 90212
Actor, comedian
Birthday: 4/29/55

Selleca, Connie
15030 Ventura Blvd., #355
Sherman Oaks, CA 91403
Actress, married to John Tesh
Birthday: 5/25/55

Semmelrogge, Martin
c/o Corina Knepper
Zur Waldkampfbahn 9
42327 Wuppertal
Germany
Actor, director of Das Boot

ServiceMaster
1 ServiceMaster Way
Downers Grove, IL 60515
Web site: http://www.svm.com
Carlos H. Cantu, CEO
Diversified outsourcing services

Service Merchandise
7100 Service Merchandise Dr.
Brentwood, TN 37027
Web site: http://
   www.servicemerchandise.com
Gary Witkin, CEO
Specialist retailers

"Sesame Street" Cast
1329 Braddock Pl.
Alexandria, VA 22314

Severance, Joan
9000 Sunset Blvd., #1200
Los Angeles, CA 90069
Actress

Seymour, Jane (Joyce Frankenberger)
PO Box 548
Agoura, CA 91376
Actress
Birthday: 2/15/51

Seymour, Stephanie
c/o IT Model Mgmt.
526 N. Larchmont Blvd.
Los Angeles, CA 90004
Model

Shaffer, Paul
1697 Broadway
New York, NY 10019
*Musical director of "The Late
   Show with David Letterman"*
Birthday: 11/28/49

Shaggy
c/o Virgin Records
338 N. Foothill Rd.
Beverly Hills, CA 90212
Singer
Birthday: 10/26/68

Shalikashvili, John
The Pentagon, #2E872
Washington, DC 20301
*Chairman of the Joint Chiefs of
   Staff*

Shandling, Garry
9150 Wilshire Blvd., #350
Beverly Hills, CA 90212
Actor, comedian
Birthday: 11/29/49

Shapiro, Joshua and Vera
9324 Home Ct.
Des Plaines, IL 60016
Web site: http://
   www.execpc.com/vjentpr/
E-mail:
   rjoshua@sprintmail.com
Metaphysical tours to sacred sites

Sharif, Omar (Michael Shaloub)
c/o Anne Alvares Correa
18 rue Troyon
75017 Paris
France
Actor
Birthday: 4/10/32

Sharp, Kevin
PO Box 888
Camino, CA 95709
Country singer

Shatner, William
PO Box 7401725
Studio City, CA 91604
Actor
Birthday: 3/22/31

Shaughnessy, Charles
534 15th St.
Santa Monica, CA 90402
Actor
Birthday: 2/9/55

Shaw Industries
616 E. Walnut Ave.
Dalton, GA 30720
Web site: http://
   www.shawinds.com
Robert E. Shaw, CEO
Textiles

Shearer, Harry
119 Ocean Park Blvd.
Santa Monica, CA 90405
Comedian, writer, director
Birthday: 12/23/43

Sheedy, Ally
PO Box 523
Topanga, CA 90290
Actress
Birthday: 6/13/62

**Sheen, Charlie (Carlos Irwin
   Estevez)**
10580 Wilshire Blvd.
Los Angeles, CA 90024
Actor
Birthday: 9/3/65

Sheldrake, Dr. Rupert
20 Willow Rd.
London NW3 1TJ
England
Biochemist

Shelton, Ricky Van
PO Box 120589
Nashville, TN 37212
Country singer

Shenandoah
PO Box 120086
Nashville, TN 37212
Music group

Shepard, Jean
Grand Ole Opry
2804 Opryland Dr.
Nashville, TN 37214
Country singer

Shepherd, Cybill
c/o Studio Fan Mail
1122 S. Robertson Blvd., #15
Los Angeles, CA 90035
Actress, model
Birthday: 2/18/50

Sheppard, T. G.
3341 Arlington, F-206
Toledo, OH 43614
Country singer

Sheridan, Jamey
c/o ICM
8942 Wilshire Blvd.
Beverly Hills, CA 90211
Actor

Sherwin-Williams
101 Prospect Ave. NW
Cleveland, OH 44115
Web site: http://
   www.sherwin-williams.com
John G. Breen, CEO
Chemicals

Shields, Brooke
2300 W. Sahara Ave., #630
Las Vegas, NV 89102
Actress, married to Andre Agassi
Birthday: 5/31/65

Shimerman, Armin
8730 Sunset Blvd., #480
Los Angeles, CA 90069
Actor, Quark of "Star Trek: Deep Space Nine"

Shirley, Mariah
c/o "The Adventure of Sinbad"
All American Television
1325 6th Ave., 6th Fl.
New York, NY 10019
Actress

Shore, Pauly
8491 Sunset Blvd., #700
W. Hollywood, CA 90069
Actor

Short, Martin
760 N. La Cienega Blvd., #200
Los Angeles, CA 90069
Actor
Birthday: 3/26/50

Shriver, Maria
3110 Main St., #300
Santa Monica, CA 90405
Broadcast journalist, wife of Arnold Schwarzenegger
Birthday: 11/6/55

Shriver, Pam
133 1st St. NE
St. Petersburg, FL 33701
Tennis player

Shue, Elisabeth
PO Box 464
South Orange, NJ 07079
Actress
Birthday: 10/6/63

Shull, Richard B.
16 Gramercy Park Pl.
New York, NY 10003
Actor

Siegfried & Roy
1639 N. Valley Dr.
Las Vegas, NV 89109
Circus act

Sierra Club National Office
730 Polk St.
San Francisco, CA 94109
Web site: http:// www.sierraclub.org
E-mail: information@sierraclub.org
Nonprofit organization that promotes conservation

Silicon Graphics
2011 N. Shoreline Blvd.
Mountain View, CA 94043
Web site: http://www.sgi.com
Richard E. Belluzzo, CEO
Computers, office equipment

Silver, Ron
c/o International Creative Mgmt.
8942 Wilshire Blvd.
Beverly Hills, CA 90211
Actor
Birthday: 7/2/46

Silverman, Jonathan
4024 Radford Ave.
Bldg. 6
Studio City, CA 91604
Actor
Birthday: 8/5/66

Silverstone, Alicia
PO Box 16539
Beverly Hills, CA 90209
Actress
Birthday: 1/4/76

Simmons, Gene (Chaim Witz)
6363 Sunset Blvd., #417
Los Angeles, CA 90028
Singer, bassist for Kiss
Birthday: 8/25/49

Simon, Paul
110 W. 57th St., #300
New York, NY 10019-3319
Singer, songwriter
Birthday: 10/13/41

Simple Minds
c/o Schoolhouse Mgmt.
63 Frederic St.
Edinburgh EH1 1LH
Scotland
Music group

Simply Red
48 Princess St.
Manchester M1 6HR
England
Music group

Sin, Jaime Cardinal
PO Box 132
10099 Manila
Philippines

Sinatra, Nancy
PO Box 69453
Los Angeles, CA 90069
Singer, Frank's daughter
Birthday: 6/8/40

Singer, Lori
c/o CAA
9830 Wilshire Blvd.
Beverly Hills, CA 90212
Actress
Birthday: 5/6/62

Singletary, Daryle
607 West Church Dr.
Sugar Land, TX 77478
Country singer

Sinise, Gary
c/o CAA
9830 Wilshire Blvd.
Beverly Hills, CA 90212
Actor
Birthday: 3/17/55

Sirhan, Sirhan
#B21014
Corcoran State Prison
Box 8800
Corcoran, CA 93212
Assassinated Robert Kennedy

Sirtis, Marina
9903 Santa Monica Blvd.
Beverly Hills, CA 90212
Actress

Sista Sista
c/o BMG Ariola Hamburg
Osterstr. 116
20095 Hamburg
Germany
Music group

Sisters with Voices
35 Hart St.
Brooklyn, NY 11206
Music group

Six Shooter
PO Box 24480
Nashville, TN 37202
Music group

Sizemore, Tom
c/o David Westberg
1724 N. Vista St.
Los Angeles, CA 90046
Actor

Skaggs, Ricky
PO Box 121799
Nashville, TN 37212-1799
Country singer

Skerritt, Tom
9560 Wilshire Blvd., #516
Beverly Hills, CA 90212
Actor
Birthday: 8/25/43

Slash
PO Box 93909
Los Angeles, CA 90093
Guitarist for Guns 'n' Roses

Slater, Christian (Christian Hawkins)
9150 Wilshire Blvd., #350
Beverly Hills, CA 90210
Actor
Birthday: 8/18/69

Slater, Kelly
c/o The Baywatch Prod. Co.
5433 Beethoven St.
Los Angeles, CA 90066
Actress
Birthday: 11/2/72

Sledge, Percy
c/o Artists International Mgmt.
9850 Sandalfoot Blvd., #458
Boca Raton, FL 33428
Singer
Birthday: 11/25/40

SLM Holding Corp.
11600 Sallie Mae Dr.
Reston, VA 20193
Web site: http://www.slma.com
Albert L. Lord, CEO
Diversified financials

Smalley, Richard E.
Dept. of Chemistry
Rice University
6100 Main St.
Houston, TX 77005
1996 Nobel Prize winner in chemistry

Smart, Jean
151 El Camino Dr.
Beverly Hills, CA 90212
Actress

Smashing Pumpkins
PO Box 578010
Chicago, IL 60657
Music group

Smith, Anna Nicole
c/o Elite Model Management
111 E. 22nd St., 2nd Fl.
New York, NY 10010
Model

Smith, Bubba
517335 N. Maple Dr., #203
Culver City, CA 90232
Actor

Smith, Connie
PO Box 2031
Brentwood, TN 37024
Country singer

Smith, Jaclyn
10398 Sunset Blvd.
Los Angeles, CA 90077
Actress
Birthday: 10/26/47

Kevin Smith Official Fan Club
9880 Magnolia Ave., #126
Santee, CA 92071
Film director

Smith, Lou
11365 Ventura Blvd., #100
Studio City, CA 91604
Widow of Wolfman Jack

Smith, Shawnee
Innovative Artists
1999 Ave. of the Stars,
  Ste. #2850
Los Angeles, CA 90069
Actress
Birthday: 7/3/70

Smith, Will
c/o Creative Artists
  Management
9830 Wilshire Blvd.
Beverly Hills, CA 90212
Actor
Birthday: 9/25/68

Smithfield Foods
999 Waterside Dr.
Norfolk, VA 23510
Joseph W. Luter III, CEO
Food company

Smithsonian Institution
1000 Jefferson Dr. SW
Washington, DC 20560

Smits, Jimmy
PO Box 49922 Barrington
Station
Los Angeles, CA 90049
Actor
Birthday: 7/9/55

Snider, Mike
Rt. 2
Gleason, TN 38229
Country singer

Snipes, Wesley
1888 Century Park E., #500
Los Angeles, CA 90067
Actor

Snow
c/o S. L. Feldman
1505 W. 2nd Ave., #200
Vancouver, BC V6H 3Y4
Canada
Singer
Birthday: 10/30/69

Snyder, Tom
c/o "The Late Late Show with
Tom Snyder"
CBS Television City
7800 Beverly Blvd., #244
Los Angeles, CA 90036
Talk show host

Sodano, Angelo Cardinal
00120 Vatican City State
Vatican

Sojourners
2401 15th St. NW
Washington, DC 20009
E-mail: sojourn@ari.net
Musical group

**Solar Energy Industries
  Association**
122 C St. NW, 4th Fl.
Washington, DC 20001
Web site: http://www.seia.org/
E-mail: seiaopps@digex.com
Dan Lenos, director
E-mail: dlenos@seia.org
*National trade association for all
  solar businesses and enterprises
  in the fields of photovoltaics,
  solar electric power, solar
  thermal power, and solar
  building products*

Solectron
777 Gibraltar Dr.
Milpitas, CA 95035
Web site: http://
  www.solectron.com
Koichi Nishimura, CEO
Electronics, electrical equipment

Somers, Suzanne
8899 Beverly Blvd., #713
Los Angeles, CA 90048
Actress
Birthday: 11/5/40

Sonat
1900 5th Ave. N.
Birmingham, AL 35203
Web site: http://www.sonat.com
Ronald L. Kuehn, Jr., CEO
Pipelines

Sonnier, Joel
PO Box 120845
Nashville, TN 37212
Singer

Sonoco
1 N. 2nd St.
Hartsville, SC 29550
Web site: http://
  www.sonoco.com
Charles W. Coker, CEO
Forest and paper products

Soraya
c/o Mercury Records
11150 Santa Monica Blvd.,
  10th Fl.
Los Angeles, CA 90025
Singer
Birthday: 3/11/69

Sorbo, Kevin
PO Box 410
Buffalo Center, IA 50424
Actor

**Kevin Sorbo International Fan
  Club**
PO Box 410
Buffalo Center, IA 50424

Sorenson, Heidi
c/o Pierce & Shelly
612 Lighthouse Ave., #275
Pacific Grove, CA 93951
Web site: http://
  www.geocities.com/
  Hollywood/Studio/9597
E-mail: HeidiSoren@aol.com
Model

Soros Foundation Network
Open Society Institute
888 7th Ave.
New York, NY 10606
Web site: http://www.soros.org
George Soros, founder
*Grant organization that supports
  research that promotes an open
  society*

Sorvino, Mira
41 W. 86th St.
New York, NY 10024
Actress

Sorvino, Paul
110 E. 87th St.
New York, NY 10128
Actor
Birthday: 4/13/49

Sothern, Ann
Box 2285
Ketchum, ID 83340
Actress
Birthday: 1/22/09

Soto, Talisa
9000 Sunset Blvd., #1200
Los Angeles, CA 90069
Model

Soundgarden
c/o Curtis Mgmt.
207½ 1st Ave. S., #300
Seattle, WA 98104
Music group

Southern
270 Peachtree St., NW
Atlanta, GA 30303
Web site: http://
  www.southernco.com
A. W. Dahlberg, CEO
Gas and electric utilities

Southwest Airlines
2702 Love Field Dr.
Dallas, TX 75235
Web site: http://
  www.iflyswa.com
Herbert D. Kelleher, CEO
Airline

**Spacek, Sissy (Mary Elizabeth
  Spacek)**
Rte. 22, #640
Cobham, VA 22929
Actress
Birthday: 12/25/49

Spacey, Kevin
151 El Camino Dr.
Beverly Hills, CA 90212
Actor
Birthday: 7/26/49

Spade, David
9150 Wilshire Blvd., #350
Beverly Hills, CA 90212
Actor

Spears, Billie Jo
Grand Ole Opry
2804 Opryland Dr.
Nashville, TN 37214
Country singer

Special Olympics International
1350 New York Ave. NW, #500
Washington, DC 20002
Web site: http://
 www.specialolympics.org/
E-mail: sdscott@juno.com
Contact: Michael Janes
E-mail: JanesmSO@aol.com
*Nonprofit, international program
 of sports training*

Spelling, Aaron
5700 Wilshire Blvd.
Los Angeles, CA 90036
Television producer

Spelling, Tori
10580 Wilshire Blvd., #59
Los Angeles, CA 90024
*Actress, daughter of Aaron
 Spelling*
Birthday: 5/16/73

Spencer, Bud
c/o Mistral Film Group
24 Via Archimede
00187 Roma
Italy
Actor

Spice Girls
35-37 Parkgate Rd., Unit 32
Ransome's Dock
London SW11 4NP
England
or
1790 Broadway, 20th Fl.
New York, NY 10019
Singing group

Spielberg, Steven
PO Box 8520
Universal City, CA 91608
Producer, director
Birthday: 12/18/47

**Sporty Spice (Melanie Jayne
 Chisholm)**
1790 Broadway, 20th Fl.
New York, NY 10019
Girl group member

Spiner, Brent
PO Box 5617
Beverly Hills, CA 90209
Actor
Birthday: 2/2/55

Springfield, Rick
c/o William Morris Agency
151 Camino Dr.
Beverly Hills, CA 90212
Singer, actor
Birthday: 8/23/49

Sprint
2330 Shawnee Mission Pkwy.
Westwood, KS 66205
Web site: http://
 www.sprint.com
William T. Esrey, CEO
Telecommunications

Squier, Billy
PO Box 1251
New York, NY 10023
Singer, musician
Birthday: 5/12/50

Squirrel Nut Zippers
c/o The Mammoth Recording
 Company
101 B St.
Carrboro, NC 27510
Music group

Stack, Robert
415 N. Camden Dr., #121
Beverly Hills, CA 90210
Actor
Birthday: 1/13/19

Stafford, Jim
PO Box 6366
Branson, MO 65616
Country singer

Stahl, Lisa
c/o Shelly & Pierce
612 Lighthouse Ave., #275
Pacific Grove, CA 93951
Actress
E-mail: LISASTAHL1@aol.com

Stallone, Sylvester
c/o White Eagle Productions
100 Universal City Pl.
Bldg. 507, #2E
Universal City, CA 91608
Actor, writer, director
Birthday: 7/6/46

Stamos, John
9255 Sunset Blvd., #1010
W. Hollywood, CA 90069
Actor, musician
Birthday: 8/19/63

Staples
1 Research Dr.
Westborough, MA 01581
Web site: http://
   www.staples.com
Thomas G. Stemberg, CEO
Specialist retailers

Stapleton, Jean
c/o Bauman, Hiller and
   Associates
5757 Wilshire Blvd., 5th Fl.
Los Angeles, CA 90036
Actress

Starr, Ringo (Richard Starkey)
1541 Ocean Ave., #200
Santa Monica, CA 90401
Drummer, actor
Birthday: 7/7/40

State Farm Companies
1 State Farm Plaza
Bloomington, IL 61710
Edward B. Rust, Jr., CEO
P & C insurance (mutual)

State Street Corp.
225 Franklin St.
Boston, MA 02110
Web site: http://
   www.statestreet.com
Marshall N. Carter, CEO
Commercial bank

Statler Brothers
PO Box 2703
Staunton, VA 24401
Music group

Staubach, Roger
6750 LBJ Frwy.
Dallas, TX 75109
Former football player

Steel, Danielle
PO Box 1637
Murray Hill Station
New York, NY 10156
Author

Steen, Jessica
c/o Somers Teitelbaum David
   (Chris Henze)
1925 Century Park E., #2320
Los Angeles, CA 90067
Web site: http://
   www.jessicasteen.com/
Actress

Steinbrenner, George
River Ave. & E. 161st St.
Bronx, NY 10451
Baseball executive

Stern, Daniel
c/o CAA
9830 Wilshire Blvd.
Beverly Hills, CA 90212
Actor
Birthday: 8/28/57

Stern, Howard
WXRK-FM
600 Madison Ave.
New York, NY 10022
Radio personality

Stevens, Brinke
8033 Sunset Blvd.
Suite 556
Hollywood, CA 90046
Actress

**Stevens, Connie (Concetta Ann
    Ingolia)**
c/o Forever Spring
8721 Sunset Blvd., PH2
Los Angeles, CA 90069
Actress, singer
Birthday: 8/8/38

Stevens, Ray (Ray Ragsdale)
1708 Grand Ave.
Nashville, TN 37212
Singer, songwriter
Birthday: 1/24/39

**Stevens, Stella (Estelle
    Eggleston)**
c/o Stellavision
1608 N. Cahuenga, #649
Hollywood, CA 90028
Actress
Birthday: 10/1/36

Stevenson, Parker
c/o Metropolitan Talent
    Agency
4526 Wilshire Blvd.
Los Angeles, CA 90010
Actor
Birthday: 6/4/51

Stewart, Patrick
PO Box 93999
Los Angeles, CA 90093
Actor, writer
Birthday: 7/13/40

Stewart, Rod
3500 W. Olive Ave., #920
Burbank, CA 91505
Singer, songwriter
Birthday: 1/10/45

Stich, Michael
c/o ProServ
1101 Wilson Blvd., Ste. 1300
Arlington, VA 22209
Professional tennis player

Stiers, David Ogden
121 N. San Vicente Blvd.
Beverly Hills, CA 90211
Actor
Birthday: 10/31/42

**Sting (Gordon Matthew
    Sumner)**
2 The Grove
Highgate Village
London N6
England
Singer, songwriter, actor
Birthday: 10/2/51

Stockwell, Dean
PO Box 6248
Malibu, CA 90264
Actor
Birthday: 3/5/35

Stone, Cliffie
PO Box 710
Los Angeles, CA 90078
Country singer

Stone, Doug
Stone Age Fan Club
PO Box 128
Orlinda, TN 37141

Stone, Sharon
PO Box 7304
N. Hollywood, CA 91603
Actress

Stone Container
150 N. Michigan Ave.
Chicago, IL 60601
Web site: http://
    www.stonecontainer.com
Roger W. Stone, CEO
Forest and paper products

Storch, Larry
330 West End Ave.
New York, NY 10023
Actor
Birthday: 1/8/23

Stowe, Madeleine
c/o Provident Financial Mgmt.
10345 W. Olympic Blvd., #200
Los Angeles, CA 90064
Actress
Birthday: 1958

Strait, George
PO Box 2119
Hendersonville, TN 37077
Country singer

Strange, Curtis
c/o Kingsman Golf Club
100 Golf Club Rd.
Williamsburg, VA 23185
Golfer

Stray Cats
113 Wardour St.
London W1
England
Music group

Streep, Meryl (Mary Louise Streep)
c/o Creative Artists Agency
9830 Wilshire Blvd.
Beverly Hills, CA 90212
Actress
Birthday: 4/22/49

Streisand, Barbra (Barbara Joan)
c/o ICM
8942 Wilshire Blvd.
Beverly Hills, CA 90211
Singer, actress, director
Birthday: 4/24/42

Stringfield, Sherry
9560 Wilshire Blvd., #516
Beverly Hills, CA 90212
Actress

Stroker, Dr. Carol
NASA—Ames Research Center
155A Moffett Park Dr.
Sunnyvale, CA 94089
NASA scientist with the Mars mission

Strugg, Kerry
17203 Bamwood Dr.
Houston, TX 77090
Gymnast

Struthers, Sally
9100 Wilshire Blvd., #1000
Beverly Hills, CA 90212
Actress
Birthday: 7/28/48

Stuart, Marty
38 Music Sq., #300
Nashville, TN 37203
Singer, songwriter

Marty Stuart Fan Club
PO Box 24180
Nashville, TN 37202

Sun
1801 Market St.
Philadelphia, PA 19103
Robert H. Campbell, CEO
Petroleum refining

Sun Microsystems
901 San Antonio Rd.
Palo Alto, CA 94303
Web site: http://www.sun.com
Scott G. McNealy, CEO
Computers, office equipment

Sunny
c/o WWF
PO Box 3859
Stamford, CT 06905
Professional wrestler

Sun Trust Bank
303 Peachtree St. NE
Atlanta, GA 30308
Web site: http://
www.suntrust.com/
index.html
James B. Williams, CEO
Commercial bank

Supermarkets General Holding
301 Blair Rd.
Woodbridge, NJ 07095
James Donald, CEO
Food and drug stores

Supernaw, Doug
PO Box 7342
Cut and Shoot, TX 77303
Country singer

Supertramp
16530 Ventura Blvd., #201
Encino, CA 91436
Music group

Supervalu
11840 Valley View Rd.
Eden Prairie, MN 55344
Web site: http://
   www.supervalu.com
Michael W. Wright, CEO
Wholesaler

Survivor
2114 W. Pico Blvd.
Santa Monica, CA 90405
Music group

Sutherland, Donald
760 N. La Cienega Blvd., #300
Los Angeles, CA 90069
Actor
Birthday: 7/17/36

Sutherland, Kiefer
c/o Intertalent Agency
9200 Sunset Blvd., Penthouse
   25
Los Angeles, CA 90069
Actor, Donald's son
Birthday: 12/18/66

Swanson, Kristy
9200 Sunset Blvd., #1232
Los Angeles, CA 90069
Actress

Swayze, Patrick
c/o Wolf/Kasteler Inc.
132 S. Rodeo Dr., #300
Beverly Hills, CA 90212
Actor
Birthday: 8/18/52

Sweethearts of the Rodeo
PO Box 160077
Nashville, TN 37216
Music group

Swing Out Sister
132 Liverpool Rd.
Islington
London N1
England
Music group

Sysco
1390 Enclave Pkwy.
Houston, TX 77077
Web site: http://www.sysco.com
Bill M. Lindig, CEO
Wholesalers

Letters blur the lines between two separate lives.

—VICKI RENTZ

Tabuchi, Shoji
HCR Rte.1, Box 755
Branson, MO 65616
Musician

Takei, George
PO Box 4395
N. Hollywood, CA 91607
Actor, Lt. Sulu of "Star Trek"

Talk Talk
121 A Revelstone N.
Wimbledon Pl.
London W15
England
Music group

Tandy
100 Throckmorton St.,
   Ste. 1800
Fort Worth, TX 76102
Web site: http://
   www.tandy.com
John V. Roach, CEO
Specialist retailers

Tarantino, Quentin
6525 Sunset Blvd., #12
Hollywood, CA 90028
Director, actor, writer
Birthday: 3/27/63

Taupin, Bernie
450 N. Maple Dr., #501
Beverly Hills, CA 90210
Songwriter

Taylor, Elizabeth
PO Box 55995
Sherman Oaks, CA 91413
Actress
Birthday: 2/27/32

Taylor, James
644 N. Doheny Dr.
Los Angeles, CA 90069
Singer, songwriter, musician
Birthday: 3/12/48

Taylor, Les
177 Northwood Dr.
Lexington, KY 40505
Country singer

Taylor, Niki
8326 Pines Blvd., #334
Hollywood, FL 33024
Model

Taylor-Young, Leigh
9229 Sunset Blvd., #710
W. Hollywood, CA 90069
Actress

Tech-Data
5350 Tech Data Dr.
Clearwater, FL 33760
Web site: http://
   www.techdata.com
Steven A. Raymund, CEO
Wholesalers

Tele-Communications
5619 DTC Pkwy.
Englewood, CO 80111
Leo J. Hindery, Jr., CEO
Telecommunications

Temple-Inland
303 S. Temple Dr.
Diboll, TX 75941
Web site: http://
    www.templeinland.com
Clifford J. Grum, CEO
Forest and paper products

Tenet Healthcare
3820 State St.
Santa Barbara, CA 93105
Web site: http://
    www.tenethealth.com
Jeffrey C. Barbakow, CEO
Health care

Tennant, Victoria
c/o Metropolitan Talent
    Agency
4526 Wilshire Blvd.
Los Angeles, CA 90010
Actress
Birthday: 9/30/53

Tenneco
1275 King St.
Greenwich, CT 06831
Web site: http://
    www.tenneco.com
Dana G. Mead, CEO
Motor vehicles and parts

Tenney, Jon
c/o U.T.A.
9560 Wilshire Blvd., #516
Beverly Hills, CA 90212
Actor

Tesh, John
14755 Ventura Blvd., #1-916
Sherman Oaks, CA 91403
Musician
Birthday: 7/1/53

Texaco
2000 Westchester Ave.
White Plains, NY 10650
Web site: http://
    www.texaco.com
Peter I. Bijur, CEO
Petroleum refining

Texas Instruments
8505 Forest Ln.
PO Box 660199
Dallas, TX 75266-0199
Web site: http://www.ti.com
Thomas J. Engibous, CEO
Electronics, semiconductors

Texas Tornados
PO Box 530
Bellaire, OH 43906
Music group

Texas Utilities
1601 Bryan St.
Dallas, TX 75201
Web site: http://www.tu.com
Erle Nye, CEO
Gas and electric utilities

Textron
40 Westminster St.
Providence, RI 02903
Web site: http://
    www.textron.com
James F. Hardymon, CEO
Aerospace

Theismann, Joe
c/o ESPN
ESPN Plaza
Bristol, CT 06010
Sportscaster

Thermo Electron
81 Wyman St.
Waltham, MA 02254
Web site: http://
    www.thermo.com
George N. Hatsopoulos, CEO
Scientific, photo, control equipment

Thiessen, Tiffani-Amber
3500 W. Olive Ave., #1400
Burbank, CA 91505
Actress

Thomas, B. J.
PO Box 120003
Arlington, TX 76012
Singer

Thomas, Dave
c/o Hildy Gottlieb
Creative Artists Agency
9830 Wilshire Blvd.
Beverly Hills, CA 90212
Actor

Thomas, Fred Dalton
c/o Thompson, Liebengood &
  Crawford
First American Ctr.
Nashville, TN 37238
Actor

Thomas, Heather
1433 San Vicente Blvd.
Santa Monica, CA 90402
Actress
Birthday: 9/8/57

Thomas, Jay
1800 Ave. of the Stars, #1400
Los Angeles, CA 90067
Actor, radio personality
Birthday: 7/12/48

Thomas, Jonathan Taylor
18711 Tiffeni Dr., #17-203
Twain Harte, CA 90212
Actor
Birthday: 9/8/81

Thomas, Kristin Scott
c/o I.C.M.
Oxford House
76 Oxford St.
London W1N 0AX
England
Actress

Thomas, Michael Phillip
c/o Miamiway Theater
12615 W. Dixie Hwy.
N. Miami, FL 33161
Actor
Birthday: 5/26/49

**Thomas Jefferson Center for
  the Protection of Free
  Expression**
400 Peter Jefferson Pl.
Charlottesville, VA 22911
Web site: http://
  www.tjcenter.org/
E-mail: RMO@virginia.edu
Norman Dorsen, chairman of
  board of trustees
*In the courts, and through
  programs in the arts and
  education, the Center seeks to
  safeguard the First Amendment
  guarantees of free speech and
  press*

Thompson, Andrea
c/o "NYPD Blue"
Steven Bochco Productions
10201 W. Pico Blvd.
Los Angeles, CA 90064
Actress

Thompson, Emma
56 King's Rd.
Kingston-upon-Thames KT2
  5HF
England
Actress

Thompson, Fred
E-mail: senator_thompson
  @thompson.senate.gov
Senator from Tennessee, actor

Thompson, Hank
5 Rushing Creek Ct.
Roanoke, TX 76262
Country singer

Thompson, Lea
PO Box 5617
Beverly Hills, CA 90210
Actress
Birthday: 5/31/62

Thompson, Sada
PO Box 490
Southbury, CT 06488
Actress
Birthday: 9/27/29

Thorne-Smith, Courtney
10100 Santa Monica Blvd.,
   Ste. 2500
Los Angeles, CA 90067
Actress

Thornton, Billy Bob
955 S. Carrillo Dr., #300
Los Angeles, CA 90048
Actor

Thurman, Uma
c/o Creative Artists Agency
9830 Wilshire Blvd.
Beverly Hills, CA 90212
Actress

TIAA-CREF
730 3rd Ave.
New York, NY 10017
John H. Biggs, CEO
*Life and health insurance
   (mutual)*

Tiegs, Cheryl
2 Greenwich Plaza, #100
Greenwich, CT 06830
Model

Tighe, Kevin
PO Box 453
Sedro Woolley, WA 98284
Actor
Birthday: 8/13/44

Tillis, Mel
48 Music Sq. E.
Nashville, TN 37203
Country singer

Tillis, Pam
PO Box 128575
Nashville, TN 37212
Country singer

Tilly, Jennifer
270 N. Canon Dr., #1582
Beverly Hills, CA 90210
Actress, Meg's sister
Birthday: 9/10/58

Tilly, Meg
321 S. Beverly Dr., #M
Beverly Hills, CA 90212
Actress
Birthday: 2/14/60

Tilton, Charlene
PO Box 1309
Studio City, CA 91614
Actress

Times Mirror
Times Mirror Sq.
Los Angeles, CA 90053
Web site: http://www.tm.com
Mark H. Willes, CEO
Publishing, printing

Time Warner
75 Rockefeller Plaza
New York, NY 10019
Web site: http://
   pathfinder.com/Corp
Gerald M. Levin, CEO
Entertainment, publishing

Tippin, Aaron
PO Box 121709
Nashville, TN 37212
Country singer

TJX
770 Cochituate Rd.
Framingham, MA 01701
Web site: http://
   tjx.stage.utopia.com
Bernard Cammarata, CEO
Specialist retailers

TLC
3350 Peachtree St., #1500
Atlanta, GA 30362
Singing group

Toblowsky, Stephen
c/o William Morris Agency
151 El Camino Dr.
Beverly Hills, CA 90212
Actor

"Today Show"
Story Ideas
30 Rockefeller Plaza, Rm. 374E
New York, NY 10112
Linda Finnell, supervising
    producer
*If your story idea is accepted they
will notify you. They do not
have a general fax number.*

Tomas Rivera Center, The
241 E. 11th St.
Steele Hall, 3rd Fl.
Scripps College
Claremont, CA 91711
E-mail: roodj@cgs.edu
*Researchers policy on
Hispanic issues in the U.S.
and Latin America*

Tomei, Marissa
151 El Camino Dr.
Beverly Hills, CA 90212
Actress
Birthday: 12/4/64

Tomlin, Lily
PO Box 27700
Los Angeles, CA 90027
Comedian, actress
Birthday: 9/1/39

**Tom Petty & the
    Heartbreakers**
PO Box 260159
Encino, CA 91426
Music group

Tork, Peter
1551 S. Robertson Blvd.
Los Angeles, CA 90035
Musician, actor
Birthday: 2/13/42

Tosco
72 Cummings Point Rd.
Stamford, CT 06902
Thomas D. O'Malley, CEO
Petroleum refining

Toys "R" Us
395 W. Passaic St.
Rochelle Park, NJ 07950
Web site: http://www.tru.com
Robert Nakasone, CEO
Specialist retailers

Tractors
PO Box 5034
Tulsa, OK 74150
Music group

Tracy, Paul
c/o Penske Motorsports
Penske Plaza
Reading, PA 19603
Race car driver

Transamerica
600 Montgomery St.
San Francisco, CA 94111
Web site: http://
    www.transamerica.com
Frank C. Herringer, CEO
Life and health insurance (stock)

Trans World Airlines
515 N. 6th St.
St. Louis, MO 63101
Web site: http://www.twa.com
Gerald Gitner, CEO
Airline

Travanti, Daniel J.
c/o Tony Howard
William Morris Agency
151 El Camino Dr.
Beverly Hills, CA 90212
Actor
Birthday: 3/7/40

Travelers Group
388 Greenwich St.
New York, NY 10013
Web site: http://
    www.travelers.com/
    index.htm
Sanford I. Weill, CEO
Diversified financials

**Travis, Randy (Randy
    Traywick)**
PO Box 121712
Nashville, TN 37212
or
PO Box 38
Ashland City, TN 37015
Country singer
Birthday: 5/4/59

Travolta, John
151 El Camino Dr.
Beverly Hills, CA 90212
Actor
Birthday: 2/18/54

Trebek, Alex
10210 W. Washington
Culver City, CA 90232
Game show host
Birthday: 7/22/40

**Official International Robert
    Trebor Fan Club, The**
Palindrome Pals
3352 Broadway Blvd., Ste. 538
Garland, TX 75043
Actor

Trends Research Institute
330 Salisbury Turnpike
Rhinebeck, NY 12572
Web site: http://
    www.trendsresearch.com/
E-mail: webmaster
    @trendsresearch.com
Gerald Celente, director
*Combines unique resources
    with its own trademarked
    methodology to help companies
    profit from trends*

Trevino, Lee
1901 W. 47th Pl., #200
Westwood, KS 66205
Professional golfer
Birthday: 12/1/39

Trevino, Rick
PO Box 500148
Austin, TX 78750
Country singer

Trevor, Claire
c/o The Pierce Hotel
2 E. 61st & 5th Ave.
New York, NY 10021
Actress

Tritt, Travis
2000 West End Ave., Ste. 1000
Nashville, TN 37203
Singer, songwriter
Birthday: 2/9/63

Travis Tritt Country Club
PO Box 2044
Hiram, GA 30141
Attn: Liz

Truck Stop
c/o Lucius B. Rechling
Quellental 14
22609 Hamburg
Germany
Country music group

**Trudeau, Garry (Garretson
    Beckman Trudeau)**
459 Columbus Ave., #113
New York, NY 10019
Cartoonist, married to Jane Pauley
Birthday: 1948

Trulli, Jarno
c/o Minardi Team S.p.A.
Via Spellanzani 21
48018 Faenza/RA
Italy
Professional Formula-1 driver

Trump, Donald
721 5th Ave.
New York, NY 10022
Real estate executive
Birthday: 6/14/46

Trump, Ivana
500 Park Ave., #500
New York, NY 10022
Author, ex-wife of Donald

TruServe
8600 W. Bryn Mawr Ave.
Chicago, IL 60631
Daniel A. Cotter, CEO
Specialist retailers

TRW
1900 Richmond Rd.
Cleveland, OH 44124
Web site: http://www.trw.com
Joseph T. Gorman, CEO
Motor vehicles and parts

Tubb, Justin
PO Box 500
Nashville, TN 37202
Country singer

Tucker, Tanya
8012 Brooks Chapel Rd.,
  Ste. 73
Brentwood, TN 37027
Country singer
Birthday: 10/10/58

Tudor, Tasha
121 Wyck St., Ste. 101
Richmond, VA 23225
Web site: www.richmond.net/
  tashatudor/index.html
E-mail: tashat@tashatudor.com
Author, illustrator

Tune, Tommy
50 E. 89th St.
New York, NY 10128
Dancer, director, actor
Birthday: 2/28/39

Turlington, Christy
344 E. 59th St.
New York, NY 10022
Model

Turner, Grant
Grand Ole Opry
2804 Opryland Dr.
Nashville, TN 37214
Country singer

**Turner, Ted (Robert Edward
  Turner III)**
1050 Techwood Dr. N.W.
Atlanta, GA 30318
*Media executive, owner of Atlanta
  Braves and Hawks*
Birthday: 11/26/39

Turner Broadcasting Systems
1 CNN Ctr., Box 105366
Atlanta, GA 30348
Ted Turner, president
Operator of cable TV networks

Turner Corp.
375 Hudson St.
New York, NY 10014
Ellis T. Gravette, Jr., CEO
Engineering, construction

Twain, Shania
PO Box 1150
Timmins, ON P4N 7H9
Canada
Country singer

Tweed, Shannon
9300 Wilshire Blvd., #410
Beverly Hills, CA 90212
Actress

Twiggy (Leslie Hornby)
4 St. George's House
15 Hanover Sq.
London W1R 9AJ
England
Model, actress
Birthday: 9/19/49

Twister Alley
Rte. 2, Box 138
Lake City, AR 72437
Music group

Twitty, Conway
1 Music Village Blvd.
Hendersonville, TN 37075
Country singer

Tyco International
1 Tyco Park
Exeter, NH 03833
Web site: http://
www.tycoint.com
L. Dennis Kozlowski, CEO
Metal products

Tyler, Liv
1999 Ave. of the Stars,
Ste. 2850
Los Angeles, CA 90067
*Actress, daughter of Aerosmith's
Steven Tyler*

**Tyler, Steven (Steven
Tallarico)**
PO Box 306
Marshfield, MA 02050
Singer for Aerosmith
Birthday: 3/26/48

Tylo, Hunter
7660 Beverly Blvd., #107
Los Angeles, CA 90036
Actress

Tyson, Cicely
315 W. 70th St.
New York, NY 10023
Actress
Birthday: 12/19/33

Tyson, Mike
c/o Don King Productions
32 E. 68th St.
New York, NY 10021
Boxer
Birthday: 7/1/66

Tyson Foods
2210 W. Oaklawn Dr.
Springdale, AR 72762
Web site: http://www.tyson.com
Leland E. Tollett, CEO
Food

It gives me the greatest pleasure to realize I have one more invisible friend at the other end of the post office. Nearly every week a new one turns up, and I feel like I am having a party, and the postman is a sort of Santa Claus every day, with letters from my new friends.

—VACHEL LINDSAY to Alice Henderson, 1913

UAL
1200 E. Algonquin Rd.
Elk Grove Township, IL 60007
Web site: http://www.ual.com
Gerald Greenwald, CEO
Airline

UB40
9247 Alden Dr.
Beverly Hills, CA 90210
Music group

UFO
10 Sutherland
London W9 24Q
England
Music group

Ullrich, Jan
c/o Team Deutsche Telekom
Königstr. 97
53115 Bonn
Germany
Winner of the Tour de France 1997
Birthday: 11/2/73

Ulrich, Skeet (Brian Ray Ulrich)
8942 Wilshire Blvd.
Beverly Hills, CA 90211
Actor
Birthday: 1/20/69

Ultramor Diamond Shamrock
6000 N. Loop 1604 W.
San Antonio, TX 78249
Web site: http://www.diasham.com
Roger Hemminghaus, CEO
Petroleum refining

Underwood, Blair
5200 Lankershim Blvd., #260
N. Hollywood, CA 91601
Actor
Birthday: 8/25/64

Unicom
10 S. Dearborn St.
Chicago, IL 60603
Web site: http://www.ceco.com
John W. Rowe, CEO
Gas and electric utilities

U96
Bernstorffst. 123
22767 Hamburg
Germany
Rock group

Union Camp
1600 Valley Rd.
Wayne, NJ 07470
Web site: http://www.unioncamp.com
W. Craig McClelland, CEO
Forest and paper products

Union Carbide
39 Old Ridgebury Rd.
Danbury, CT 06817
Web site: http://
www.unioncarbide.com
William H. Joyce, CEO
Chemicals

Union of Concerned Scientists
1616 P St. NW, #310
Washington, DC 20036
Web site: http://
www.ucsusa.org/
Henry Kendall, chair of board
of directors
*Nonprofit alliance of scientists and
citizens working for a healthy
environment and a safe world:
researches and promotes clean
energy and transportation
technologies*

Union Pacific
1717 Main St., Ste. 5900
Dallas, TX 75201
Web site: http://www.up.com
Richard K. Davidson, CEO
Railroads

Unisource
1100 Cassatt Rd.
Berwyn, PA 19312
Web site: http://
www.unisourcelink.com
Ray B. Mundt, CEO
Wholesalers

Unisys
Township Line & Union Mtg.
Rds.
Blue Bell, PA 19424
Web site: http://
www.unisys.com
Lawrence A. Weinbach, CEO
Computer and data services

Unitas, Johnny
c/o Pro Football Hall of Fame
2121 George Halas Dr. NW
Canton, OH 44708
Former football player

United HealthCare
9900 Bren Rd. E.
Minnetonka, MN 55343
Web site: http://
www.unitedhealthcare.com
William W. McGuire, CEO
Health care

United Parcel Service
55 Glenlake Pkwy. NE
Atlanta, GA 30328
Web site: http://www.ups.com
James P. Kelly, CEO
Mail, package, freight delivery

**United Services Automobile
Association**
9800 Fredericksburg Rd., F-3-E
San Antonio, TX 78288
Robert T. Herres, CEO
P & C insurance (stock)

**United States Chamber of
Commerce**
1615 H St. NW
Washington, DC 20062

**United States Student
Association**
1612 K St. NW, #510
Washington, DC 20006
Web site: http://
www.essential.org/ussa./
E-mail: ussafdir@essential.org

United Technologies
1 Financial Plaza
Hartford, CT 06101
Web site: http://www.utc.com
George David, CEO
Aerospace

United We Stand America
7616 LBJ Frwy. #727
Dallas, TX 75221
Political organization

Universal Tobacco
1501 N. Hamilton St.
Richmond, VA 23230
Henry H. Harrell, CEO
Tobacco

Unocal
2141 Rosecrans Ave., Ste. 4000
El Segundo, CA 90505
Web site: http://
   www.unocal.com
Roger C. Beach, CEO
Mining, crude-oil production

Unser, Al, Jr.,
PO Box 25047
Albuquerque, NM 87125
Race car driver

Unum
2211 Congress St.
Portland, ME 04122
Web site: http://
   www.unum.com
James F. Orr III, CEO
Life and health insurance (stock)

Upshaw, Gene
c/o Pro Football Hall of Fame
2121 George Halas Dr. NW
Canton, OH 44708
Professional football player

Urban Institute
2100 M St. NW
Washington, DC 20037
Web site: http://www.urban.org
Jill Marsteller, researcher
Len M. Nichols, researcher
Stephen Zuckerman,
   researcher
*Nonprofit economic, social, and
   policy research organization*

Urich, Robert
10061 Riverside Dr., #1026
Toluca Lake, CA 91602
Actor
Birthday: 12/19/47

US Airways Group
2345 Crystal Dr.
Arlington, VA 22227
Web site: http://
   www.usairways.com
Stephen M. Wolf, CEO
Airline

U.S. Bancorp
601 2nd Ave. S.
Minneapolis, MN 55402
Web site: http://www.fbs.com/
   home.html
John F. Grundhofer, CEO
Commercial bank

USF&G
6225 Centennial Way
Baltimore, MD 21209
Web site: http://www.usfg.com
Norman P. Blake, Jr., CEO
P & C insurance (stock)

USG
125 S. Franklin St.
Chicago, IL 60606
Web site: http://www.usg.com
William C. Foote, CEO
Building materials, glass

U.S. Office Products
1025 T. Jefferson St. NW
Washington, DC 20007
Web site: http://www.usop.com
Thomas Morgan, CEO
Wholesalers

U.S. Term Limits
1511 K St. NW, #540
Washington, DC 20005
Web site: http://
   www.termlimits.org/
E-mail: admin@termlimits.org
Paul Jacob, executive director
*Organization devoted to setting
   term limits for elected officials*

US West
7800 E. Orchard Rd.
Englewood, CO 80111
Web site: http://
   www.uswest.com
Richard D. McCormick, CEO
Telecommunications

USX
600 Grant St.
Pittsburgh, PA 15219
Thomas J. Usher, CEO
Petroleum refining

UtiliCorp United
20 W. 9th St.
Kansas City, MO 64105
Web site: http://
  www.utilicorp.com
Richard C. Green, Jr., CEO
Gas and electric utilities

U2
c/o Upfront Mgmt.
4 Windmill Ln.
Dublin, 2
Ireland
or
119 Rockland Ctr., #350
Nanuet, NY 10954
Rock band

La Lettre, l'epitre, qui n'est pas un genre mais tous les genres, la littérature même.

The letter, the epistle, which is not a genre but all the genres, literature itself.

—Jacques Derrida, *"La Carte Postale"*

Valasquez, Patricia
c/o Ford Model Management
344 E. 59th St.
New York, NY 10022
Model

Van Buren, Abigail
PO Box 69440
Los Angeles, CA 90069
Dear Abby

Van Buren, Steve
c/o Pro Football Hall of Fame
2121 George Halas Dr. NW
Canton, OH 44708
Football player

Vance, Courtney B.
c/o CAA
9830 Wilshire Blvd.
Beverly Hills, CA 90212
Actress

Van Damme, Jean-Claude
PO Box 4149
Chatsworth, CA 91313
Actor, martial arts expert
Birthday: 10/18/60

Vendela
344 E. 59th St.
New York, NY 10022
Model

Van Dien, Casper
3500 Olive Ave., #1400
Burbank, CA 91505
Actor, grandson of Robert Mitchum
Birthday: 1/18/68

Vandross, Luther
PO Box 5542
Beverly Hills, CA 90209
Singer

Van Dyke, Dick
c/o William Morris Agency
151 El Camino Dr.
Beverly Hills, CA 90212
Actor

Van Dyke, Jerry
145 S. Fairfax Ave., #130
Los Angeles, CA 90036
Actor, Dick's brother
Birthday: 7/27/32

Van Dyke, Leroy
Rte. 1, Box 271
Smithton, MO 65350
Country singer

Vangelis
195 Queens Gate
London W1
England
Music group

Van Halen
10100 Santa Monica Blvd.,
  Ste. 2460
Los Angeles, CA 90067
Rock group

Van Horn, Patrick
c/o Writers & Artists Agency
924 Westwood Blvd., #900
Los Angeles, CA 90024
Actor

Vanilla Ice
1290 Ave. of the Americas, #4
New York, NY 10104
Rapper

Van Peebles, Mario
9560 Wilshire Blvd., #516
Beverly Hills, CA 90212
Actor, writer, director
Birthday: 1/15/57

Van Shelton, Ricky
PO Box 120589
Nashville, TN 37212
Country singer

Vargas, Elizabeth
c/o ABC-TV News Dept.
77 W. 66th St.
New York, NY 10023
Journalist

Varney, Jim
c/o Cosden & Sherry
1200 McGovock St.
Nashville, TN 37203
Actor
Birthday: 6/15/49

Vaughan, Greg
c/o Pierce & Shelly
612 Lighthouse Ave., #275
Pacific Grove, CA 93951
Web site: http://
  www.geocities.com/
  Hollywood/Boulevard/5539
E-mail: GREGV000@aol.com
Actor

Vedder, Eddie
c/o Pearl Jam
PO Box 4570
Seattle, WA 98104
Singer, songwriter
Birthday: 12/23/64

Vencor
400 W. Market St.
Louisville, KY 40202
Web site: http://
  www.vencor.com
W. Bruce Lunsford, CEO
Health care

Vereen, Ben
200 W. 57th St.
New York, NY 10019
Actor
Birthday: 1/13/25

Verstappen, Jos
c/o Tyrrell Racing
  Organisation Ltd.
Long Reach
Ockham
Woking
Surrey GU23 6PE
England
Professional Formula-1 driver

**Veterans of Foreign Wars
  (VFW) Political Action
  Committee**
200 Maryland Ave. NE
Washington, DC 20002
Web site: http://www.vfw.org/
E-mail: info@vfw.org
*Organization dedicated to securing
  the rights and benefits of
  veterans*

VF
Mackey J. McDonald
1047 N. Park Rd.
Wyomissing, PA 19610
Web site: http://www.vfc.com
Apparel

Viacom
1515 Broadway
New York, NY 10036
Sumner M. Redstone, CEO
Entertainment

Victim Services
2 Lafayette St., 3rd Fl.
New York, NY 10007
Web site: http://
  www.victimservices.org/
E-mail:
  feedback@victimservices.org
Chris Whipple, executive
  director
*Direct service, research, and
  advocacy organization for
  domestic violence, rape, child
  abuse, assault victims, and
  survivors of homicide*

Vietnam Veterans of America
1224 M St. NW
Washington, DC 20005
Web site: http://www.vva.org/
E-mail:
  71154.702@compuserve.com
Mokie Pratt Porter,
  communications director
*National veterans service
  organization*

Vigoda, Abe
8500 Melrose Ave., #208
W. Hollywood, CA 90069
Actor
Birthday: 2/24/21

Vila, Bob
10877 Wilshire Blvd., #900
Los Angeles, CA 90024
TV host

Villeneuve, Jacques
c/o Williams GP Engineering
  Ltd.
Grove
Wantage
Oxfordshire OX12 0DQ
England
*Professional Formula-1 driver,
  World Cup winner 1997*

Vincent, Jan-Michael
11693 San Vincente Blvd.,
  #296
Los Angeles, CA 90049
Actor
Birthday: 7/15/44

Vincent, Rhonda
PO Box #31
Greentop, MO 63546
Country singer

Vincent, Rick
Box #323
1336 North Moorpark Rd.
Thousand Oaks, CA 91360
Country singer

Vinton, Bobby
PO Box 6010
Branson, MO 65615
Singer
Birthday: 4/16/35

Visitor, Nana
PO Box 5617
Beverly Hills, CA 90210
*Actress, Major Kira of "Deep
  Space Nine"*
Birthday: 2/26/57

Vitale, Dick
c/o ESPN Plaza
935 Middle Street
Bristol, CT 06010
Sportscaster

Voluntary Euthanasia Society of England & Wales (EXIT)
13 Prince of Wales Ter.
Kensington
London W8 5PG
England
Web site: http://
   dialspace.dial.pipex.com/
   ves.london/
E-mail:
   ves.london@dial.pipex.com
John Oliver, executive director

Voorhies, Lark
10635 Santa Monica Blvd., Ste.
   130
Los Angeles, CA 90025
Actress
Birthday: 3/25/74

Vrankovic, Stojko
c/o L.A. Sports Arena
3939 S. Figueroa St.
Los Angeles, CA 90037
Basketball player
Birthday: 1/22/64

W

Dear Pamela, the value of a letter can't be measured quantitatively. If you haven't time to write what you call a "real" letter, then write a few lines. I don't expect anyone to compose longwinded epistles, as I sometimes do. I write letters because I enjoy doing it. It doesn't matter too much whether the recipient takes pleasure in reading what I write; I've had my pleasure.

— *"In Absentia"*

Wachovia
100 N. Main St.
Winston-Salem, NC 27150
Web site: http://
    www.wachovia.com
Leslie M. Baker, Jr., CEO
Commercial bank

Wade, Virginia
1 Erieview Pl.
Cleveland, OH 44114
Former tennis player

Wagner, Lindsay
PO Box 5002
Sherman Oaks, CA 91403
Actress
Birthday: 6/22/49

Wagner, Robert
PO Box 93339
Los Angeles, CA 90093
Actor
Birthday: 2/10/30

Wagoner, Porter
PO Box 290785
Nashville, TN 37229
Country singer

Wai-hing, Emily Lau
No. 12–13, g/f
Hok Sam House
Lung Hang Estate
Shatin, New Territories
Hong Kong
E-mail: Elau@hknet.com
*Hong Kong legislator and
    democracy advocate*
Birthday: 1/2/52

Waits, Tom
PO Box 498
Valley Ford, CA 94972
Singer, songwriter, actor
Birthday: 12/7/49

Walgreen
200 Wilmot Rd.
Deerfield, IL 60015
Web site: http://
    www.walgreens.com
L. Daniel Jorndt, CEO
Food and drug stores

Walker, Ally
7920 Sunset Blvd., #400
Los Angeles, CA 90046
Actress

Walker, Billy
PO Box 618
Hendersonville, TN 37077
Country singer

Walker, Charlie
Grand Ole Opry
2804 Opryland Dr.
Nashville, TN 37214
Country singer

Walker, Clay
PO Box 1304
Nederland, TX 77627
Country singer

Walker, Jerry Jeff
PO Box 39
Austin, TX 78767
Country singer, songwriter

Walker, Jimmy
11365 Ventura Blvd., #100
Studio City, CA 91604
Comedian, actor
Birthday: 6/25/48

Walker, Marcy
9107 Wilshire Blvd., #700
Beverly Hills, CA 90210
Birthday: 11/26/61
Actress

Walker, Mort
c/o King Features
235 E. 45th St.
New York, NY 10017
Cartoonist

Wallach, Eli
200 W. 57th St., #900
New York, NY 10019
Actor
Birthday: 12/7/15

Wallflowers, The
8900 Wilshire Blvd., #300
Beverly Hills, CA 90211
Music group

Wal-Mart
702 S.W. 8th St.
Bentonville, AR 72716
Web site: http://
   www.wal-mart.com
David D. Glass, CEO
General merchandisers

Walsh, John
E-mail: feedback@amw.com
TV host

Walston, Ray
423 S. Rexford Dr., #205
Beverly Hills, CA 90212
Actor
Birthday: 11/2/24

Walt Disney
500 S. Buena Vista St.
Burbank, CA 91521
Web site: http://
   www.disney.com
Michael D. Eisner, CEO
Entertainment

Walters, Barbara
c/o "20/20"
ABC
77 W. 66th St.
New York, NY 10023
TV hostess
Birthday: 9/25/31

Wang, Garret
PO Box 13767
Sacramento, CA 95853
*Actor, Ensign Harry Kim on "Star
   Trek: Voyager"*

Ward, Megan
c/o Innovative Artists
1999 Ave. of the Stars, #2850
Los Angeles, CA 90067
Actress
Birthday: 9/24/69

Ward, Rachel
110 Queen St.
Woollahra, NSW 2025
Australia
Actress
Birthday: 9/12/57

Wariner, Steve
PO Box 1667
Franklin, TN 37065
Country singer

Warlock, Billy
9229 Sunset Blvd., #315
Los Angeles, CA 90069
Actor
Birthday: 3/26/60

Warner, Julie
c/o Creative Artists Agency
9830 Wilshire Blvd.
Beverly Hills, CA 90212
Actress
Birthday: 1965

Warner, Malcolm-Jamal
15303 Ventura Blvd., #1100
Sherman Oaks, CA 91403
Actor

Warner-Lambert
201 Tabor Rd.
Morris Plains, NJ 07950
Web site: http://
    www.warner-lambert.com
Melvin R. Goodes, CEO
Pharmaceuticals

Washington, Denzel
8942 Wilshire Blvd.
Beverly Hills, CA 90211
Actor
Birthday: 12/28/54

Washington Mutual
1201 3rd Ave.
Seattle, WA 98101
Kerry K. Killinger, CEO
Savings institution

Waste Management
3003 Butterfield Rd.
Oak Brook, IL 60523
Web site: http://
    www.wastemanagement.com
Robert Steve Miller, CEO
Waste management

Waters, John
ICM
8942 Wilshire Blvd.
Los Angeles, CA 90211
Actor, director, writer
Birthday: 4/22/49

Waters, Roger
c/o Ten Tenth Mgmt.
106 Gifford St.
London N1 0DF
England
Musician
Birthday: 9/6/44

Waterston, Sam
RR1, Box 232
West Cornwall, CT 06796
Actor
Birthday: 11/15/40

Watson, Gene
PO Box 2210
Nashville, TN 37202
Country singer

Weathers, Carl
10960 Wilshire Blvd., #826
Los Angeles, CA 90024
Actor
Birthday: 1/14/48

Weaver, Dennis
PO Box 257
Ridgeway, CO 81432
Actor
Birthday: 6/4/25

Weaver, Sigourney
200 W. 57th St.
New York, NY 10019
Actress

Webber, Andrew Lloyd
725 5th Ave.
New York, NY 10022
Composer, producer
Birthday: 3/22/48

Weber, Steven
c/o ICM
8942 Wilshire Blvd.
Beverly Hills, CA 90211
Actor

Weinger, Scott
9255 Sunset Blvd., #1010
W. Hollywood, CA 90069
Actor

Welch, Kevin
Warner Bros.
1815 Division
Nashville, TN 37212
Country singer

Welch, Racquel (Racquel Tejada)
9903 Santa Monica Blvd., #514
Beverly Hills, CA 90212
Actress
Birthday: 9/5/40

WellPoint Health Networks
21555 Oxnard St.
Woodland Hills, CA 91367
Web site: http://
   www.wellpoint.com
Leonard D. Schaeffer, CEO
Health care

Wells, Dawn
11365 Ventura Blvd., #100
Studio City, CA 91604
Actress, Mary Ann of "Gilligan's Island"

Wells, Kitty
240 Old Hickory Blvd.
Madison, TN 37115
Country singer

Wells Fargo & Co.
420 Montgomery St.
San Francisco, CA 94163
Web site: http://
   www.wellsfargo.com
Paul Hazen, CEO
Commercial bank

Wenders, Wim
c/o Wim Wenders Produktion
Segitzdamm 2
10969 Berlin
Germany
Director
Birthday: 8/14/45

Wendt, George
9150 Wilshire Blvd.
Beverly Hills, CA 90212
Actor
Birthday: 10/17/48

West, Adam
11365 Ventura Blvd., #100
Studio City, CA 91604
or
PO Box 3477
Ketchum, ID 83340
Actor, TV's Batman
Birthday: 9/19/29

West, Jerry
c/o Basketball Hall of Fame
1150 W. Columbia Ave.
Springfield, MA 01101
Former basketball player

Western Atlas
10205 Westheimer Rd.
Houston, TX 77042
Web site: http://
   www.westatlas.com
John R. Russell, CEO
Industrial and farm equipment

Western Digital
8105 Irvine Center Dr.
Irvine, CA 92618
Web site: http://www.wdc.com.
Charles A Haggerty, CEO
Computer peripherals

Westvaco
299 Park Ave.
New York, NY 10171
Web site: http://
    www.westvaco.com
John A. Luke, Jr., CEO
Forest and paper products

Wet Wet Wet
c/o Precious Organisation
Pet Sound Studio
24 Gairbraid Ave. #6-B
Maryhill
Glasgow G20 1XX
Scotland
Music group

Weyerhaeuser
33663 Weyerhaeuser Way S.
Federal Way, WA 98003
Web site: http://
    www.weyerhaeuser.com
Steven R. Rogel, CEO
Forest and paper products

Whalley-Kilmer, Joanne
c/o ICM
Oxford House
76 Oxford St.
London, W1N 0AX
England
*Actress, formerly married to Val
    Kilmer*
Birthday: 8/25/64

Wheaton, Wil
c/o Innovative Artists
1999 Ave. of the Stars,
    Ste. 2850
Los Angeles, CA 90067
Actor

Whirlpool
2000 N. M-63
Benton Harbor, MI 49022
Web site: http://
    www.whirlpool.com
David R. Whitwam, CEO
Electronics, electrical equipment

White, Betty
PO Box 491965
Los Angeles, CA 90049
Actress
Birthday: 1/17/22

White, Bryan
International Fan Club
PO Box 120162
Nashville, TN 37212
Country singer

White, Jaleel
c/o William Morris Agency
151 El Camino Dr.
Beverly Hills, CA 90212
Actor
Birthday: 1/26/76

White, Joy Lynn
1101 17th Ave. S.
Nashville, TN 37212
Country singer

White, Lari
c/o J. Willoughby
PO Box 120086
Nashville, TN 37212
Country singer

White, Michael
1116 Douglas Pl.
Gallatin, TN 37066
Country singer

White, Reggie
c/o Green Bay Packers
PO Box 10628
Green Bay, WI 54307
Football player

White, Vanna (Vanna Rosich)
10202 W. Washington Blvd.
Culver City, CA 90232
TV personality
Birthday: 2/8/57

White House for Kids
Web site: http://
    www.whitehouse.gov/WH/
    kids/html/
*Answers children's questions about
    the White House*

Whites, The
15 Music Sq. W.
Nashville, TN 37203
Music group

Whitman
3501 Algonquin Rd.
Rolling Meadows, IL 60008
Web site: http://
www.whitmancorp.com
Bruce S. Chelberg, CEO
Beverages

Whitman, Christine Todd
E-mail: cwhitman@rutgers.edu
Governor of New Jersey

Whitman, Slim
221 W. 57th St., 9th Fl.
New York, NY 10019
Singer

Wilburn, Teddy
Grand Ole Opry
2804 Opryland Dr.
Nashville, TN 37214
Country singer

Wilder, Gene (Jerome Silberman)
1511 Sawtelle Blvd., #155
Los Angeles, CA 90025
Actor, writer, director
Birthday: 6/11/35

Wilderness Society, The
900 17th St. NW
Washington, DC 20006
Web site: http://
www.wilderness.org/
Bill Meadows, president
*Devoted primarily to public lands
protection and management
issues*

Wild Rose
PO Box 121705
Nashville, TN 37212
Music group

Willamette Industries
1300 S.W. 5th Ave.
Portland, OR 97201
Web site: http://www.wii.com
William Swindells, CEO
Forest and paper products

HRH Prince William
Highgrove House
Gloucestershire
England
Son of Prince Charles

Williams
1 Williams Ctr.
Tulsa, OK 74172
Web site: http://www.twc.com
Keith E. Bailey, CEO
Pipelines

Williams, Andy
2500 W. Hwy. 76
Branson, MO 65616
Singer
Birthday: 12/30/30

Williams, Don
1103 16th Ave. S.
Nashville, TN 37212
Country singer

Williams, Hank, Jr.,
PO Box 850
Paris, TN 38242
*Country singer, son of Hank
Williams*

Williams, Hank, III
PO Box 121736
Nashville, TN 37212
*Country singer, grandson of Hank
Williams*

Williams, Jason D.
819 18th Ave. S.
Nashville, TN 37203
Country singer

Williams, Jett
PO Box 177
Hartsville, TN 37074
Country singer

Williams, Jobeth
9911 West Pico Blvd.
Penthouse #1
Los Angeles, CA 90035
Actress
Birthday: 1953

Williams, John
Tanglewood Symphony Hall
Lenox, MA 01240
Composer, conductor
Birthday: 2/8/32

Williams, Robin
9830 Wilshire Blvd.
Beverly Hills, CA 90212
Actor, comedian
Birthday: 7/21/52

Williams, Treat (Richard Williams)
215 W. 78th St., #10A
New York, NY 10024
Actor
Birthday: 12/1/51

Williams, Vanessa
PO Box 858
Chappaqua, NY 10514
Singer
Birthday: 3/18/63

Williams, Walter E.
George Mason University
4400 University Dr.
Fairfax, VA 22030-4444
Web site: http://www.gmu.edu/
    departments/economics/
    williams.htm
E-mail:
    wwilliam@wpgate.gmu.edu
*John M. Olin Distinguished
    Professor of Economics, author
    of* Do the Right Thing: The
    People's Economist Speaks

Williams & Ree
24 Music Sq. W.
Nashville, TN 37203
Music group

Willis, Bruce (Walter Bruce Willis)
1122 S. Robertson Blvd., #15
Los Angeles, CA 90035
Actor
Birthday: 3/19/55

Wilson, Carnie
13601 Ventura Blvd., #286
Sherman Oaks, CA 91423
Singer
Birthday: 4/29/68

Wilson, Katharina
c/o Puzzle Publishing
PO Box 230023
Portland, OR 97281-0023
Author of The Alien Jigsaw, *a
    book about alien abduction*

Wilson, Mara
3500 W. Olive Ave., #1400
Burbank, CA 91506
Actress

Wilson, Rita
9830 Wilshire Blvd.
Beverly Hills, CA 90212
Actress

Windom, William
c/o Film Artists Associates
7080 Hollywood Blvd., #1118
Hollywood, CA 90028
Actor
Birthday: 9/28/23

Winfrey, Oprah
PO Box 909715
Chicago, IL 60690
Talk show host, actress
Birthday: 1/29/54

Winger, Debra (May Debra Winger)
PO Box 9078
Van Nuys, CA 91409
Actress
Birthday: 5/17/55

Winkler, Henry
PO Box 49914
Los Angeles, CA 90049
Actor (the Fonz), director
Birthday: 10/30/45

Winn-Dixie
5050 Edgewood Ct.
Jacksonville, FL 32254
A. Dano Davis, CEO
Food and drug stores

Winslet, Kate
9830 Wilshire Blvd.
Beverly Hills, CA 90212
or
503/504 Lotts Rd.
The Chambers
Chelsea Harbour
London SW10 OXF
England
E-mail: webmaster
@pde.paramount.com
Actress

Winter, Alex
107 W. 25th St., #6B
New York, NY 10001
Actor

Winwood, Steve
9200 Sunset Blvd., PH 15
Los Angeles, CA 90069
Musician

Witt, Katarina
c/o Arts and Promotion
Bergerstr. 295
60385 Frankfurt
Germany
Actress, Figure Skater
Birthday: 12/3/65

Wolf, Scott
10390 Santa Monica Blvd.,
Ste. 300
Los Angeles, CA 90025
Actor

Wonder, Stevie
4616 Magnolia Blvd.
Burbank, CA 91505
Singer, songwriter

Wong, B. D.
c/o Innovative Artists
1999 Ave. of the Stars, #2850
Los Angeles, CA 90067
Actor

Woo, John
c/o Garth Productions
20th Century Fox
10201 W. Pico Blvd.
Los Angeles, CA 90064
Director

Wood, Elijah
9150 Wilshire Blvd., #350
Beverly Hills, CA 90212
Actor
Birthday: 1/28/81

Woodard, Alfre
c/o ICM
8942 Wilshire Blvd.
Beverly Hills, CA 90211
Actress

Woods, James
760 N. La Cienega Blvd.
Los Angeles, CA 90069
Actor
Birthday: 4/18/47

● **Woods, Tiger**
c/o International Management
Group
1 Erieview Plz., Ste. #1300
Cleveland, OH 44114
Professional golfer

Woodward, Joanne
c/o ICM
40 W. 57th St.
New York, NY 10019
Actress, married to Paul Newman
Birthday: 10/27/30

Wooley, Sheb
123 Walton Ferry Rd., 2nd Fl.
Hendersonville, TN 37075
Singer

F. W. Woolworth Co.
233 Broadway
New York, NY 10279
Roger N. Farah, CEO
Specialist retailers

Wopat, Tom
PO Box 128031
Nashville, TN 37212
Country singer

World Com
515 E. Amite St.
Jackson, MS 39201
Web site: http://
www.wcom.com
Bernard J. Ebbers, CEO
Telecommunications

**World Federation of Right to
Die Societies**
61 Minterne Ave.
Norwood Green
Southhall
Middlesex UB2 4HP
England
Malcolm Hurwitt, secretary

World Future Society
7910 Woodmont Ave., #450
Bethesda, MD 20814
Web site: http://www.wfs.org/
E-mail: schley@wfs.org
*Nonprofit educational and
scientific organization for people
interested in how social and
technological developments are
shaping the future*

Worley, Joanne
PO Box 2054
Toluca Lake, CA 91610
Actress

W. R. Grace
1 Town Center Rd.
Boca Raton, FL 33486
Web site: http://www.grace.com
Albert J. Costello, CEO
Chemicals

Wright, Bobby
PO Box 477
Madison, TN 37116
Country singer

Wright, Johnny
PO Box 477
Madison, TN 37116
Country singer

Wright, Michelle
PO Box 152
Morpeth, ON NOP 1X0
Canada
Country singer

Wu-Tang Clan
c/o BMG Music
1540 Broadway
New York, NY 10036
Music group

W. W. Grainger
455 Knightsbridge Pkwy.
Lincolnshire, IL 60069
Web site: http://
www.grainger.com
Richard L. Keyser, CEO
Wholesalers

Wyman, Bill
c/o H. Siegel
410 Park Ave., 10th Fl.
New York, NY 10022-4407
*Former bass player for the Rolling
Stones*
Birthday: 10/24/36

Wyman, Jane
PO Box 1317
Elfers, FL 34680
Actress, formerly married to Ronald
Reagan
Birthday: 1/4/14

X

I see you understand the pleasure that can be got from writing letters. In other centuries this was taken for granted. Not any longer. Only a few people carry on true correspondences. No time, the rest will tell you. Quicker to telephone. Like saying a photograph is more satisfying than a painting. There wasn't all that much time for writing letters in the past, either, but time was found, as it generally can be for whatever gives pleasure.

—ANONYMOUS

Official "Xena: Warrior Princess" Fan Club
c/o Creation Entertainment
664A W. Broadway
Glendale, CA 91204

Xerox
800 Long Ridge Rd.
Stamford, CT 06904
Web site: http://
  www.xerox.com
Paul A. Allaire, CEO
Office equipment

"The X-Files"
c/o Fox
PO Box 900
Beverly Hills, CA 90213
TV series

X-Perience
c/o WEA Records
Postfach 761260
22062 Hamburg
Germany
Music group

Y

But I want music and intellectual companionships and affection. Well, perhaps I'll get all that one day. And in the meantime there are little things to look forward to, letters and the unexpected.

—ANONYMOUS

Yasbeck, Amy
c/o William Morris Agency
151 S. El Camino Dr.
Beverly Hills, CA 90212
Actress

Yearwood, Trisha
PO Box 65
Monticello, GA 31064
Country singer

Yell4You
c/o Nady
Postfach 303
74345 Lauffen/N.
Germany
Music group

Yello
c/o Dieter Meier
Aurastraße 78
8031 Zürich
Switzerland
Music group

Yellow
10990 Roe Ave.
Overland Park, KS 66211
Web site: http://
  www.yellowcorp.com
A. Maurice Myers, CEO
Trucking

Yellowjackets
9220 Sunset Blvd., #320
Los Angeles, CA 90069
Music group

Yeltsin, Boris
The Kremlin
Moscow
Russia
or
Belij Dom
Kraschnopresnenskaj nab. 2
103274 Moscow
Russia
President of Russia
Birthday: 2/1/31

Yes
9 Hillgate St.
London W8 7SP
England
Music group

Yoakam, Dwight
15030 Ventura Blvd., #770
Sherman Oaks, CA 91403
or
1250 6th St., #401
Santa Monica, CA 90401
Country singer

York, Michael
c/o International Creative
  Management
8942 Wilshire Blvd.
Beverly Hills, CA 90211
Actor
Birthday: 3/27/42

York International
631 S. Richland Ave.
York, PA 17403
Web site: http://www.york.com
Robert N. Pokelwaldt, CEO
Industrial and farm equipment

Young, Burt
6233 Wilshire Blvd.
Los Angeles, CA 90048
Actor

Young, Faron
1300 Division
Nashville, TN 37203
Country singer

Young, John
c/o NASA
Houston, TX 77058
Astronaut

Young, Neil
1026 S. Robertson Blvd., #200
Los Angeles, CA 90035
Singer, songwriter

Young, Nina
c/o Narrow Road Company
22 Poland St.
London W1V 3DD
England
Actress

Young, Sean
PO Box 20547
Sedona, AZ 86341
Actress
Birthday: 11/20/59

I have now attained the true art of letter writing, which, we are always told, is to express on paper exactly what one would say to the same person by word of mouth; I have been talking to you almost as fast as I could the whole of this letter.

—JANE AUSTEN

Zaca Creek
PO Box 237
Santa Ynez, CA 93460
Music group

Zadora, Pia
9560 Wilshire Blvd.
Beverly Hills, CA 90212
Actress, singer
Birthday: 5/4/56

Zahn, Steve
2372 Veteran Ave., #102
Los Angeles, CA 90064
Actor

Zane, Billy
450 N. Rossmore Ave.,
Ste. 1001
Los Angeles, CA 90004
Actor
Birthday: 2/24/66

Zappa, Dweezil
PO Box 5265
N. Hollywood, CA 91616
Musician, Frank Zappa's son
Birthday: 9/5/69

Zappa, Moon Unit
PO Box 5265
N. Hollywood, CA 91616
Actress, singer, Frank Zappa's daughter, Dweezil's sister
Birthday: 9/28/68

Zeman, Jackie
c/o "General Hospital"
ABC-TV
4151 Prospect Ave.
Los Angeles, CA 90027
Soap opera actress

Zemeckis, Robert
1880 Century Park E., Ste. 900
Los Angeles, CA 90067
Director, producer, screenwriter
Birthday: 5/14/51

Zero Population Growth (ZPG)
1400 16th St. NW, #320
Washington, DC 20036
Web site: http://www.zpg.org
Peter H. Kostmayer, executive director
Nation's largest grass-roots organization concerned with the impacts of rapid population growth and wasteful consumption

Zero to Three
National Center for Clinical
  Infant Programs
200 14th St. N., #380
Arlington, VA 22201
Web site: http://
  www.zerotothree.org/
E-mail:
  webmaster@cyberserv.com
Kathryn E. Barnard, board of
  directors
*National nonprofit dedicated to the
  healthy development of infants,
  toddlers, and their families, with
  information for parents and
  professionals*

Ziering, Ian
1122 S. Robertson Blvd., #15
Los Angeles, CA 90035
Actor

Zimbalist, Stephanie
16255 Ventura Blvd., #1011
Encino, CA 91436
Actress

Zucchero
c/o Prima Pagina
Via Hayech 41
20100 Milano
Italy
Singer

Zuniga, Daphne
c/o Contellation
PO Box 1249
White River Junction, VT
  05001
Actress

• **ZZ Top**
PO Box 19744
Houston, TX 77229
Music group

SENATE MAILING ADDRESS

The Honorable [Name of Senator]
United States Senate
Washington, DC 20510

Dear Senator_____

SENATE E-MAIL ADDRESSES

Spencer Abraham (R-MI)
michigan
@abraham.senate.gov

John Ashcroft (R-MO)
john_ashcroft
@ashcroft.senate.gov

Max Baucus (D-MT)
max@baucus.senate.gov

Robert Bennett (R-UT)
senator@bennett.senate.gov

Joseph Biden (D-DE)
senator@biden.senate.gov

Jeff Bingaman (D-NM)
senator_bingaman
@bingaman.senate.gov

Kit Bond (R-MO)
kit_bond@bond.senate.gov

Barbara Boxer (D-CA)
senator@boxer.senate.gov

John Breaux (D-LA)
senator@breaux.senate.gov

Dale Bumpers (D-AR)
senator@bumpers.senate.gov

Conrad Burns (R-MT)
conrad_
burns@burns.senate.gov

John Chafee (R-RI)
senator_
chafee@chafee.senate.gov

Thad Cochran (R-MS)
senator@cochran.senate.gov

Paul Coverdell (R-GA)
senator_coverdell
@coverdell.senate.gov

Larry Craig (R-ID)
larry_craig@craig.senate.gov

Thomas Daschle (D-SD)
tom_
daschle@daschle.senate.gov

Mike DeWine (R-OH)
senator_
dewine@dewine.senate.gov

Christopher Dodd (D-CT)
sen_dodd@dodd.senate.gov

Pete Domenici (R-NM)
senator_domenici
@domenici.senate.gov

Byron Dorgan (D-ND)
senator@dorgan.senate.gov

Russell Feingold (D-WI)
senator@feingold.senate.gov

Dianne Feinstein (D-CA)
senator@feinstein.senate.gov

Wendell Ford (D-KY)
wendell_
ford@ford.senate.gov

William Frist (R-TN)
senator_frist@frist.senate.gov

Slade Gorton (R-WA)
senator_
gorton@gorton.senate.gov

Bob Graham (D-FL)
bob_
graham@graham.senate.gov

Rod Grams (R-MN)
mail_
grams@grams.senate.gov

Charles Grassley (R-IA)
chuck_
grassley@grassley.senate.gov

Judd Gregg (R-NH)
mailbox@gregg.senate.gov

Tom Harkin (D-IA)
tom_
harkin@harkin.senate.gov

Orrin Hatch (R-UT)
senator_
hatch@hatch.senate.gov

Jesse Helms (R-NC)
jesse_
helms@helms.senate.gov

Ernest Hollings (D-SC)
senator@hollings.senate.gov

Kay B. Hutchison (R-TX)
senator
@hutchinson.senate.gov

James Jeffords (R-VT)
vermont@jeffords.senate.gov

Dirk Kempthorne (R-ID)
dirk_kempthorne
@kempthorne.senate.gov

Edward Kennedy (D-MA)
senator@kennedy.senate.gov

Robert Kerrey (D-NE)
bob@kerrey.senate.gov

John Kerry (D-MA)
john_kerry@kerry.senate.gov

Herb Kohl (D-WI)
senator_
kohl@kohl.senate.gov

Jon Kyl (R-AZ)
info@kyl.senate.gov

Patrick Leahy (D-VT)
senator_
leahy@leahy.senate.gov

Carl Levin (D-MI)
senator@levin.senate.gov

Joseph Lieberman (D-CT)
senator_lieberman
@lieberman.senate.gov

John McCain (R-AZ)
senator_
mccain@mccain.senate.gov

Mitch McConnell (R-KY)
senator
@mcconnell.senate.gov

Barbara Mikulski (D-MD)
senator@mikulski.senate.gov

Daniel Moynihan (D-NY)
senator@dpm.senate.gov

Don Nickles (R-OK)
senator@nickles.senate.gov

Harry Reid (D-NV)
senator_reid@reid.senate.gov

Charles Robb (D-VA)
senator@robb.senate.gov

John Rockefeller (D-WV)
senator
@rockefeller.senate.gov

Rick Santorum (R-PA)
senator
@santorum.senate.gov

Paul Sarbanes (D-MD)
senator@sarbanes.senate.gov

Jeff Sessions (R-AL)
senator@sessions.senate.gov

Richard Shelby (R-AL)
senator@shelby.senate.gov

Bob Smith (R-NH)
opinion@smith.senate.gov

Arlen Specter (R-PA)
senator_
specter@specter.senate.gov

Ted Stevens (R-AK)
senator_
stevens@stevens.senate.gov

Fred Thompson (R-TN)
senator_thompson
@thompson.senate.gov

Strom Thurmond (R-SC)
senator
@thurmond.senate.gov

John Warner (R-VA)
senator@warner.senate.gov

Paul Wellstone (D-MN)
senator
@wellstone.senate.gov

HOUSE OF REPRESENTATIVES MAILING ADDRESS

The Honorable [Name of Representative]
U.S. House of Representatives
Washington, DC 20515

Dear Representative_____

HOUSE OF REPRESENTATIVES E-MAIL ADDRESSES

Sonny Callahan (R-AL, 1st)
callahan@hr.house.gov

Terry Everett (R-AL, 2nd)
everett@hr.house.gov

Robert B. Cramer (D-AL, 5)
budmail@hr.house.gov

Spencer Bachus (R-AL, 6th)
sbachus@hr.house.gov

Don Young (R-AK, AL)
dyoung@hr.house.gov

Mat Salmon (R-AZ, 1st)
salmon@hr.house.gov

Ed Pastor (D-AZ, 2nd)
ed.pastor@mail.house.gov

John Shadegg (R-AZ, 4th)
jshadegg@hr.house.gov

Jim Kolbe (R-AZ, 5th)
jimkolbe@hr.house.gov

J. D. Hayworth (R-AZ, 6th)
hayworth@hr.house.gov

Vic Snyder (D-AR, 2nd)
snyder.congress
@mail.house.gov

Asa Hutchinson (R-AR, 3rd)
asa.hutchinson
@mail.house.gov

Jay Dickey (R-AR, 4th)
jdickey@hr.house.gov

John Doolittle (R-CA, 4th)
jdoolitt@hr.house.gov

Robert Matsui (D-CA, 5th)
ca05@hr.house.gov

Lynn Woolsey (D-CA, 6th)
woolsey@hr.house.gov

George Miller (D-CA, 7th)
gmiller@hr.house.gov

Nancy Pelosi (D-CA, 8th)
sf.nancy@mail.house.gov

Ellen Tauscher (D-CA, 10th)
ellen.
taucher@mail.house.gov

Tom Lantos (D-CA, 12th)
talk2tom@hr.house.gov

Pete Stark (D-CA, 13th)
petemail@hr.house.gov

Anna Eshoo (D-CA, 14th)
annagram@hr.house.gov

Tom Campbell (R-CA, 15th)
campbell@hr.house.gov

Zoe Lofgren (D-CA, 16th)
zoegram@lofgren.house.gov

Sam Farr (D-CA, 17th)
samfarr@mail.house.gov

Gary Condit (D-CA, 18th)
gcondit@hr.house.gov

G. Radanovich (R-CA, 19th)
george@hr.house.gov

Buck McKeon (R-CA, 25th)
tellbuck@hr.house.gov

David Dreier (R-CA, 28th)
cyberrep@mail.house.gov

Juanita McDonald (D-CA, 37th)
millender-mcdonald
@hr.house.gov

Steve Horn (R-CA, 38th)
stephen.
horn@mail.house.gov

George Brown (D-CA, 42nd)
talk2geb@hr.house.gov

Dana Rohrabacher (R-CA, 45)
sjohnso4@hr.house.gov

Christopher Cox (R-CA, 47)
chriscox@hr.house.gov

Ron Packard (R-CA, 48th)
rpackard@hr.house.gov

Brian Bilbray (R-CA, 49th)
bilbray@hr.house.gov

Diana DeGette (D-CO, 1st)
degette@mail.house.gov

Bob Schaffer (R-CO, 4th)
bob.schaffer@mail.house.gov

Dan Schaefer (R-CO, 6th)
rep.dan.schaefer
@mail.house.gov

Sam Gejdenson (D-CT, 2nd)
bozrah@hr.house.gov

Rosa DeLauro (D-CT, 3rd)
delauro@hr.house.gov

Christopher Shays (R-CT, 4th)
cshays@hr.house.gov

Michael Castle (R-DE, AL)
delaware@hr.house.gov

Joe Scarborough (R-FL, 1st)
FL01@hr.house.gov

Karen Thurman (D-FL, 5th)
kthurman@hr.house.gov

Cliff Stearns (R-FL, 6th)
cstearns@hr.house.gov

John Mica (R-FL, 7th)
mica@hr.house.gov

Michael Bilirakis (R-FL, 9th)
fl09@hr.house.gov

Charles Canady (R-FL, 12th)
canady@hr.house.gov

Dan Miller (R-FL, 13th)
miller13@hr.house.gov

David Weldon (R-FL, 15th)
fla15@hr.house.gov

Mark Foley (R-FL, 16th)
mfoley@hr.house.gov

Peter Deutsch (D-FL, 20th)
pdeutsch@hr.house.gov

Alcee Hastings (D-FL, 23rd)
hastings@hr.house.gov

Michael Collins (R-GA, 3rd)
rep3mac@hr.house.gov

Newt Gingrich (R-GA, 6th)
georgia6@hr.house.gov

Bob Barr (R-GA, 7th)
bbarr@hr.house.gov

Saxby Chambliss (R-GA, 8th)
saxby@hr.house.gov

Charles Norwood (R-GA, 10th)
ga10@hr.house.gov

John Linder (R-GA, 11th)
jlinder@hr.house.gov

Robert Underwood (D-GU, AL)
guamtodc@hr.house.gov

Neil Abercrombie (D-HI, 1st)
neil@abercrombie.house.gov

Jim Leach (R-IA, 1st)
leach.ia01@mail.house.gov

Jim Nussle (R-IA, 2nd)
nussleia@hr.house.gov

Greg Ganske (R-IA, 4th)
ganske@hr.house.gov

Tom Latham (R-IA, 5th)
latham@hr.house.gov

Helen Chenoweth (R-ID, 1st)
askhelen@hr.house.gov

Bobby Rush (D-IL, 1st)
brush@hr.house.gov

Luis Gutierrez (D-IL, 4th)
luisg@hr.house.gov

Jerry Weller (R-IL, 11th)
jweller@hr.house.gov

Jerry Costello (D-IL, 12th)
JFCIL12@hr.house.gov

Harris Fawell (R-IL, 13th)
hfawell@hr.house.gov

Dennis Hastert (R-IL, 14th)
dhastert@hr.house.gov

Ray LaHood (R-IL, 18th)
lahood18@hr.house.gov

John Shimkus (R-IL, 20th)
shimkus@midwest.net

David McIntosh (R-IN, 2nd)
mcintosh@hr.house.gov

Tim Roemer (D-IN, 3rd)
troemer@hr.house.gov

Mark Souder (R-IN, 4th)
souder@hr.house.gov

John Hostettler (R-IN, 8th)
johnhost@hr.house.gov

Julia Carson (D-IN, 10th)
jcarson@indy.net

Todd Tiahrt (R-KS, 4th)
tiahrt@hr.house.gov

Edward Whitfield (R-KY, 1st)
edky01@hr.house.gov

Jim McCrery (D-LA, 4th)
mccrery@hr.house.gov

Thomas Allen (D-ME, 1st)
rep.tomallen
@mail.house.gov

John Baldacci (D-ME, 2nd)
baldacci@hr.house.gov

Robert Ehrlich (R-MD, 2nd)
ehrlich@hr.house.gov

Benjamin Cardin (D-MD, 3rd)
cardin@hr.house.gov

Albert Wynn (D-MD, 4th)
alwynn@hr.house.gov

John Olver (D-MA, 1st)
olver@hr.house.gov

Richard Neal (D-MA, 2nd)
wtranghe@hr.house.gov

Martin Meehan (D-MA, 5th)
mtmeehan@hr.house.gov

John Tierney (D-MA, 6th)
tierney@usal.com

Joe Moakley (D-MA, 9th)
jmoakley@hr.house.gov

Bart Stupak (D-MI, 1st)
stupak@hr.house.gov

Peter Hoekstra (R-MI, 2nd)
tellhoek@hr.house.gov

Vernon Ehlers (R-MI, 3rd)
rep.ehlers@mail.house.gov

Dave Camp (R-MI, 4th)
davecamp@hr.house.gov

James Barcia (D-MI, 5th)
jbarcia@hr.house.gov

Fred Upton (R-MI, 6th)
talk2fsu@hr.house.gov

Nick Smith (R-MI, 7th)
repsmith@hr.house.gov

Dale Kildee (D-MI, 9th)
dkildee@hr.house.gov

Sander Levin (D-MI, 12th)
slevin@hr.house.gov

Lynn Rivers (D-MI, 13th)
lrivers@hr.house.gov

John Conyers (D-MI, 14th)
jconyers@hr.house.gov

Gil Gutknecht (R-MN, 1st)
gil@hr.house.gov

David Minge (D-MN, 2nd)
dminge@hr.house.gov

Jim Ramstad (R-MN, 3rd)
mn03@hr.house.gov

Bruce Vento (D-MN, 4th)
vento@hr.house.gov

Martin O. Sabo (D-MN, 5th)
martin.sabo@mail.house.gov

Bill Luther (D-MN, 6th)
tell.bill@mail.house.gov

Collin Peterson (D-MN, 7th)
tocollin.peterson
@mail.house.gov

James Oberstar (D-MN, 8th)
oberstar@hr.house.gov

James Talent (R-MO, 2nd)
rep.talent@mail.house.gov

Richard Gephardt (D-MO, 3rd)
gephardt@hr.house.gov

JoAnn Emerson (R-MO, 8th)
jemerson@hr.house.gov

Rick Hill (R-MT, AL)
rick.hill@mail.house.gov

Charles Bass (R-NH, 2nd)
cbass@hr.house.gov

Robert Andrews (D-NJ, 1st)
randrews@hr.house.gov

Frank LoBiondo (R-NJ, 2nd)
lobiondo@hr.house.gov

Bob Franks (R-NJ, 7th)
franksnj@hr.house.gov

Bill Pascrell (D-NJ, 8th)
bill@pascrell.org

R. Frelinghuysen (R-NJ, 11th)
njeleven@hr.house.gov

Michael Forbes (R-NY, 1st)
mpforbes@hr.house.gov

Rick Lazio (R-NY, 2nd)
lazio@hr.house.gov

Peter King (R-NY, 3rd)
pete.king@mail.house.gov

Jerrold Nadler (D-NY, 8th)
nadler@hr.house.gov

Carolyn Maloney (D-NY, 14th)
cmaloney@hr.house.gov

Charles Rangel (D-NY, 15th)
rangel@hr.house.gov

Jose Serrano (D-NY, 16th)
jserrano@hr.house.gov

Eliot Engel (D-NY, 17th)
engeline@hr.house.gov

Nita Lowey (D-NY, 18th)
nitamail@hr.house.gov

Sue Kelly (R-NY, 19th)
dearsue@hr.house.gov

Benjamin Gilman (R-NY, 20th)
robert.becker
@mail.house.gov

Michael McNulty (D-NY, 21st)
mmcnulty@hr.house.gov

Sherwood Boehlert (R-NY, 23rd)
boehlert@hr.house.gov

James Walsh (R-NY, 25th)
jwalsh@hr.house.gov

Maurice Hinchey (D-NY, 26th)
hinchey@hr.house.gov

Louise Slaughter (D-NY, 28th)
louiseny@hr.house.gov

Amo Houghton (R-NY, 31st)
houghton@hr.house.gov

Eva Clayton (D-NC, 1st)
eclayton@hr.house.gov

David Price (D-NC, 4th)
david.price@mail.house.gov

Richard Burr (R-NC, 5th)
richard.burrNC05
camail.house.gov

Howard Coble (R-NC, 6th)
howard.coble
@mail.house.gov

Sue Myrick (R-NC, 9th)
myrick@hr.house.gov

Cass Ballenger (R-NC, 10th)
cassmailcahr.house.gov

Charles Taylor (R-NC, 11th)
chtaylor@hr.house.gov

Melvin Watt (D-NC, 12th)
melmail@hr.house.gov

Earl Pomeroy (D-ND, AL)
epomeroy@hr.house.gov

Rob Portman (R-OH, 2nd)
portmail@hr.house.gov

Michael Oxley (R-OH, 4th)
oxley@hr.house.gov

John Kasich (R-OH, 12th)
budget@hr.house.gov

Sherrod Brown (D-OH, 13th)
sherrod@hr.house.gov

Deborah Pryce (R-OH, 15th)
pryce15@hr.house.gov

James Traficant (D-OH, 17th)
telljim@hr.house.gov

Bob Ney (R-OH, 18th)
bobney@hr.house.gov

J. C. Watts (R-OK, 4th)
rep.jcwatts@mail.house.gov

Ernest Istook (R-OK, 5th)
istook@hr.house.gov

Earl Blumenaurer (D-OR, 3rd)
earl@mail.house.gov

Peter DeFazio (D-OR, 4th)
pdefazio@hr.house.gov

Robert Borski (D-PA, 3rd)
rborski@hr.house.gov

Curt Weldon (R-PA, 7th)
curtpa7@hr.house.gov

James Greenwood (R-PA, 8th)
jim.greenwood
@mail.house.gov

Bud Shuster (R-PA, 9th)
shuster@hr.house.gov

Paul Kanjorski (D-PA, 11th)
paul.kanjorski
@mail.house.gov

John Murtha (D-PA, 12th)
murtha@hr.house.gov

Paul McHale (D-PA, 15th)
mchale@hr.house.gov

Mark Sanford (R-SC, 1st)
sanford@hr.house.gov

John Spratt (D-SC, 5th)
jspratt@hr.house.gov

James Clyburn (D-SC, 6th)
jclyburn@hr.house.gov

John Duncan (R-TN, 2nd)
jjduncan@hr.house.gov

Van Hilleary (R-TN, 4th)
hilleary@hr.house.gov

Bob Clement (D-TN, 5th)
clement@hr.house.gov

Bart Gordon (D-TN, 6th)
bart@hr.house.gov

John Tanner (D-TN, 8th)
john.tanner@mail.house.gov

Harold Ford (D-TN, 9th)
hford@hr.house.gov

Jim Turner (D-TX, 2nd)
tx02@mail.house.gov

Sam Johnson (R-TX, 3rd
sam.tx03@mail.house.gov

Ralph Hall (D-TX, 4th)
rmhall@hr.house.gov

Joe Barton (R-TX, 6th)
barton06@hr.house.gov

Lloyd Doggett (D-TX, 10th)
doggett@hr.house.gov

Ron Paul (R-TX, 14th)
rep.paul@mail.house.gov

Charlie Stenholm (D-TX, 17th)
texas17@hr.house.gov

Sheila J. Lee (D-TX, 18th)
tx18@lee.house.gov

Henry Gonzalez (D-TX, 20th)
bnkgdems@hr.house.gov

Lamar Smith (R-TX, 21st)
lamars@hr.house.gov

Tom Delay (D-TX, 22nd)
thewhip@mail.house.gov

Martin Frost (D-TX, 24th)
frost@hr.house.gov

Ken Bentson (D-TX, 25th)
bentsen@hr.house.gov

Gene Green (D-TX, 29th)
ggreen@hr.house.gov

Eddie B. Johnson (D-TX, 30th)
ejohnson@hr.house.gov

Merrill Cook (R-UT, 2nd)
merrill.cook@mail.house.gov

Christopher Cannon (R-UT, 3rd)
cannon.ut03
@mail.house.gov

Owen Pickett (D-VA, 2nd)
opickett@hr.house.gov

Bob Goodlatte (R-VA, 6th)
talk2bob@hr.house.gov

James Moran (D-VA, 8th)
jim.moran@mail.house.gov

Rick Boucher (D-VA, 9th)
ninthnet@hr.house.gov

Thomas Davis (R-VA, 11th)
tomdavis@hr.house.gov

Bernard Sanders (I-VT, AL)
bernie@hr.house.gov

George Nethercutt (R-WA, 5th)
grnwa05@hr.house.gov

Jennifer Dunn (R-WA, 8th)
dunnwa08@hr.house.gov

Robert Wise (D-WV, 2nd)
bobwise@hr.house.gov

Nick J. Rahall (D-WV, 3rd)
nrahall@hr.house.gov

Jerry Klecska (D-WI, 4th)
jerry4wi@hr.house.gov

Tom Barrett (D-WI, 5th)
telltom@hr.house.gov

Thomas Petri (R-WI, 6th)
tompetri@hr.house.gov

James Sensenbrenner (R-WI, 9th)
sensen09@hr.house.gov

CONSULATES GENERAL

Argentina
5055 Wilshire Blvd., Ste. 210
Los Angeles, CA 90036

Australia
2049 Century Park E., 19th Fl.
Century City, CA 90067

Austria
11859 Wilshire Blvd., Ste. 501
W. Los Angeles, CA 90025

Barbados
3440 Wilshire Blvd., Ste. 1215
Los Angeles, CA 90010

Belgium
6100 Wilshire Blvd., Ste. 1200
Los Angeles, CA 90048

Botswana
333 S. Hope St., 38th Fl.
Los Angeles, CA 90071

Brazil
8484 Wilshire Blvd., Ste. 730
Beverly Hills, CA 90211

Canada
300 S. Grand Ave. Ste. 1000
Los Angeles, CA 90071

Chile
1900 Ave. of the Stars, Ste.
2450
Century City, CA 90067

China
44 Shatto Pl.
Los Angeles, CA 90020

Costa Rica
3540 Wilshire Blvd., Ste. 404
Los Angeles, CA 90010

Denmark
10877 Wilshire Blvd., Ste. 1105
Westwood, CA 90024

Finland
1900 Ave. of the Stars,
Ste. 1025
Century City, CA 90067

France
10990 Wilshire Blvd., Ste. 300
Westwood, CA 90024

Germany
6222 Wilshire Blvd., Ste. 500
Los Angeles, CA 90048

Great Britain
11766 Wilshire Blvd., Ste. 400
W. Los Angeles, CA 90025

Greece
12424 Wilshire Blvd., Ste. 800
W. Los Angeles, CA 90025

Guatemala
2975 Wilshire Blvd., Ste. 101
Los Angeles, CA 90010

Honduras
3450 Wilshire Blvd., Ste. 230
Los Angeles, CA 90010

Indonesia
3457 Wilshire Blvd., 4th Fl.
Los Angeles, CA 90010

Israel
6380 Wilshire Blvd., Ste. 1700
Los Angeles, CA 90048

Italy
12400 Wilshire Blvd. Ste. 300
W. Los Angeles, CA 90025

Japan
350 S. Grand Ave., Ste. 1700
Los Angeles, CA 90071

Kenya
9150 Wilshire Blvd., Ste. 160
Beverly Hills, CA 90212

Korea
3243 Wilshire Blvd.
Los Angeles, CA 90010

Malaysia
350 S. Figueroa St., Ste. 400
Los Angeles, CA 90071

Mexico
2401 W. 6th St.
Los Angeles, CA 90057

The Netherlands
11766 Wilshire Blvd., Ste. 1150
W. Los Angeles, CA 90025

New Zealand
12400 Wilshire Blvd., Ste. 1150
W. Los Angeles, CA 90025

Nicaragua
2500 Wilshire Blvd., Ste. 915
Los Angeles, CA 90057

Peru
3460 Wilshire Blvd., Ste. 1005
Los Angeles, CA 90010

Philippines
3660 Wilshire Blvd., Ste. 900
Los Angeles, CA 90010

Russian Federation
2790 Green St.
San Francisco, CA 94123

Saudi Arabia
2045 Sawtelle Blvd.
W. Los Angeles, CA 90025

South Africa
50 N. La Cienega Blvd.,
   Ste. 300
Beverly Hills, CA 90211

Spain
5055 Wilshire Blvd. Ste. 960
Los Angeles, CA 90036

Sweden
530 Broadway Ave., Ste. 1106
San Diego, CA 92101

Switzerland
11766 Wilshire Blvd., Ste. 1400
W. Los Angeles, CA 90025

Thailand
801 N. La Brea Ave.
Hollywood, CA 90038

Turkey
4801 Wilshire Blvd., Ste. 310
Los Angeles, CA 90010

Uruguay
429 Santa Monica Blvd.,
   Ste. 400
Santa Monica, CA 90401

MAJOR LEAGUE BASEBALL ADDRESSES

Office of the Commissioner
350 Park Ave., 17th Fl.
New York, NY 10022
Web site: MLB@BAT

American League
350 Park Ave., 18th Fl.
New York, NY 10022

National League
350 Park Ave.
New York, NY 10022

AMERICAN LEAGUE

Anaheim Angels
Office:
2000 Gene Autry Way
Anaheim, CA 92806

Mailing address:
PO Box 200
Anaheim, CA 92803
Web site: http://
   www.angelsbaseball.com/

Baltimore Orioles
333 W. Camden St.
Baltimore, MD 21201
Web site: http://
   www.theorioles.com/

Boston Red Sox
Fenway Park
4 Yawkey Way
Boston, MA 02215
Web site: http://
   www.redsox.com/

Chicago White Sox
333 W. 35th St.
Chicago, IL 60616
Web site: http://
   www.chisox.com/

Cleveland Indians
Jacobs Field
2401 Ontario St.
Cleveland, OH 44115
Web site: http://
   www.indians.com/

Detroit Tigers
Tiger Stadium
2121 Trumbull Ave.
Detroit, MI 48216
Web site: http://
   www.detroittigers.com/

Kansas City Royals
Office:
1 Royal Way
Kansas City, MO 64129

Mailing Address:
PO Box 419969
Kansas City, MO 64141
Web site: http://
   www.kcroyals.com/

Minnesota Twins
34 Kirby Puckett Pl.
Minneapolis, MN 55415
Web site: http://www.wcco.com/
   sports/twins/

New York Yankees
Yankee Stadium
161st St. & River Ave.
Bronx, NY 10451
Web site: http://
   www.yankees.com/

Oakland Athletics
7677 Oakport St., Ste. 200
Oakland, CA 94621
Web site: http://
   www.oaklandathletics.com/

Seattle Mariners
Office:
83 S. King St.
Seattle, WA 98104

Mailing address:
PO Box 4100
Seattle, WA 98104
Web site: http://
www.mariners.org./

Tampa Bay Devil Rays
Tropicana Field
1 Tropicana Dr.
St. Petersburg, FL 33705
Web site: http://
www.devilray.com

NATIONAL LEAGUE

Arizona Diamondbacks
Office:
401 E. Jefferson St.
Phoenix, AZ 85004

Mailing Address:
PO Box 2095
Phoenix, AZ 85001
Web site: http://
www.azdiamondbacks.com/

Atlanta Braves
Office:
755 Hank Aaron Dr.
Atlanta, GA 30315

Mailing address:
PO Box 4064
Atlanta, GA 30302
Web site: http://
www.atlantabraves.com/

Chicago Cubs
Wrigley Field
1060 W. Addison St.
Chicago, IL 60613
Web site: http://www.cubs.com/

Texas Rangers
Office:
1000 Ballpark Way
Arlington, TX 76011

Mailing address:
PO Box 90111
Arlington, TX 76004
Web site: http://
www.texasrangers.com/

Toronto Blue Jays
1 Blue Jays Way
Ste. 3200, Skydome
Toronto, ON M5V 1J1
Canada
Web site: http://
www.bluejays.ca/

Cincinnati Reds
100 Cinergy Field
Cincinnati, OH 45202
Web site: http://
www.cincinnatireds.com/

Colorado Rockies
2001 Blake St.
Denver, CO 80205
Web site: http://
www.coloradorockies.com/

Florida Marlins
Pro Player Stadium
2267 N.W. 199th St.
Miami, FL 33056
Web site: http://
www.flamarlins.com/

Houston Astros
Office:
8400 Kirby Dr.
Houston, TX 77054

Mailing address:
PO Box 288
Houston, TX 77001
Web site: http://
www.astros.com/

Los Angeles Dodgers
1000 Elysian Park Ave.
Los Angeles, CA 90012
Web site: http://
www.dodgers.com/

Milwaukee Brewers
Stadium:
201 S. 46th St.
Milwaukee, WI 53214

Mailing address:
PO Box 3099
Milwaukee, WI 53201
Web site: http://
www.milwaukeebrewers.com

Montreal Expos
Office:
4549 Pierre-de-Courbertin Ave.
Montreal, QC H1V 3N7

Mailing address:
PO Box 500, Station M
Montreal, QC H1V 3P2
Canada
Web site: http://
www.montrealexpos.com/

New York Mets
Shea Stadium
123-01 Roosevelt Ave.
Flushing, NY 11368

Philadelphia Phillies
Veterans Stadium
3501 S. Broad St.
Philadelphia, PA 19148

Mailing address:
PO Box 7575
Philadelphia, PA 19101
Web site: http://
www.phillies.com

Pittsburgh Pirates
600 Stadium Circle
Pittsburgh, PA 15212

Mailing address:
PO Box 7000
Pittsburgh, PA 15212
Web site: http://
www.pirateball.com/

St. Louis Cardinals
250 Stadium Plaza
St. Louis, MO 63102
Web site: http://
www.stlcardinals.com/

San Diego Padres
Office:
Jack Murphy Stadium
8880 Rio San Diego Dr.,
Ste. 400
San Diego, CA 92108

Mailing address:
PO Box 2000
San Diego, CA 92112
Web site: http://
www.padres.org/

San Francisco Giants
3Com Park at Candlestick
Point
San Francisco, CA 94124
Web site: http://
www.sfgiants.com/

BASEBALL TEAM SPRING TRAINING ADDRESSES

AMERICAN LEAGUE

Anaheim Angels
Tempe Diable Stadium
2200 W. Alameda
Tempe, AZ 85282

Baltimore Orioles
Fort Lauderdale Stadium
5301 N.W. 12th Ave.
Ft. Lauderdale, FL 33309

Boston Red Sox
City of Palm Park
2201 Edison Ave.
Fort Myers, FL 33901

Chicago White Sox
Tucson Electric Park
2500 E. Ao Way
Tucson, AZ 85713

Cleveland Indians
Chain of Lakes Park
Winter Haven, FL 33880

Detroit Tigers
2125 N. Lake Ave.
Lakeland, FL 33805

Kansas City Royals
Baseball City Stadium
300 Stadium Way
Davenport, FL 33837

Minnesota Twins
Hammond Stadium
14100 Six Mile Cypress Pkwy.
Fort Myers, FL 33912

NATIONAL LEAGUE

Arizona Diamondbacks
Tucson Electric Park
2500 E. Ao Way
Tucson, AZ 85713

Atlanta Braves
700 S. Victory Way
Kissimmee, FL 34744

Chicago Cubs
HoHoKam Park
1235 N. Center St.
Mesa, AZ 85201

Cincinnati Reds
12th St. & Tuttle Ave.
Sarasota, FL 34237

New York Yankees
3802 W. Martin Luther King
Blvd.
Tampa, FL 33614

Oakland Athletics
Phoenix Municipal Stadium
5999 E. Van Buren St.
Phoenix, AZ 85008

Seattle Mariners
Peoria Sports Complex
PO Box 999
Peoria, AZ 85380-0999

Tampa Bay Devil Rays
Al Lang Stadium
180 2nd Ave. SE
St. Petersburg, FL 33701

Texas Rangers
Rangers Complex
2300 El Jobean Rd.
Port Charlotte, FL 33948

Toronto Blue Jays
PO Box 957
Dunedin, FL 34697

Colorado Rockies
Hi Corbett Field
3400 E. Camino Campestre
Tucson, AZ 85716

Florida Marlins
Space Coast Stadium
5800 Stadium Pkwy.
Melbourne, FL 32940

Houston Astros
PO Box 422229
Kissimmee, FL 34742-2229

Los Angeles Dodgers
Holman Stadium at
Dodgertown
PO Box 2887
Vero Beach, FL 32961

Milwaukee Brewers
Maryvale Baseball Park
3600 N. 51st Ave.
Phoenix, AZ 85031

Montreal Expos
PO Box 8976
Jupiter, FL 33468

New York Mets
525 N.W. Peacock Blvd.
Port St. Lucie, FL 34986

Philadelphia Phillies
PO Box 10336
Clearwater, FL 34617

Pittsburgh Pirates
Pirate City
PO Box 1359
Bradenton, FL 34206

St. Louis Cardinals
PO Box 8929
Jupiter, FL 33468

San Diego Padres
Peoria Sports Complex
16101 N. 83rd Ave.
Peoria, AZ 85382

San Francisco Giants
Scottsdale Stadium
7408 E. Osborn Rd.
Scottsdale, AZ 85251

NATIONAL BASKETBALL ASSOCIATION TEAMS

National Basketball Association
Olympic Tower
645 5th Ave.
New York, NY 10022
Web site: http://www.nba.com/

Atlanta Hawks
1 CNN Ctr.
Ste. 405, South Tower
Atlanta, GA 30303

Boston Celtics
151 Merrimac St., 4th Fl.
Boston, MA 02114

Charlotte Hornets
100 Hive Dr.
Charlotte, NC 28217

Chicago Bulls
1901 W. Madison
Chicago, IL 60612

Cleveland Cavaliers
Gund Arena
1 Center Ct.
Cleveland, OH 44115

Dallas Mavericks
Reunion Arena
777 Sports St.
Dallas, TX 75207

Denver Nuggets
1635 Clay St.
Denver, CO 80204

Detroit Pistons
The Palace of Auburn Hills
2 Championship Dr.
Auburn Hills, MI 48326

Golden State Warriors
Oakland Coliseum Arena
7000 Coliseum Way
Oakland, CA 94621

Houston Rockets
10 Greenway Plaza
Houston, TX 77046

Indiana Pacers
Market Square Arena
300 E. Market St.
Indianapolis, IN 46204

Los Angeles Clippers
L.A. Sports Arena
3939 S. Figueroa St.
Los Angeles, CA 90037

Los Angeles Lakers
Great Western Forum
PO Box 10
Inglewood, CA 90306

Miami Heat
Sun Trust International Cr.
1 S.E. 3rd Ave., Ste. 2300
Miami, FL 33131

Milwaukee Bucks
1001 N. 4th St.
Milwaukee, WI 53203

New Jersey Nets
Nets Champion Center
390 Murray Hill Parkway
East Rutherford, NJ 07073

New York Knicks
4 Penn Plaza
New York, NY 10001

Orlando Magic
8701 Maitland Summit Blvd.
Orlando, FL 32810

Philadelphia 76ers
3601 South Broad Street
Philadelphia, PA 19148

Phoenix Suns

201 East Jefferson Street
Pheonix, AZ 85001

Portland Trailblazers
1 Center Court
Portland, OR 97227

Sacramento Kings
1515 Sports Drive
Sacramento, CA 95834

San Antonio Spurs
100 Montana Street
San Antonio, TX 78203

Seattle SuperSonics
190 Queen Anne North
Seattle, WA 98188

Toronto Raptors
20 Bay Street
Toranto
CANADA M5M 2C9

Utah Jazz
5 Triad Center
Salt Lake City, UT 84108

Vancouvers Grizzlies
800 Griffiths Way
Vancouver BC V6B

Washington Wizards
601 F Street NW
Washington, DC 20004

WOMEN'S NATIONAL BASKETBALL ASSOCIATION TEAMS

Charlotte Sting
3308 Oak Lake Blvd., Ste. B
Charlotte, NC 28208

Cleveland Rockers
Gund Arena
1 Center Ct.
Cleveland, OH 44115

Detroit Shock
The Palace of Auburn Hills
2 Championship Dr.
Auburn Hills, MI 48326

Houston Comets
2 Greenway Plaza, Ste. 400
Houston, TX 77046

Los Angeles Sparks
PO Box 10
Inglewood, CA 90306

New York Liberty
Madison Square Garden
2 Pennsylvania Plaza, 14th Fl.
New York, NY 10121

Phoenix Mercury
America West Arena
201 E. Jefferson
Phoenix, AZ 85004

Sacramento Monarchs
1 Sports Pkwy.
Sacramento, CA 95834

Utah Starzz
Delta Center
301 W. South Temple
Salt Lake City, UT 84101

Washington Mystics
1 Harry S. Truman Dr.
Landover, MD 20785

AMERICAN BASKETBALL LEAGUE TEAMS

American Basketball League
1900 Embarcadero Rd., Ste. 110
Palo Alto, CA 94303
Web site: http://
   www.ableague.com/
E-mail:hoops@ableague.com

Atlanta Glory
2100 Powers Ferry Rd., Ste. 400
Atlanta, GA 30339
Web site: http://
   www.atlantaglory.com
E-mail: info@atlantaglory.com

Colorado Xplosion
800 Grant St., Ste. 410
Denver, CO 80203
Web site: http://
   www.xplosion.com
E-mail: info@xplosion.com

Columbus Quest
7451 State Rte. 161
Dublin, OH 43016
Web site: http://
   www.columbusquest.com

Long Beach Stingrays
1 World Trade Ctr., Ste. 202
Long Beach, CA 90831
Web site: http://
   www.lbstingrays.com

New England Blizzard
179 Allyn St., Ste. 403
Hartford, CT 06103
Web site: http://
   www.neblizzard.com
E-mail: info@neblizzard.com

Portland Power
439 N. Broadway
Portland, OR 97227
Web site: http://
   www.portlandpower.com

Philadelphia Rage
123 Chestnut St., 4th Fl.
Philadelphia, PA 19106
Web site: http://
   www.phillyrage.com/

San Jose Lasers
1530 Parkmoor Ave., Ste. A
San Jose, CA 95128
Web site: http://
   www.sjlasers.com

Seattle Reign
400 Mercer St., Ste. 408
Seattle, WA 98109
Web site: http://
   www.settlereign.com
E-mail: reign@seattlereign.com

CONTINENTAL BASKETBALL ASSOCIATION TEAMS

Continental Basketball Association
2 Arizona Ctr.
400 N. 5th St., Ste. 1425
Phoenix, AZ 85004
Web site: http://
www.cbahoops.com/
E-mail: cbagc@netcom.com

Connecticut Pride
21 Waterville Rd.
Avon, CT 06001

Idaho Stampede
90 S. Cole Rd.
Franklin Business Park
Boise, ID 83709

Fort Wayne Fury
1010 Memorial Way, Ste. 210
Fort Wayne, IN 46805

Grand Rapids Hoops
190 Monroe NW, Room 222
Grand Rapids, MI 49503

La Crosse Bobcats
200 Main St. Ste. 200
PO Box 1717
La Crosse, WI 54602

Quad City Thunder
7800 14th St. W.
Rock Island, IL 61201

Rockford Lightning
3660 Publisher's Dr.
Rockford, IL 61109

Sioux Falls Skyforce
330 N. Main Ave., #101
Sioux Falls, SD 57102

Yakima Sun Kings
PO Box 2626
Yakima, WA 98907

NATIONAL FOOTBALL LEAGUE TEAMS

National Football League
410 Park Ave.
New York, NY 10022
Web site: http://www.nfl.com

Arizona Cardinals
PO Box 888
Phoenix, AZ 85001-0888

Atlanta Falcons
2745 Burnette Rd.
Suwanee, GA 30174

Baltimore Ravens
11001 Owings Mills Blvd.
Owings Mills, MD 21117

Buffalo Bills
1 Bills Dr.
Orchard Park, NY 14127

Carolina Panthers
227 W. Trade St., Ste. 1600
Charlotte, NC 28202

Chicago Bears
250 N. Washington Rd.
Lake Forest, IL 60045

Cincinnati Bengals
200 Riverfront Stadium
Cincinnati, OH 45202

Dallas Cowboys
1 Cowboys Pkwy.
Irving, TX 75063

Denver Broncos
13655 Broncos Pkwy.
Englewood, CO 80112

Detroit Lions
Pontiac Silverdome
1200 Featherstone Rd.
Pontiac, MI 48342

Green Bay Packers
1265 Lombardi Ave.
Green Bay, WI 54304

Houston Oilers
6910 Fannin St.
Houston, TX 77030

Indianapolis Colts
PO Box 535000
Indianapolis, IN 46253

Jacksonville Jaguars
1 Stadium Pl.
Jacksonville, FL 32202

Kansas City Chiefs
1 Arrowhead Dr.
Kansas City, MO 64129

Miami Dolphins
2269 N.W. 199th St.
Miami, FL 33056

Minnesota Vikings
9520 Viking Dr.
Eden Prairie, MN 55344

New England Patriots
60 Washington St.
Foxboro, MA 02035
Web site: http://
   www.patriots.com/

New Orleans Saints
6928 Saints Dr.
Metairie, LA 70003

New York Giants
Giants Stadium
East Rutherford, NJ 07073

New York Jets
1000 Fulton Ave.
Hempstead, NY 11550

Oakland Raiders
332 Center St.
El Segundo, CA 90245

Philadelphia Eagles
3501 S. Broad St.
Philadelphia, PA 19148

Pittsburgh Steelers
300 Stadium Cir.
Pittsburgh, PA 15212

St. Louis Rams
100 N. Broadway
St. Louis, MO 63102

San Francisco 49ers
4949 Centennial Blvd.
Santa Clara, CA 95054

San Diego Chargers
PO Box 609609
San Diego, CA 92160

Seattle Seahawks
11220 N.E. 53rd St.
Kirkland, WA 98033

Tampa Bay Buccaneers
1 Buccaneer Pl.
Tampa, FL 33607

Washington Redskins
21300 Redskin Park Dr.
Ashburn, VA 22011

NATIONAL HOCKEY LEAGUE TEAMS

National Hockey League
1251 Ave. of the Americas
New York, NY 10020

Web site: http://www.nhl.com/

Toronto office:
75 International Blvd., Ste. 300
Rexdale, ON M9W 6L9
Canada

Montreal office:
1800 McGill College Ave., Ste. 2600
Montreal, QC H3A 3J6
Canada

The Mighty Ducks of Anaheim
2695 E. Katella Ave.
PO Box 61077
Anaheim, CA 92803

Boston Bruins
FleetCenter
Boston, MA 02114

Buffalo Sabres
Marine Midland Arena
1 Seymour Knox III Plaza
Buffalo, NY 14203

Calgary Flames
Canadian Airlines Saddledome
PO Box 1540, Station M
Calgary, AB T2P 3B9
Canada

Carolina Hurricanes
5000 Aerial Center, Ste. 1000
Morrisville, NC 27560

Chicago Blackhawks
United Center
1901 W. Madison St.
Chicago, IL 60612

Colorado Avalanche
McNichols Sports Arena
1635 Clay St.
Denver, CO 80204

Dallas Stars
Star Center
211 Cowboys Pkwy.
Irving, TX 75063

Detroit Red Wings
Joe Louis Arena
600 Civic Center
Detroit, MI 48226

Edmonton Oilers
11230 110th Ave.
Edmonton, AB T5G 3G8
Canada

Florida Panthers
100 N.E. 3rd Ave., 10th Fl.
Ft. Lauderdale, FL 33301

Los Angeles Kings
3900 W. Manchester Blvd.
PO Box 10
Inglewood, CA 90305

Montreal Canadiens
Molson Centre
1260, rue de la Gauchetiere O
Montreal, QC H3B 5E
Canada

New Jersey Devils
Continental Airlines Arena
PO Box 504
East Rutherford, NJ 07073

New York Islanders
Nassau Coliseum
Uniondale, NY 11553

New York Rangers
Madison Square Garden
4 Pennsylvania Plaza
New York, NY 10001

Ottawa Senators
Corel Center
1000 Palladium Dr.
Kanata, ON K2V 1A5
Canada

Philadelphia Flyers
CoreStates Center
1 CoreStates Complex
Philadelphia, PA 19148

Phoenix Coyotes
1 Renaissance Sq.
2 N. Central, Ste. 1930
Phoenix, AZ 85004

Pittsburgh Penguins
Civic Arena
Gate 9
Pittsburgh, PA 15219

St. Louis Blues
Kiel Center
1401 Clark Ave.
St. Louis, MO 63103

San Jose Sharks
San Jose Arena
525 W. Santa Clara St.
San Jose, CA 95113

Tampa Bay Lightning
Ice Palace
401 Channelside Dr.
Tampa, FL 33602

Toronto Maple Leafs
Maple Leaf Gardens
60 Carlton St.
Toronto, ON M5B 1L1
Canada

Vancouver Canucks
General Motors Pl.
800 Griffiths Way
Vancouver, BC V6B 6G1
Canada

Washington Capitals
U.S. Airways Arena
Landover, MD 20785

AMERICAN HOCKEY LEAGUE TEAMS

American Hockey League
425 Union St.
W. Springfield, MA 01089
Web site: http://www.canoe.ca/
   AHL/

Adirondack Red Wings
1 Civic Center Plaza
Glens Falls, NY 12801

Albany River Rats
Knickerbocker Arena
51 S. Pearl St.
Albany, NY 12207

Cincinnati Mighty Ducks
2250 Seymour Ave.
Cincinnati, OH 45212

Fredericton Canadiens
Aitken University Centre
PO Box HABS
Fredericton, NB E3B 4Y2
Canada

Hamilton Bulldogs
85 York Blvd.
Hamilton, ON L8R 3L4

Hartford Wolf Pack
196 Trumbull St., 3rd Fl.
Hartford, CT 06103

Hershey Bears
PO Box 866
Hershey, PA 17033

Kentucky Thoroughblades
410 W. Vine St.
Lexington, KY. 40507

Beast of New Haven
275 Orange St.
New Haven, CT 06510

Philadelphia Phantoms
The CoreStates Spectrum
1 CoreStates Complex
Philadelphia, PA 19148

Portland Pirates
Cumberland County Civic
   Center
85 Free St.
Portland, ME 04101

Providence Bruins
Providence Civic Center
1 LaSalle Sq.
Providence, RI 02903

Rochester Americans
50 South Ave.
Rochester, NY 14604

Saint John Flames
PO Box 4040, Station B
Saint John, NB E2M 5E6
Canada

St. John's Maple Leafs
6 Logy Bay Rd.
St. John's NF A1A 1J3
Canada

Springfield Falcons
PO Box 3190
Springfield, MA 01101

Syracuse Crunch
Onondaga County War
   Memorial
800 S. State St.
Syracuse, NY 13202

Worcester Ice Cats
303 Main St.
Worcester, MA 01608

CENTRAL HOCKEY LEAGUE TEAMS

Central Hockey League
5840 S. Memorial Dr., Ste. 302
Tulsa, OK 74145

Columbus Cottonmouths
PO Box 1886
Columbus, GA 31902-1886

Fayetteville Force
121 E. Mountain Dr., Rm. 22B
Fayetteville, NC 28306
Web site: http://
   www.fayettevilleforce.com

Fort Worth Fire
University Centre
1300 S. University, Ste. 515
Fort Worth, TX 76107
Web site: http://
   www.fwfire.com/

Huntsville Channel Cats
Von Braun Center
700 Monroe St.
Huntsville, AL 35801
Web site: http://
   www.channelcats.com

Macon Whoopee
Macon Centreplex
200 Coliseum Dr.
Macon, GA 31201
Web site: http://
   www.maconwhoopee.com

Memphis RiverKings
Mid-South Coliseum
The Fairgrounds
Memphis, TN 38104

Nashville Ice Flyers
PO Box 190595
Nashville, TN 37219

Oklahoma City Blazers
119 N. Robinson, Ste. 230
Oklahoma City, OK 73102
Web site: http://
   www.okcblazers.com/

Tulsa Oilers
613 S. Mingo
Tulsa, OK 74133

Wichita Thunder
505 W. Maple, Ste. 100
Wichita, KS 67213

EAST COAST HOCKEY LEAGUE TEAMS

East Coast Hockey League
125 Village Blvd., Ste. 210
Princeton, NJ 08540
Web site: http://www.echl.org/

Baton Rouge Kingfish
PO Box 2142
Baton Rouge, LA 70821

Birmingham Bulls
PO Box 1506
Birmingham, AL 35201

Charlotte Checkers
2700 E. Independence Blvd.
Charlotte, NC 28205

Columbus Chill
7001 Dublin Park Dr.
Dublin, OH 43016

Dayton Bombers
Ervin J. Nutter Center
3640 Colonel Glenn Hwy.,
  Ste. 417
Dayton, OH 45435

Hampton Roads Admirals
PO Box 299
Norfolk, VA 23501

Huntington Blizzard
763 3rd Ave.
Huntington, WV 25701

Jacksonville Lizard Kings
5569-7 Bowden Rd.
Jacksonville, FL 32216

Johnstown Chiefs
326 Napoleon St.
Johnstown, PA 15901

Knoxville Cherokees
500 E. Church St.
Knoxville, TN 37915

Louisiana IceGators
444 Gajundome Blvd.
Lafayette, LA 70506

Louisville RiverFrogs
PO Box 36407
Louisville, KY 40233

Mississippi Sea Wolves
2350 Beach Blvd.
Biloxi, MS 39531

Mobile Mysticks
PO Box 263
Mobile, AL 36601

Pensacola Ice Pilots
Civic Center
201 E. Gregory St. Rear
Pensacola, FL 32501

Peoria Rivermen
201 S. W. Jefferson
Peoria, IL 61602

Raleigh IceCaps
4000 W. Chase Blvd., Ste. 110
Raleigh, NC 27607

Richmond Renegades
601 E. Leigh St.
Richmond, VA 23219

Roanoke Express
4502 Starkey Rd. SW, Ste. 211
Roanoke, VA 24014

South Carolina Stingrays
3107 Firestone Rd.
N. Charleston, SC 29418

Tallahassee Tiger Sharks
505 W. Pensacola St., Ste. 1
Tallahassee, FL 32301

Toledo Storm
1 Main St.
Toledo, OH 43605

Wheeling Nailers
PO Box 6563
Wheeling, WV 26003-0815

WESTERN PROFESSIONAL HOCKEY LEAGUE TEAMS

Western Professional Hockey League
14040 N. Cave Creek Rd., Ste. 100
Phoenix, AZ 85022
Web site: http://
www.wphlhockey.com
E-mail: wphl@netzone.com

Amarillo Rattlers
320 S. Polk St., Ste. 800
Amarillo, TX 79101
Web site: http://www.
wphl-rattlers.com

Austin Ice Bats
7311 Decker Ln.
Austin, TX 78724

Central Texas Stampede
600 Forest Dr.
Belton, TX 76513

El Paso Buzzards
4100 E. Paisano Dr.
El Paso, TX 79905

Fort Worth Bramahs
PO Box 470606
Fort Worth, TX 76147

Lake Charles Ice Pirates
900 Lakeshore Dr., 2nd Fl.
Lake Charles, LA 70602

Monroe Moccasins
2102 Louisville Ave.
Monroe, LA 71201

New Mexico Scorpions
1101 Cardenas Plaza, Ste. 201
Albuquerque, NM 87110

Odessa Jackalopes
PO Box 51187
Midland, TX 79710

San Angelo Outlaws
3260 Sherwood Way
San Angelo, TX 76901

Shreveport Mudbugs
3701 Hudson St., 2nd Fl.
Shreveport, LA 71109

Waco Wizards
2040 N. Valley Mills Dr.
Waco, TX 76710

MAJOR LEAGUE SOCCER TEAMS

Major League Soccer
110 E. 42nd St., 10th Fl.
New York, NY 10017
Web site: http://
www.mlsnet.com

Chicago Fire
311 W. Superior, Ste. 444
Chicago, IL 60610
Web site: http://
www.chicago-fire.com

Colorado Rapids
555 17th St., Ste. 3350
Denver, CO 80202
Web site: http://
www.coloradorapids.com
E-mail: Rapids@mlsnet.com

Columbus Crew
77 E. Nationwide Blvd.
Columbus, OH 43215
Web site: http://
www.thecrew.com/
E-mail: crew2739@aol.com

Dallas Burn
2602 McKinney, Ste. 200
Dallas, TX 75204
Web site: http://
www.burnsoccer.com
E-mail: mail@burnsoccer.com

DC United
13832 Redskin Dr.
Herndon, VA 22071
Web site: http://
www.dcunited.com
E-mail: united-fan@mlsnet.com

Kansas City Wizards
706 Broadway St., Ste. 100
Kansas City, MO 64105
Web site: http://
www.kcwizards.com/
E-mail: ctaylor@mlsnet.com

Los Angeles Galaxy
1640 S. Sepulveda Blvd.,
Ste. 114
Los Angeles, CA 90025

Miami Fusion
2200 Commercial Blvd.,
Ste. 104
Ft. Lauderdale, FL 33309
Web site: http://
www.miamifusion.com

New England Revolution
Foxboro Stadium
60 Washington St., Rte. 1
Foxboro, MA 02035
Web site: http://
www.nerevolution.com/

NY/NJ MetroStars
1 Harmon Plaza, 8th Fl.
Secaucus, NJ 07094
Web site: http://
www.metrostars.com/
E-mail: MetroFan@mlsnet.com

San Jose Clash
1265 El Camino Real, 2nd Fl.
Santa Clara, CA 95050
Web site: http://www.clash.com/
E-mail: clash@clash.com

Tampa Bay Mutiny
1408 Westshore Blvd.,
Ste. 1004
Tampa, FL 33607
Web site: http://
www.tampabaymutiny.com/
E-mail:
mutinymail@mlsnet.com

NATIONAL PROFESSIONAL SOCCER LEAGUE TEAMS

**National Professional Soccer
League**
115 Dewalt Ave. NW, 5th Fl.
Canton, OH 44702
E-mail: NPSL1@aol.com

Baltimore Spirit
201 W. Baltimore St.
Baltimore, MD 21201
Web site: http://
www.baltimorespirit.com
E-mail: spiritsoccer
@baltimorespirit.com

Buffalo Blizzard
Marine Midland Arena
1 Seymour Knox III Plaza
Buffalo, NY 14203
Web site: http://
www.buffaloblizzard.com

Cincinnati Silverbacks
537 E. Pete Rose Way, 2nd Fl.
Cincinnati, OH 45202

Cleveland Crunch
34200 Solon Rd.
Solon, OH 44139

Detroit Rockers
600 Civic Center Dr.
Detroit, MI 48226
E-mail: rockersoc@aol.com

Edmonton Drillers
11230 110th St.
Edmonton, AB T5G 3G8
Canada
Web site: http://
www.edmontondrillers.com
E-mail:
drillers@compusmart.ab.ca

Harrisburg Heat
PO Box 60123
Harrisburg, PA 17106
Web site: http://
www.heatsoccer.com/
E-mail: heatsoccer@aol.com

Kansas City Attack
1800 Genessee
Kansas City, MO 64102

Milwaukee Wave
10201 N. Port Washington Rd.,
Ste. 200
Mequon, WI 53092
Web site: http://
www.wavesoccer.com

Montreal Impact
8000 Langelier, Ste. 104
St. Leonard, QC H1P 3K2
Canada
Web site: http://
www.impactmtl.com
E-mail: Info@impact.usisl.com

Philadelphia Kixx
CoreStates Spectrum
1 CoreStates Complex
Philadelphia, PA 19148-9727
Web site: http://
kixx.phillynews.com
E-mail: kixxsoccer@aol.com

St. Louis Ambush
7547 Ravensridge
St. Louis, MO 63119

Wichita Wings
500 S. Broadway
Wichita, KS 67202
Web site: http://
www.wichita-wings.com

THE A-LEAGUE HOCKEY TEAMS

The A-League
14497 N. Dale Mabry, Ste. 211
Tampa, FL 33618

California Jaguars
12 Clay St.
Salinas, CA 93901

Atlanta Ruckus
1131 Alpharetta St.
Roswell, GA 30075

Carolina Dynamo
3517 W. Wendover Ave.
Greensboro, NC 27407

Charleston Battery
4401 Belle Oaks Dr., Ste. 450
Charleston, SC 29405

Colorado Foxes
6200 Dahlia St.
Commerce City, CO 80022

Connecticut Wolves
PO Box 3196
Veterans Memorial Stadium
New Britain, CT 06050-3196

El Paso Patriots
6941 Industrial
El Paso, TX 79915

Hershey Wildcats
100 W. Hersheypark Dr.
Hershey, PA 17033

Jacksonville Cyclones
9428 Bay Meadows Rd.,
   Ste. 175
Jacksonville, FL 32256

Long Island Rough Riders
1670 Old Country Rd.,
   Ste. 227
Plainview, NY 11803

Milwaukee Rampage
Uihlein Soccer Park
7101 W. Good Hope Rd.
Milwaukee, WI 53223

Minnesota Thunder
1700 105th Ave. NE
Elaine, MN 55449

Montreal Impact
8000 Langelier, Ste. 104
St. Leonard, QC H1P 3K2
Canada

Nashville Metros
7115 S. Spring Dr.
Franklin, TN 37067-1616

New Orleans Riverboat Gamblers
5690 Eastover Dr.
New Orleans, LA 70128

Orange County Zodiac
c/o Unicor
14210 Quail Ridge Dr.
Riverside, CA 92503

Orlando Sundogs
1 Citrus Bowl Pl.
Orlando, FL 32805

Raleigh Flyers
130 Wind Chime Ct.
Raleigh, NC 27615

Richmond Kickers
2320 W. Main St.
Richmond, VA 23220

Rochester Raging Rhinos
333 N. Plymouth Ave.
Rochester, NY 14608

Seattle Sounders
10838 Main St.
Bellevue, WA 98004

Toronto Lynx
c/o HIT Pro Soccer Inc.
55 University Ave., Ste. 506
Toronto, ON M5J 2H7
Canada

Vancouver 86ers
1126 Douglas Rd.
Burnaby, BC V5C 4Z6
Canada

Worcester Wildfire
500 Main St., Ste. 515
Worcester, MA 01608

Write to Me

The Address Book is updated every two years, and you can play an active role in this process. If you are notable in any field or know someone who is, send the name, mailing address, and some documentation of the notability (newspaper clippings are effective) for possible inclusion in our next edition.

Also, we are very interested in learning of any success stories resulting from *The Address Book.*

During the last few years, I have received tens of thousands of letters, ranging from loving to vituperative, from owners of *The Address Book.* Despite the overwhelming task of answering this mail, I really enjoy the letters.

But, please, remember a couple of rules if you write:

- Remember to include a *self-addressed stamped envelope.* For reasons of both time and expense, this is the only way I can respond to mail; so, unfortunately, I've had to draw the line—no SASE, no reply.
- I need your comments. While I confess I'm partial to success stories, comments from purchasers of the book have helped me a great deal for updating editions; so fire away.
- Many people have written to request addresses of people not listed in the book. As much as I would like to, I simply can't open up this can of worms. Requests for additional addresses are carefully noted and considered for future editions.

Receiving a photo from someone who writes adds an entirely new dimension to the letter, so feel free. That's right, enclose a photo of yourself. After all, from the photo on the back cover, you know what I look like, and I'm rather eager to see you.

Keep those cards and letters coming.

Michael Levine
5750 Wilshire Blvd., #555
Los Angeles, CA 90036